Michael T Buchanan

# Managing Curriculum Change in Religious Education

## An inside Perspective from School Leaders in Religious Education

**LAP LAMBERT** Academic Publishing

## Impressum/Imprint (nur für Deutschland/ only for Germany)

Bibliografische Information der Deutschen Nationalbibliothek: Die Deutsche Nationalbibliothek verzeichnet diese Publikation in der Deutschen Nationalbibliografie; detaillierte bibliografische Daten sind im Internet über http://dnb.d-nb.de abrufbar.

Alle in diesem Buch genannten Marken und Produktnamen unterliegen warenzeichen-, marken- oder patentrechtlichem Schutz bzw. sind Warenzeichen oder eingetragene Warenzeichen der jeweiligen Inhaber. Die Wiedergabe von Marken, Produktnamen, Gebrauchsnamen, Handelsnamen, Warenbezeichnungen u.s.w. in diesem Werk berechtigt auch ohne besondere Kennzeichnung nicht zu der Annahme, dass solche Namen im Sinne der Warenzeichen- und Markenschutzgesetzgebung als frei zu betrachten wären und daher von jedermann benutzt werden dürften.

Coverbild: www.ingimage.com

Verlag: LAP LAMBERT Academic Publishing GmbH & Co. KG
Dudweiler Landstr. 99, 66123 Saarbrücken, Deutschland
Telefon +49 681 3720-310, Telefax +49 681 3720-3109
Email: info@lap-publishing.com

Herstellung in Deutschland:
Schaltungsdienst Lange o.H.G., Berlin
Books on Demand GmbH, Norderstedt
Reha GmbH, Saarbrücken
Amazon Distribution GmbH, Leipzig
ISBN: 978-3-8433-6554-3

## Imprint (only for USA, GB)

Bibliographic information published by the Deutsche Nationalbibliothek: The Deutsche Nationalbibliothek lists this publication in the Deutsche Nationalbibliografie; detailed bibliographic data are available in the Internet at http://dnb.d-nb.de.

Any brand names and product names mentioned in this book are subject to trademark, brand or patent protection and are trademarks or registered trademarks of their respective holders. The use of brand names, product names, common names, trade names, product descriptions etc. even without a particular marking in this works is in no way to be construed to mean that such names may be regarded as unrestricted in respect of trademark and brand protection legislation and could thus be used by anyone.

Cover image: www.ingimage.com

Publisher: LAP LAMBERT Academic Publishing GmbH & Co. KG
Dudweiler Landstr. 99, 66123 Saarbrücken, Germany
Phone +49 681 3720-310, Fax +49 681 3720-3109
Email: info@lap-publishing.com

Printed in the U.S.A.
Printed in the U.K. by (see last page)
ISBN: 978-3-8433-6554-3

# Contents

Ministry?

2

# *Acknowledgements*

There are many people I would like to acknowledge who have had a significant influence over my thinking and in one way or another contributed to the research or writing of this book. In particular I would especially like to acknowledge my colleagues from the Australian Catholic University – I am sincerely grateful to Kath Engebretson who has been my mentor for her excellent and invaluable advice, support and encouragement. In particular I am deeply appreciative of the personal interest in this research as well as her meticulous attention to detail. I would also like to express my grateful appreciation to Marian de Souza for her continuous encouragement and invitations to push the boundaries pertaining to my research endeavours.

I am also appreciative of the generous support and encouragement given to me by several other colleagues and past colleagues from Australian Catholic University –Peta Goldburg, Catherine McCahill, Patricia Hacker, Helga Neidhart, Brendan Hyde and Richard Rymarz. I especially thank them for their tireless reading and commenting on various sections of this work.

This research could not have taken place without the consent of the Director of Catholic Education Melbourne, who exercises educational leadership over the third largest Catholic diocese in the world and one of the largest education systems in Australia. I am also appreciative of all the Principals of Catholic secondary schools in Melbourne, Australia. Each one supported this research by allowing me the opportunity to invite the Religious Education Coordinator in their respective school to participate in the study. To the Religious Education Coordinators who have one of the most important and most misunderstood leadership roles in Catholic education, I express my sincere appreciation and gratitude for your willingness to participate in this study and share your insights, experiences and expertise regarding the management of curriculum change in religious education. Your insights have underpinned the focus of this research. This book portrays the way in which you manage curriculum change and conveys to the education community and broader community how this important role is carried out from your perspective.

Finally I would like to express my deeply felt thanks and appreciation to those who complete my joy for life – Sake`, Meiko, Mum, Dad, Nanna and Nannu. You inspire me in ways that cannot be explained. Your guidance and love encourages me in so many ways.

# *Preface*

Catholic education is imbued within a 2000 year religious tradition and has a long history of being at the service of the broader international community. Throughout Australia approximately 20 per cent of the student population are educated in Catholic schools. Catholic education systems throughout the country are the main provider of a faith-based education and compulsory religious education programs are taught from the preparatory years through to Year 12 (the final year of schooling).

Since the Second Vatican Council (1962-1965) a key leadership role in Catholic schools has emerged to help foster the religious and faith dimension of the school. This role has been commonly referred to as Religious Education Coordinator (REC) and in some dioceses Assistant Principal Religious Education (APRE). The role has been conceived in many different ways over the decades and perceptions of the role are incredibly diverse. This is particularly so in Melbourne where the appointment criteria for the position of REC is determined at the school level by the principal. Consequently it is virtually impossible to achieve a uniform agreement as to what the role actually entails. Much research has attested to the importance of the role and recent studies have explored the nature of the role and in so doing exposed many of the complexities associated with it. An ongoing debate has gained momentum in recent times regarding whether the REC role is in fact a role within the Church or a role within education (or a role within both Church and education).

As educators the RECs in Catholic schools hold a key leadership position within the school. They are appointed from the community of trained and professionally qualified teachers. In writing this book my focus was oriented towards exploring a specific educational dimension of the role. One key role the REC is responsible for is curriculum leadership in religious education. While some studies have indicated that given the complex demands of the role curriculum leadership was one area of the role that RECs tend to ignore. However in contrast, my own research into the RECs management of curriculum change provided an amazing insight into the ways in which RECs exercise curriculum leadership in the wake of curriculum change. The research which forms the basis of this book reveals insights into how curriculum changed in religious education is managed by RECs.

In writing this book I hope to do justice to the RECs who helped to provide an understanding of how curriculum change is managed from their perspective, as they are responsible for curriculum leadership.

I offer *Managing Curriculum Change in Religious Education* as a guide for RECs and other educational leaders as well as others who wish to study and understand the complexities and dynamics associated with this very important dimension of leadership in religious education within the school context.

# *Introduction*

This study analyses the religious education coordinators' (RECs') management of a particular curriculum change in religious education in Catholic secondary schools in the Archdiocese of Melbourne. The role of the REC[1] is regarded as a key leadership position in Australian Catholic schools, and it requires leadership and coordination of all aspects of the religious education curriculum. Leadership and coordination in religious education is concerned with curriculum issues within the formal classroom setting as well as activities beyond the formal classroom, such as liturgy and prayer, retreats, social action groups, community service programmes and pastoral care (Engebretson, Fleming & Rymarz, 2002, p. 19). The diverse nature of the role of REC in Catholic schools has been reported on in two major Australian studies (Crotty, 2002; Fleming, 2002). Both studies explored the multi-dimensional nature of the role and alluded to the difficulties associated with defining the role given the broad range of responsibilities related to the position (Crotty, 2002; Fleming, 2002). This study is concerned with a certain aspect of the role of the REC, that is responsibilities regarding the formal classroom curriculum in religious education, and it is specifically concerned with how RECs managed a particular curriculum change initiative.

The change initiative which was the focus of this study was instigated by the former Archbishop of Melbourne, now Cardinal George Pell in 1999. By 2001, Cardinal Pell directed all schools in the Archdiocese to implement a "text-based curriculum" (Pell, 2001, p. 5) and it was founded on a new series of religious education textbooks written for the Archdiocese and entitled *To Know Worship and Love*. Although he had referred to this curriculum initiative as a "text-based curriculum", no official interpretation or explanation of the term was provided or documented by the Archdiocesan authorities. It is arguable that the term "text-based curriculum" referred to each school developing its own religious education curriculum based on the contents and topics outlined in the *To Know Worship and Love* textbook series. Traditionally each school in the Archdiocese had been responsible for writing its own curriculum in religious education based on the curriculum guidelines produced by the Catholic Education Office, Melbourne.[2] Catholic schools in the Archdiocese continued to write school based curricula, however now these were to be underpinned by the student textbook series instead of the curriculum guidelines that had been previously developed by the Catholic Education Office, Melbourne (1995).

---

[1] Chapter two of this book provides a comprehensive explanation and overview of the role of the REC in several Australian Catholic dioceses.

[2] Throughout the 1970s, 1980s and 1990s the Catholic Education Office, Melbourne had produced a series of curriculum statements entitled, *Guidelines for religious education of students in the Archdiocese of Melbourne* (1973; 1975; 1977; 1984; 1995). The curriculum statements were to be considered by each Catholic school in the process of developing the formal classroom curriculum in religious education.

This initiative was a "top down" (Morris, 1995; see also, Marsh & Bowman, 1987) approach as it was directed by the Head of the Archdiocese, that is, the Archbishop. In the late 1990s prior to giving this direction, Cardinal Pell had established an Episcopal Vicariate for Religious Education which was responsible for the production and distribution of the religious education textbook series, which contained textbooks relevant to each year level of schooling from preparatory to year ten.

## The Problem to be Investigated

This study was undertaken to explore an aspect of the RECs' curriculum role concerning the management of a particular classroom curriculum change. In order to determine the impact of this facet of the RECs' curriculum role, this study investigated the RECs' perspectives on curriculum change.

The aims of the study were:

a) To study the perspectives of RECs' in secondary schools in the Archdiocese of Melbourne regarding their management of a particular curriculum change in religious education.

b) To identify factors which assisted and impeded their management of the curriculum change.

c) To analyse the theory generated from research questions a and b against existing knowledge about curriculum change in education.

d) To propose some recommendations for future directions and practices concerning the management of curriculum change in religious education in Catholic schools.

The RECs themselves who were responsible for managing the text-based curriculum initiative and the empirical component of this research explored the RECs' perspectives on the management of the curriculum change. Although this "top down" (Morris, 1995) curriculum change occurred in both Catholic primary and secondary schools this study focussed on RECs within Catholic secondary schools within the Archdiocese of Melbourne. There were several reasons for focussing solely on this change in the Catholic secondary school context.

To begin with, the process of managing the change to a text-based curriculum differed significantly between the primary school sector and the secondary schools. In managing the change in the Catholic primary school sector a team approach was fostered. Professional support was provided to the leadership teams of each primary school by the Catholic Education Office, Melbourne. In contrast in the secondary schools, the Catholic Education Office, Melbourne targeted their support directly to the RECs rather than the leadership teams.

Secondly, in the primary schools, RECs work mainly with all generalist classroom teachers who are more likely to have responsibility for the total educational program and the duty of care for their class throughout the school day. In contrast the REC in the secondary school coordinates a formal classroom curriculum in religious education where not all teachers within the school are likely to be involved.

Thirdly, the primary school textbooks in the *To Know Worship and Love* textbook series were written by a team of curriculum advisers from the Catholic Education Office, Melbourne. The theoretical position of the primary textbooks in the *To Know Worship and Love* textbook series

8

differed from that of the secondary textbooks. The theoretical position of the primary textbooks emanated from a catechetical doctrinal overview authorised by the Episcopal Vicariate for Religious Education (Elliott, 2001c, pp. 231-240). The doctrinal overview was based on the teachings in the *Catechism of the Catholic Church* (1994). The secondary school textbooks however, were written by two academics from Australian Catholic University who had adopted a theoretical position influenced by typology (Habel and Moore, 1982). A theoretical understanding of the typological approach to learning and teaching in religious education is discussed at length in Chapter one of this book. The various differences in the texts and their development from the primary and secondary sectors made it necessary to select only one of these sectors for study.

## The Significance of this Study

There have been two major Australian studies on the role of the REC. Fleming (2002) explored perceptions of the role of the REC in the Melbourne Archdiocese and Crotty (2002) examined the role of the REC in terms of religious leadership in Catholic schools in the Archdiocese of Sydney. Some minor research projects have been undertaken which provide a context for understanding aspects of the role of the REC. Johnson (1989) explored the role of the REC in terms of mission and ministry. Her research commented on the educational demands of the role concerning curriculum leadership and suggested that this aspect of the role received less attention by the RECs than the ministerial demands of the role. Blahut and Bezzina (1998) explored the role demands of the REC in the primary school context. The impetus for their research came from concerns about the constant turnover of REC personnel. Other minor studies have provided a context for understanding the dimensions and demands of the role (Buchanan, 2005b; Crotty, 1998, 2005; D' Orsa, 1998; Engebretson, 1998, Fleming, 2004; Johnson, 1998; Liddy, 1998; Paxton, 1998; McCarthy, 2004; Rymarz, 1998). Aside from Smith and Lovat (2003) and the researcher's own investigations into factors that assist curriculum change and factors that impede curriculum change in religious education (Buchanan, 2006c; 2006d) there is very little published literature concerning the role of the REC in relation to the management of curriculum change in religious education in the Australian context. This study takes into account what the limited research has found in regard to the diverse and complex demands of role of the REC, and aims to contribute understandings about a specific aspect of the role, that being curriculum change management.

Since 2001 major curriculum change initiatives have been underway in several Australian dioceses. The limited published research concerning how RECs manage curriculum change has serious implications for understanding this phenomenon and the associated responsibilities for managing curriculum change in religious education. Given the scarcity of such research in an Australian context, this study is significant. It has attempted to provide some insights into how RECs manage curriculum change. Fundamental to the research design and research methodology has been the intention of obtaining from the RECs their perspective on the management of this particular change to a text-based curriculum. The management of curriculum change concerning the formal classroom curriculum is an important aspect of the role that is sometimes ignored (Fleming, 2002; Johnson, 1989). This is the first major study concerning the management of a particular curriculum change in religious education in an Australian context. It makes a significant contribution to the literature concerning change management in a highly specialised field.

## Structure of the Book

The introduction of this book presents the background and purpose of this study. It outlines the problem to be investigated and explains the significance of this research within the context of the Archdiocese of Melbourne. Exact definitions of terms, assumptions and limitations of this study are not presented separately, but rather are made as the research unfolds.

Chapter one outlines relevant national and international approaches to religious education which have informed learning and teaching in this field in Catholic schools in the Melbourne Archdiocese. Grimmitt (2000) has argued that each new approach is a successor of those approaches which have gone before it. Therefore the change to a text-based curriculum is situated within the context of preceding approaches to religious education in the Archdiocese of Melbourne. The approaches are presented chronologically as a means by which to mark the progression and development of each approach and its relevance to the text-based curriculum initiative which is the focus of this study.

Chapter two provides a review of literature from two broad areas relevant to this research. One area draws from literature about change and in particular curriculum change. It also explores literature regarding educational change as it applies to curriculum change. The other broad area explored in this chapter concerns literature on the REC in an Australian context. The literature focuses on the various dimensions of the role to provide a framework for contextualising and understanding curriculum aspects of the role.

Chapter three reviews literature concerned with the part textbooks play in the curriculum and how this may be applied to the role of textbooks in the religious education curriculum. A broad overview of the literature concerning textbooks in education is presented followed by a summary of the literature concerning textbooks in religious education.

Chapter four outlines the epistemology, theoretical perspective and methodology for this qualitative research. It situates this study within a constructivist and constructionist paradigm and outlines the use of interpretivism with a specific focus on symbolic interactionism and social interactionism to form the theoretical perspective. There is a description and justification of grounded theory as the preferred methodology along with a detailed explanation of the use of unstructured in-depth interviews as the preferred interview method. Techniques for determining the plausibility of the theory generated such as comments from experts and the voice of the researcher are discussed.

Chapter five presents the theory generated from the categories that emerged from the in-depth interviews with the RECs involved in this study. Analyses of the five major categories reported on in this chapter are discussed in the context of the literature reviewed.

Chapter six presents the generation of additional theories that reveal the RECs' perspectives on the factors that they perceived to impede and assist the change to a text-based curriculum. An analysis of the two categories reported in this chapter and discussed in the context of the literature reviewed.

Chapter seven provides a further level of analysis of the theory generated and reported on in Chapters four and Chapter five. This is achieved by exploring the views of outside informants such as leading experts in the area of religious education and curriculum and the researcher's voice. The views of the outside expert informants help to develop the theory emerging from the in-depth interviews beyond thick description (Goulding, 2002, p. 43) as well as contribute to a deeper level of analysis. Within a constructivist paradigm the views of the leading experts in religious education and curriculum help to establish the plausibility of the study (Guba and Lincoln, 1994).

Chapter eight begins by providing a synthesis of the theory generated concerning the RECs' perspectives on the management of the change to a text-based curriculum. It then proceeds to make some recommendations for curriculum management in the area of religious education in Catholic education.

# CHAPTER ONE
# Context for Understanding the Text-based Curriculum Change

The primary focus of this chapter is to provide a context for understanding the text-based curriculum initiative and the theoretical framework underpinning it. The significance of this change can be understood by situating it within the context of preceding approaches that have informed learning and teaching in religious education in the Archdiocese of Melbourne. Grimmitt (2000) has suggested that an awareness of the interrelatedness associated with each approach provides a means by which to understand the relevance of a particular change initiative.

> Each pedagogy owes much to those that have preceded it and while significant shifts of focus or orientation have occurred and re-interpretations of former insights and principles have been frequent, there is a sense in which each new pedagogy is a direct response to, and therefore a successor of, those that have gone before it. (Grimmitt, 2000, p. 25)

This chapter situates the text-based curriculum initiative within the context of previous yet interrelated approaches to religious education. An understanding of the interrelatedness associated with each approach to religious education will provide a crucial framework in which to understand the shift of focus to a text-based curriculum. Therefore the following approaches that have informed learning and teaching in the Archdiocese of Melbourne are outlined in their historical context.[3]

## The Doctrinal Approach

The doctrinal approach was concerned with learning and teaching from the magisterium of the Church. From the time of European settlement in Australia until the early 1960s, religious education in Catholic schools had an emphasis on teaching and learning the doctrines of the Church via a catechism (Ryan, 1997, p. 23). The style of the catechisms of the nineteenth and twentieth centuries was a series of doctrinal questions and answers outlining "all the necessary truths of the Roman Catholic Church ranging from beliefs about God and who made the world, through moral

---

[3] Parts of this chapter have been published in:
Buchanan, M.T. (2003). Survey of current writings on trends in religious education. *Journal of Religious Education, 51* (4), 22-30.
Buchanan, M. T. (2004). An outcomes based educational approach to using *To Know Worship and Love* in religious education in the Archdiocese of Melbourne. *Catholic School Studies: A Journal of Catholic Education, 77* (1), 36-40.
Buchanan, M. T. (2005a). Pedagogical drift: The evolution of new approaches and paradigms in religious education. *Religious Education, 100* (1), 20-37.
Buchanan, M. T. (2006a). A brief history of approaches to RE in Catholic schools. In R. Rymarz, (Ed.). *Leadership in Religious Education* (pp. 11-29). Australia: St Paul Publication.

obligations to God and even beliefs about one's fundamental identity as Catholics" (Lovat, 1989, p. 5). In Australia, a local catechism commonly known as the *Red Catechism*, was produced and it contained 236 short questions and answers regarding the teachings of the Church or Church doctrine. Figure 1 provides an example of three doctrinal questions and answers from the *Red Catechism*.

---

**Chapter 8. –SIN: CONTRITION: PURGATORY**

**82.    What is sin?**
Sin is any wilful thought, word, deed, or omission against the law of God.
**83.    How many kinds of sin can a person commit?**
A person can commit two kinds of sin, mortal sin and venial sin.
**84.    What is mortal sin?**
Mortal sin is breaking God's law in a serious way. (Mannix, 1937, pp. 26-27)

*Figure 1.* An example of the contents contained in the *Red Catechism*. Note the presentation of Church doctrine in question and answer style.

---

The doctrinal approach that influenced religious education in Australia can be understood by exploring the development of the catechism in Europe.

## *The Reformation*

The Reformation in the early 1500s pushed the Catholic Church into a very strong reactionary mode and contributed to one third of all western Christians denouncing allegiance to the Pope and the authority of the Catholic Church (Lovat, 1989). Luther had written two catechisms in 1529, one for Protestant pastors and teachers and the other for children. This shift in faith commitment along with Luther's reaching out to children concerned Catholic authorities.

In the wake of the Protestant Reformation an ecumenical council, the Council of Trent, was held from 1545-1563 (McBrien, 1995, p. 1267). The Council of Trent mandated bishops for the first time to provide catechesis for children each Sunday and on holy days of obligation. Catechesis in the Church was concerned with the ministry of the word of God. It involved instruction to adults and children before their baptism in order to awaken, nourish and deepen their Christian faith and identity (McBrien, 1995, p. 235). The Council argued that the survival of the Church depended not only on adults but also on children being instructed thoroughly in the doctrines of the Church (Jungmann, 1957, pp. 19-20, Schroder, 1941, p. 26).

A series of devotional Catholic catechisms appeared as early as 1530, but it was not until the Council of Trent that a catechism was designed specifically for the purpose of instruction on Church doctrine. In 1566, during the reign of Pope Pius V, a Catechism entitled *Catechismus ex Decretis Concilii Tridentini ad Parochos*, (commonly known as *Catechismus Romanus*) was produced. This catechism was intended to help pastors provide religious instruction to both adults and youths (Jungmann, 1957, p. 24). Towards the end of the 1500s Pope Clement VIII commissioned the Bishop of Capan, Bishop Robert Bellarmine, to write a catechism. It was published in 1598 under the title of *Dottrina Cristiana Breve da Imparasi a Mente* (Brodrik, 1928, p. 390) and it became one of the most prominent catechisms in Catholicism (Ryan, 1997, p. 16). This doctrinal catechism was considered so influential that during the sessions of the Vatican Council of 1870 (Vatican Council I), plans were discussed to produce a universal catechism based on Bellarmine's model (Jungmann, 1957, p. 23).

Catholic catechisms originated in reaction to the Protestant Reformation and were established by bishops as an acceptable means of catechetical instruction on the teachings of the Catholic faith tradition for both adults and children.

## Eighteenth Century

The introduction of universal compulsory school attendance towards the latter part of the eighteenth century projected catechesis directly into the learning environment of the school (Jungmann, 1957, p. 27), and a catechism was used as the main learning and teaching instrument. Catechisms were originally designed by bishops to assist priests in the instruction of adults who requested further understanding of Church teachings. During the eighteenth century, however, they were used in schools as the official learning resource in religious instruction for children.

It was presumed that because children had been baptised and therefore initiated into the Catholic faith that is was theologically acceptable to use the Catechism in Catholic schools (Jungman, 1957). Such a presumption did not take into account that children baptised as infants did not share the same freedom as adults to choose or request more knowledge about the faith and the teachings of the Church. A 'siege mentality' (Lovat, 2002) emerged within Catholic schooling, and the catechism was used as a means of instructing children in order to armour them against the dangers of turning to Protestantism. This mentality influenced the Catholic Church's approach to religious education in Catholic schools from the time of the Protestant Reformation until the Second Vatican Council (1962-1965) (Lovat, 1989).

During the nineteenth century in Australia, concerns about teaching doctrine and the effectiveness of the catechism as a tool for the religious education of children began to emerge.

## The Catechism in Australia

As early as 1804 attempts were made in Sydney Cove, New South Wales, to establish a Catholic school and to provide religious instruction based on the catechism. However it was not until 1820, with the arrival of Father John Therry in Sydney, that permanent Catholic schools began to be established. The prominence of religious education in Catholic schools was largely a result of the views held and encouraged by bishops and other leaders of the Catholic community. They believed that the Catholic school was the "surest and most effective means of providing religious education" (Ryan, 1997, p. 19). Religious education taught from the catechism was a daily event in the school day. In the nineteenth century concerns about this approach to religious education in Catholic schools emerged. The Marist Brothers, a French religious teaching order with schools in Sydney and Melbourne, had identified some of the limitations of the use of the catechism. As a pedagogical instrument they found it limiting and suggested reforms to the catechism such as making it more appealing to young people in terms of presentation and layout (Doyle, 1972).

The 1885 agenda of the First Plenary Council of Australasian Bishops included the issue of producing an Australian Catholic Catechism. The outcome of the Council was a directive by the bishops that all dioceses adopt a catechism based on a style similar to the Irish Maynooth Catechism. This became known as the *Penny Catechism* (Ryan, 1997, p. 26) and was the foundation of religious content in Catholic schools in Australia. It shaped and influenced the religious development of Catholic children for almost eighty years. "The catechism was a complete map of religious life, and knowing it by heart was the means both to avoid danger and to find certainty and security" (O' Farrell, 1992, p. 242). The catechism was considered an authority on Church teachings and its questions and answers contained everything that was considered necessary to know.

Dissatisfaction with the influence of a dogmatic catechism on the formation of young Catholics reached its zenith in the twentieth century. The sense of repression and duty many Catholics felt was perceived as unhealthy. The stress on obedience and focus on correct conduct were seen as obstacles to a person's ability to develop free and critical thinking skills. The moral and religious growth of a person was measured by the prescribed criteria stemming from the contents of the catechism. There was concern that it was out of step with new understandings relating to stages of faith development. The catechism aimed to produce an adult level of faith, which could not be fully appreciated by children (Lovat, 1989, pp. 6-7, Ryan, 1997, pp. 31-32).

In the twentieth century, the dilemmas of the modern world challenged the way many Catholics would come to terms with God, Church authority, religion and their place in the world. Factors such as world wars, economic depression and the rise of communism challenged the Church's authority and credibility. The dogmatic, authoritarian, pedagogical approach associated with teaching religious education via the catechism was losing credibility (Jungmann, 1957, pp. 27-64; Lovat, 1989, pp. 6-7; Ryan, 1997, pp. 29-33). Consideration of new methods of learning and teaching religious education began to gain momentum in many countries, including Australia. The innovative pedagogical ideas emanating from the criticisms related to doctrinal teachings from the catechism emerged in a new approach to teaching and learning in religious education. This approach was the kerygmatic approach.

## The Kerygmatic Approach

The kerygmatic approach focussed strongly on the salvific message of Christianity. Its orientation was towards encouraging students to encounter Jesus as a personal saviour. Kerygma is derived from the Greek word for proclaiming the message (Engebretson et al., 2002, p. 7). By the 1930s and 1940s some European theologians interested in the liturgy of the early Christian Church began to explore the kerygmatic approach to catechesis. A German born, Austrian Jesuit and theologian, Joseph Jungmann, "considered that too much store had been placed on intellectual assent to the truths of the Church expressed in theological propositions" (Ryan, 1997, p. 36; see also Jungmann, 1957). Jungmann (1957) argued that the catechism was not the most effective pedagogical method for catechesis of young children. He considered sacramental and liturgical catechesis to be more effective in the religious formation of the child than catechesis experienced through the doctrinal focus contained in various catechisms (Jungmann, 1957, pp. 284 - 294). Jungmann believed that the salvific message contained within the scriptures was a key to evoking experiences of glory and joy similar to those commonly associated with the experience of catechesis in the early Christian period. The kerygmatic approach challenged the Catholic Church and religious educators to bring the joyful salvific message into the classroom.

A pupil of Jungmann's and a fellow Jesuit, Johannes Hofinger (1966) believed that Jungmann's kerygmatic approach to catechesis could be developed effectively for children. Supporters of the kerygmatic approach acknowledged that doctrine must be known but the kerygma must be proclaimed. This marked a clear distinction between the doctrinal approach and the kerygmatic approach. Hofinger (1966) argued that catechesis needed to be systematic and that children needed to encounter a personal understanding of the joyful message of salvation. Scripture would feature significantly in this spiritual process. It was assumed that once children had been inculcated in this process they would be better prepared to learn Church doctrine as presented in the catechism (Hofinger, 1966, pp. 44-45). The kerygmatic approach was an innovation adopted worldwide and regarded by Jungmann (1957) as a key step in the formation of Christians. Once students have come to know Jesus and the joyful message of salvation, their Christian formation could be advanced further by the doctrinal teachings contained within a catechism. Hofinger visited Australia in the early 1960s (Engebretson, et al., 2002, p. 7). He was instrumental in bringing the kerygmatic approach to catechesis to the consciousness of religious educators in Australia. The response in Australia was marked by the production of a textbook series based on kerygmatic principles. The textbooks were to be used in schools and parishes throughout Australia. In 1962 under the direction of the Australian Bishops, Father John Kelly and a team of catechists began to produce this textbook series titled, *My Way To God*.

The pedagogical initiatives suggested by the Marist Brothers and other critics of the catechism had drifted into the pedagogical techniques associated with the kerygmatic approach. What emerged in the design of the *My Way To God* series was an interactive learning approach that engaged students through story, song, prayers and colourful pictorial presentations. Figure 2 contains an excerpt from *My Way To God Book 2*, of a story designed to help students come to know the salvific message of Jesus.

Jesus came on earth to lead us to the Father. The best way to please our Heavenly Father is to be like His Son. We are sure to get to heaven if we do what He tells us.

We cannot see Him, but we have learnt about Him. We try to do things the way He would have done them. Often we pray to our Heavenly Father with the greatest love we can give.

When we meet other boys and girls and grown-ups we are kind to them because Jesus was always kind and thoughtful. We love everyone because He loves them.

Jesus was always obedient. That was one thing they wrote about Jesus as a boy. We please God when we do what we are told happily and cheerfully and quickly.

Jesus calls us to follow Him. With all the love of our hearts we will answer that call and give ourselves to Him fully. (Australian Catholic Bishops,1964, p. 55)

*Figure 2.* An example of the kerygmatic approach reflected in *My Way To God Book 2* (Australian Catholic Bishops, 1964).

There was an integral connection between the kerygmatic approach and learning the doctrines through the catechism. Supporters of the kerygmatic approach argued that once students had come to know Jesus as their personal saviour then they would be able to learn the doctrines of the Church. The pedagogical techniques commonly associated with the kerygmatic approach in Australia can be seen as a response to the recommendations to modify the pedagogy of the catechism. The underlying intention of the kerygmatic approach was that the focus on Jesus as God, as presented in scripture, would help students develop a life of faith in the community of the Church (Engebretson, et al., 2002, p. 7). The popularity of the kerygmatic approach extended to the whole of Australia. "The texts [*My Way to God*] were prescribed for use in all Australian Catholic schools by the Australian Catholic Bishops' Committee for Education in September 1962" (Ryan, 1997, p. 40).

The *My Way to God* series represented the culmination of the hopes of those many critics of the traditional question and answer catechisms who called for bright and cheerful presentations of catechetical material. The books were large in format, brightly coloured with a systematic presentation of the Church's story, which included some Australian references. The books contained songs, which could be learned and performed by the class, striking graphs and drawings and biblical references. (Ryan, 1997, pp. 39-40)

Regardless of its popularity, the kerygmatic approach to catechesis was comparatively short lived. There were educational reasons as well as theological and magisterial developments occurring in the Church and in society in the 1960s that contributed to the short existence of the kerygmatic approach. Teachers in Australia were generally not adequately prepared for the new content and pedagogical focus associated with the kerygmatic approach. They had insufficient preparation in the areas of scripture and Church history. The kerygmatic approach disengaged many parents and grandparents in their efforts to reinforce religious learning. They had come to know their faith through the doctrinal approach, and the kerygmatic approach was foreign to their understanding of religious education (Ryan, 1997, pp. 35-49).

The Second Vatican Council (1962-1965) marked a shift in Church thinking, and the Church's teaching on revelation was indicative of this. The influential document on revelation that emerged from the Second Vatican Council (1962-1965) was the *Dogmatic Constitution on Divine Revelation* (Abbott, 1966, pp. 107-132), commonly known as *Dei Verbum*. Prior to the Second Vatican Council (1962-1965), scripture and Church tradition were considered to be sources of revelation and, in light of this understanding, it was the teachers' role to hand on the truths of the faith. *Dei Verbum* made it clear that scripture and Church tradition were not sources of revelation, but rather witnesses to it. The Constitution stressed that God was the only source of divine revelation and that revelation was an ongoing process that God initiated (Abbott, 1966, p. 113). The Second Vatican Council (1962-1965) supported the view that God was not only revealed in past events but also through the present events experienced in ordinary life. The sacred and secular world needed to be understood as integral rather than separate in order to understand this enlightened view of revelation. With this perspective at the fore of current thinking, catechesis was seen as much broader than proclaiming the Church's salvation story. "If catechesis was to be meaningful for contemporary students in Australian Catholic Schools, it would need to emphasise and take account of the life experience and interests of students" (Ryan, 1997, p. 48).

## The Life-centred Approach

A key factor influencing the short life of the kerygmatic approach was the Second Vatican Council (1962-1965). The Catholic Church's authority and credibility had been called into question by many of the troubles of the twentieth century including "a worldwide economic depression, two world wars and the emergence of fascism and communism in the Church's backyard" (Lovat, 2002, p. 5). The aim of the Council was to deal with the problems facing the Church and to refocus the Church and renew its relationship with the modern world. The opening session of the Second Vatican Council in 1962 expressed this aim.

> In this assembly, under the guidance of the Holy Spirit, we wish to inquire how we ought to renew ourselves, so that we may be found increasingly faithful to the gospel of Christ. Coming together in unity from every nation under the sun, we carry in our hearts the hardships, and hopes of all the people entrusted to us. (Abbott, 1966, pp. 3-5)

Pope John XXIII wanted the Second Vatican Council (1962-1965) to consider some of the modern thinking coming from biblical scholars, theologians, social scientists and others. It was believed that embracing such new ideas would help to bring the Church into harmony with the modern world. The enlightened understanding of revelation portrayed in *Dei Verbum* was one way of strengthening the nexus between the Church and the modern world. It provided a platform for considering ways of encountering God through life experience.

*Dei Verbum* challenged catechetical theorists to consider new ways of teaching religious education. In the early 1970s religious educators in Australia were strongly influenced by the Jesuit theologian Amalorpavadass. He visited Australia in 1973, and his understanding of revelation was a major influence in developing a life-centred pedagogical approach to religious education. He argued that,

> Revelation calls for faith. Faith is a personal and living encounter with the living God, a total acceptance of the revealing and giving person by a loving surrender of one's life according to His word. All this should result in the sealing of a covenant and the realisation of a fellowship in love. Therefore our inter-personal relationship is one of dialogue, covenant and fellowship. Therefore man's [*sic*] response or reaction to God's revelation will be essentially attention and responsibility, expectation and listening, openness and acceptance, and reciprocal self-gift in a total surrender and dedication of oneself. This is what we call faith. (Amalorpavadass, 1973, p. 19)

The life-centred approach emphasised "the sharing of life experiences between students and teacher, reflection on this life experience, and the linking of this reflection with growth in knowledge and affective understanding of faith content" (Engebretson, 2002, p. 38). Catholic education leaders in Australia became convinced that the catechetical developments promoted by Amalorpavadass were valid. Their support of this approach was strengthened by the publication of the Australian Episcopal Conference's translation of the Italian document, *The Renewal of Education of Faith* (1970). Carlo Colombo, President of the Episcopal Commission of the Doctrine of the Faith and Catechesis, stressed in the preface of the Australian translation of the document support for the life-centred approach and the importance of personal reflection on life experiences (Colombo, 1970, p. xvi). The life-centred approach to religious education has been significantly entrenched in the Archdiocese of Melbourne since the early 1970s. The 1973, 1984 and 1995 *Guidelines for Religious Education for Students in the Archdiocese of Melbourne,* (*Guidelines*) have emphasised a pedagogical methodology which embodied this approach. This catechetical approach hinged on the understanding that catechesis was best explored through the life experiences of the students because God is revealed in their experiences. *Guidelines* systematised an interactive process consisting of four movements in the act of catechesis. The schema for the four-point plan consisted of the following teaching and learning process:

- Experience shared (we share our experiences)
- Reflection deepened (we reflect together)
- Faith expressed (we come to know our Catholic faith)
- Insights reinforced (we gain further insights and respond) (Catholic Education Office, Melbourne, 1995, p. 27; Engebretson, 2002, p. 38).

The Catholic Education Office produced a series of student resources for use in secondary and primary school religious education classes. *Come Alive* was produced for use in secondary schools and *Let's Go Together* was used widely in Catholic primary schools for the teaching of religious education. Figure 3 provides an excerpt from *Let's Go Together*. This highlighted the emphasis on the student's experience in the educative process.

**MY FIRST DAY**

I am really very happy
And it isn't hard to guess
'Cos mummy has been busy
And I am wearing my new dress.

I'm feeling very happy
And I hope that you are too
I've made a lot of friends today
And most of them are new.

I've got a brand new teacher
And another room as well
We're in a brand new family
So everything is swell.

---

What do you know about your new class?
How many boys are in your class?
How many girls are in your class?
How many children is that all together?
What is the name of your new teacher?

(Catholic Education Office, Melbourne, 1972, p. 4)

*Figure 3.* An excerpt from *Let's Go Together* which draws on the life experience of a student commencing a new class.

---

Engebretson et al., (2002) contextualised the emergence of the life-centred approach within the teachings emanating out of Second Vatican Council (1962-1965). They stated that:

> There were two main springboards for the life-centred approach to catechesis. In the Catholic Church the springboard was theological and came from the formulation of the doctrine of Revelation (*Dogmatic Constitution on Divine Revelation, Dei Verbum* 1965). The understanding of revelation stressed that God was revealed in people and in the events of life. There was also renewed emphasis on God as revealed in the here and now. Religious education integrated these broad understandings of God's revelation into a new emphasis in religious education that had life experience as the focus. (p. 8)

The life-centred approach to catechesis presumed that students were ready and willing to be incorporated into the life of the Church. As such, its starting point was theological and catechetical. The underlying assumption implied that students had an understanding of Church teaching and the person of Christ. The pedagogical techniques of the doctrinal and kerygmatic approaches had drifted into the consciousness of those promoting the life-centered approach. Such a presumption was unfounded for the many students populating Catholic schools in Australia from the 1970s onwards. Immigration patterns had diversified the population in Catholic schools to the extent that there was no longer a homogeneous expression of the Catholic faith. For many people in Australia the Church was no longer an unquestioned authority. Increasingly students and even their families were not involved in the faith life of the Church (Ryan, 1997, p. 63). Many students in Catholic schools were disconnected from faith and parish life and this made it very difficult to consider the revelation of God through their experiences. The lack of understanding of Church teaching and a personal relationship with Christ made it challenging for students and teachers to always make the link between life experience and faith. Attempts were made to bridge the gap by contextualizing the life experiences of the students within a particular framework. One approach which gained popular attention was shared Christian praxis (Groome, 1980), which saw the catechetical and theological focus of the life experience approach drift into an approach distinguished by critical educational rationale.

## The Shared Christian Praxis Approach

Groome (1991) defined shared Christian praxis as,

> ... a participative and dialogical pedagogy in which people reflect critically on their own historical agency in time and place and on their socio-cultural reality, have access together to Christian Story/Vision, and personally appropriate in community with the creative intent of reviewed praxis in Christian faith towards God's reign for all creation (p. 135).

In contrast to the life-centred approach, which was based on the theological and catechetical rationale of Amalorpavadass (1971, p. 16), shared Christian praxis was based on critical educational theories (Engebretson, 1997, p. 27) and was a response to the growing quest for human freedom. This quest was perceived as one of the major contemporary challenges facing the Christian tradition. The response within educational circles was to employ strategies where skills in critical self-reflection could be developed. "The goal of religious education, then, was not to deliver static 'truths', nor to determine certain attitudes, but to create critical participants to the ongoing life of the Christian community" (Lovat, 2002, pp. 24-25). Groome (1980) recommended a five -step religious education program known as the Shared Christian praxis model. The five steps were identified as:

- Naming the Present Action: (to reflect on present events and make distinctions between what was really happening and what should be happening)
- The Participants' Stories and Visions: (the beginning of critical reflection on the factors that led to the present situation. It was concerned with the 'why' questions: for example: Why do we do as we do?)
- The Christian Community Story and Vision: (aspects of the Christian story were remembered and told. Participants were provided with an opportunity to see their own experience in light of the Christian vision)

- Dialogue between the Inspirational Story and Participants: (in light of remembering the Christian story the participants' experiences were examined in light of what 'should be' as well as what actually 'is')
- A Decision for Future Action: (out of an understanding of the way it was and the way it should have been can emerge a decision to close the gap between the lived experience and the Christian vision. At this point praxis was considered to have developed) (Lovat, 2002, pp. 25-26; Ryan, 1997, p. 73).

In relation to general academic standards, shared Christian praxis was "as academically rigorous and challenging as any other approach" (Groome, 1991, p. 276) in that it emphasised critical self-reflection by initiating groups and individuals to think in a praxis model, rather than to learn theories. This could be achieved by providing a model that encouraged participants to reflect on their own feelings and actions, rather than what they should think or are told to think. The aim of the shared Christian praxis approach was to engage the whole person. It was more than an exercise in learning the cognitive dimensions of religious education. It also emphasised the development of faith. According to Groome (1991), shared Christian praxis,

> ...engages a person's whole 'being'; it subsumes cognition, affection and volition in synthesis as a self-in community who reflects and realises Christian identity and agency. Christian conation means 'being' and becoming Christian. (Groome, 1991, p. 30)

Shared Christain praxis has been very influential in Australia since the late 1980s. The Diocese of Parramatta in New South Wales has used the shared Christian praxis model in its religious education curriculum, and through particular practitioners, it has had an influence in other dioceses in Victoria (Ballarat, Sale and Sandhurst), Tasmania, South Australia and the Northern Territory (Bezzina, Gahan, McLenaghan & Wilson, 1997, p. 3).

The potential for shared Christian praxis to meet the requirements of religious education in Catholic schools was questioned by experts and practitioners (Lovat, 2002; see also, Engebretson, 2002; Liddy, 2002; Rossiter, 1988). Groome argued that it is inappropriate to separate 'education' from 'faith formation' in a religious education program (1991, p. 194), However, Rossiter (1988) argued that the separation was necessary in light of the diverse populations in Catholic schools where not all students are willing to participate at a personal faith level.

> The most appropriate slant or context for classroom religious education is to base it within an intellectual study ... In practice, one of the most stifling influences on a student's personal involvement in religious education is a perceived 'requirement' that they participate at a personal level. (Rossiter, 1988, p. 266)

Rossiter claimed that shared praxis,

> ... is an authentic catechesis for adults or youth commitment groups. Because the natural context for shared Christian praxis is different from a classroom with about 30 adolescents who attend religion lessons as part of the school's required core curriculum, the approach needs adaptation for classroom use. (1988, p. 269)

While Groome (1991) did not specifically associate catechesis with his shared Christian praxis model, Lovat argued that shared Christian praxis does take on some of the inaccurate assumptions of catechesis when applied to the classroom (2002, p. 31). Some similarities and differences between shared Christian praxis and the life-centred approach have been debated by Groome (1991) and Lovat (2002). Engebretson (1997) indicated that shared Christian praxis was based on educational rationale and the life-centred approach was based on theological principles. The paradigm of shared Christian praxis presented another pedagogical approach that grappled with the interplay between the educational and catechetical dynamic often associated with religious education.

## The Phenomenological Approach

An important factor contributing to the popularity of Groome's shared Christian praxis approach in Catholic schools was its ability to fit within an academic or educational context. An approach to religious education situated within an academic or educational context irrelevant to catechesis was known as the phenomenological approach. This approach which was wide-spread in Britain would eventually impact on religious education in Australia. A brief account of the British approach to religious education in schools is outlined with the intention of placing the Australian application of this approach in context with international trends. Unlike the social background influencing religious education in Australia, the education system in Britain enshrined Christian teaching in legislation.

The 1944 Education Act in the United Kingdom mandated the daily act of religious worship and instruction in all schools (Hull, 1984, pp. 5-7). Until the 1960s the teaching of religion in British schools was perceived as a confession of Christian faith or an application of Christian faith in the classroom (Hull, 1984, p. 29). From the 1960s the ethnic, cultural and religious diversity of the British population challenged the effectiveness of compulsory religious education taught from a Christian faith perspective. A wave of agreed syllabi in religious education appeared in the late 1960s, all with a central focus on Christianity. It was not until 1975 that a major breakthrough in teaching religious education from a phenomenological perspective was cemented in law. The *Birmingham Agreed Syllabus* and accompanying *Handbook* were published in that year and were based on Smart's phenomenological approach (Smart, 1968). The *Birmingham Agreed Syllabus* abandoned any intention to foster the faith of any particular religion. It focussed on the critical understanding of religion and it was taught and understood in the context of secular ideologies. Contrasting and comparing various religious traditions and non-religious alternatives such as humanism and communism was intended to shape a pupil's understanding of religion. The intention of the *Birmingham Agreed Syllabus* was that religious studies be impartial between the religions and the secular ideologies. The teacher was required to teach each religion represented in his or her classroom or school with the same spirit of thoughtful courteous appreciation and inquiry (Hull, 1984, pp. 29-34).

The legislation establishing and promoting education in Australia ensured that it remain a secular institution. However, concern about the value of teaching religious education in government schools gained momentum during the 1970s. During the 1970s and 1980s several state government inquiries in Australia were set up to review state education. The study of religion in Australian schools, it was argued, would help to promote tolerance in a population made up of people from diverse religious and cultural backgrounds. The government inquiries resulted in the following reports being tabled in various state parliaments: The Steinle Report (1973) of South Australia, the Nott Report (1977) of Western Australia, the Russell Report (1974) of Victoria, and the Rawlinson Report (1980) of NSW. By the 1980s each of the above mentioned states had commenced the process of implementing the study of religion in state schools. Opportunities for Australia's citizens to develop religious literacy began to be promoted through the state education systems. The philosophy behind most of the reports suggested that there was value in learning about religion in general and about the diverse religions present in Australian society (Lovat, 2002, pp. 33-34). The development of studies in religion in state schools had to take into consideration the inter-faith and secular composition of the student population. An approach to teaching and learning religion was employed that would respond to the diversity of inter-faith and secular populations present in schools. The phenomenological approach that was favoured in Britain and shaped the *Birmingham Agreed Syllabus* had a significant influence on school curricula in religious education in Australia.

Smart was the author of the phenomenological approach as it applied to the study of religion (Smart, 1968, 1974a, 1974b, 1978, 1979; see also Engebretson, et al., 2002, p. 10; Lovat, 1995, p. 8; Ryan, 1997, p. 102). The approach focussed on the content of what should be taught. It was concerned with the logic of religious education and with the consequences of that logic in a secular or religiously neutralist society (Smart, 1968, p. 7). The approach was founded on the theory that religion can be studied from the 'outside'. That is, one does not have to belong to the religious tradition or any religious tradition in order to learn about religion. A student taught by this method could gain an understanding of religious beliefs and in so doing become literate in the language of religion but would not be required to accept or approve of those beliefs. The phenomenological approach held the view that,

> … religion was a legitimate object of study because it developed distinctive skills and encouraged particular insights. Religion offered a view of the ways people organise and interpret their spiritual experiences and form systems by which to contain and communicate these to each other and to succeeding generations. (Lovat, 2002, p. 45)

The phenomenological approach to religious education had intentions that were clearly different from earlier theories of teaching and learning in religious education. The catechetical approach, including the catechism, the kerygmatic approach, the life-centred approach, and the shared Christian praxis approach were all associated with faith formation through catechesis. The phenomenological approach stood clearly in contrast, as its intention was to study religion objectively as a means of gaining insights about a religion from an outsider's perspective. It did not require that a student should have a personal commitment to a particular creed in order to have a deep understanding and appreciation of religion. Acceptance or approval of religious beliefs was not a requirement for understanding such beliefs. Smart (1979) identified a structure for the study of a religion. His work indicated that, from a phenomenological perspective, a religion could be studied through the examination of phenomena such as rites of passage, myths, holy times, holy places, symbols, pilgrimages, scriptures, temples and priests. Studying religion from a phenomenological perspective would enable a student to gain insight into the world of religion.

Shared Christian praxis provided opportunities for students to explore knowledge about religious issues within the context of a Christian faith tradition. The phenomenological approach placed an emphasis on knowledge as part of social education.

24

The phenomenological approach to the study was extremely influential in Britain, Europe and Australia, where it presented a non-judgemental way of studying religions as phenomena of human existence, and thus of contributing to greater understanding and tolerance of religious groups within a local community. (Engebretson, 2004, p. 4)

Habel and Moore (1982) applied, tried, tested and adapted Smart's phenomenological approach in Australia and another distinguishable yet interrelated approach to religious education emerged.

## The Typological Approach

Smart was not concerned with how religion should be taught in schools. He was concerned with decisions about what content should be taught (Smart, 1968, p. 7), and such decisions would have implications about teaching methodology. Habel and Moore (1982), two Australian academics, focussed on the "how" question. They developed a theory that identified how Smart's phenomenological approach could be implemented in the formal religion classroom. Habel and Moore's typological approach was based on the understanding that "the modern world forces people increasingly to confront others with varying religious and cultural beliefs to their own" (Ryan, 1997, p. 105). Social cohesion could be more effective if students gained an understanding of the religious backgrounds of their neighbours. In this context the study of religion was perceived to have a social significance that could influence the views of many human beings. Habel and Moore (1982) held the view that students would benefit from learning about the types of component phenomena associated with religions. Habel and Moore's (1982) theory outlined eight 'types' or components shared by religious traditions which students were able to study in order to gain an insight into understanding a religion. The study of certain types or components originally identified by Habel and Moore were: beliefs, texts, stories, ethics, ritual, symbols, social structure and experience (1982, p. 71). Habel and Moore had developed Smart's phenomenological theory and applied it in a practical way for teachers and curriculum developers to implement in a classroom situation (Ryan, 1997, pp. 13-15).

During the 1970s and 1980s state governments responded to the pressure to introduce state accredited courses in religion in schools. "The intention was to offer courses of study that would be equivalent in intellectual rigour and standing to other curriculum areas" (Ryan, 1997, p. 106). State accredited courses in religion were required not to presume a confessional commitment from the students or teacher and to uphold that no one religion would be held in favour over another (Engebretson, 1991, pp. 9-11). Such an approach to religious education underpinned the phenomenological approach. In Australia, the theories of Smart, and Habel and Moore strongly influenced the design of the schema for state accredited courses in religion. By 1992 two courses in religion were fully accredited and implemented in Victoria. One course was called *Religion and Society* and the other *Texts and Traditions*. Both accredited courses in religion consisted of four semester units that could be studied. These courses relied heavily upon the phenomenological approach and the typological approach developed by Habel and Moore (Ryan, 1997, pp. 105-108). Phenomenology and typology have not only shaped the Victorian state accredited courses in religion but they have also formed the basis of the learning schema of the Melbourne Archdiocesan textbook series *To Know Worship and Love* at the secondary level. These Church sponsored textbooks which have been directed for use in Catholic schools are the focus of the curriculum change managed by the religious education coordinators involved in this study.

## A Text-based Educational Approach

This section of the chapter contextualises the text-based curriculum which is the focus of this study within an educational paradigm. The first part of this section explains the emergence of an educational approach to religious education in the Melbourne Archdiocese. This explanation provides a background for understanding the shift to a text-based curriculum which is underpinned by a strong knowledge-centred educational approach to learning and teaching in religious education. Therefore the second part of this section briefly outlines some of the issues that marked a shift towards an outcome based text-based curriculum. The following section explores the theoretical position underpinning the text-based curriculum in the Archdiocese and the relevance of outcomes based learning and teaching in religious education. Against this background this researcher will offer evidence to suggest that the text-based curriculum is theoretically situated within a knowledge-centred outcomes based educational paradigm. A detailed explanation of the theoretical position underpinning the text-based curriculum is vital as it provides a context for understanding the focus of this study that is the RECs' perspective about the management of change to this text-based curriculum.

## *The Emergence of an Educational Approach in the Melbourne Archdiocese*

The life-centred approach (early 1970s through to late 1990s) was situated within a catechetical framework. However during this time Rummery (1975) argued that a systematic approach to teaching the educational dimensions of religious education was paramount. In the following years Rossiter (1988) also emphasised that the intellectual study of religion was the most appropriate approach to use when teaching religious education in the formal religious education classroom (p. 266). These views were in contrast with catechesis which underpinned the life-centred approach.

Educational approaches to learning and teaching religious education similar to the phenomenological approach (Smart, 1978) and the typological approach (Habel and Moore, 1982) emphasised the cognitive dimension of learning. Unlike the catechetical approaches, the educational approaches did not assume that students or teachers subscribed to a particular religion or faith tradition. Knowledge about religion or a religious tradition could be taught neutrally and as an academic discipline (Grimmitt, 2000; Jackson, 2004).

As noted earlier, during the late 1970s and 1980s various state governments in Australia began to introduce state accredited religious education courses of study for senior secondary students. In Victoria, two state accredited courses were introduced in Catholic secondary schools, *Religion and Society* and *Texts and Traditions* (Engebretson, 1991, p. 9). The design of these courses, were strongly influenced by two educational approaches also discussed earlier in this chapter, the phenomenological approach (Smart, 1978) and the typological approach (Habel and Moore, 1982).

From the late 1970s until the introduction of the *To Know Worship and Love* textbook series in 2001 and 2002, two approaches underpinned religious education in Catholic schools in

26

Melbourne. One approach the life-centred approach was catechetical in its design and placed much emphasis on reflecting on life experience as a means to form students in the Catholic faith tradition. Alongside this approach students in Catholic secondary schools had an opportunity to study more academically rigorous state accredited religious education courses at senior level.

The Board of Studies (now the Victorian Curriculum & Assessment Authority, VCAA) had approved two state accredited courses, *Religion and Society* and *Texts and Traditions* and these courses were popular amongst senior students in Catholic secondary schools (Engebretson, 1991). It is arguable that the popularity of these courses stemmed from the fact that they were based on Habel and Moore's (1982) typological theory and promoted an educational approach thus enabling the study of religion to be equally accessible to all students regardless of their background. During the late 1980s and into the 1990s concerns about a student's ability to cope with the intellectual demands of these courses were expressed. Teachers and parents argued that senior students were barely literate in religion despite the compulsory nature of the subject at all levels of Catholic schooling (Constable, 1992). The life-centred approach with its emphasis on sharing life experiences had not adequately prepared students in Catholic schools for the rigorous academic challenges required in undertaking a state accredited religious education course (Constable, 1992). In order to prepare senior students to successfully undertake state based religious studies "a great deal of work had to be done with students to help them be academically ready for its intellectual demands" (Engebretson, 2002, p. 39). Against this background the introduction of knowledge-centred textbooks provided a vehicle to help prepare students and it also marked a shift in the approach to religious education in Catholic schools.

## *Towards an Outcomes Based Text-based Curriculum*

The decision to move towards an outcomes based text-based curriculum in religious education was not the result of one particular factor. There were various influences contributing towards this shift. Among these influences were a changing clientele in Catholic schools, the introduction of state accredited courses in religious education, and the Victorian government's emphasis on a general curriculum that emphasised outcomes based learning across the curriculum (VCAA, 2001).

Migration had a significant impact upon the changing clientele in Catholic schools. Resulting from immigration trends from the 1950s onwards the students populating Catholic schools were no longer a homogeneous group of Catholics inculcated in the ministerial and ecclesial life of the Church. Since the Second Vatican Council (1962-65) the populations that make up most Catholic schools in Australia have come from diverse religious and secular backgrounds (Engebretson, 2002; Liddy; 2002; Lovat, 2002; Rossiter; 1988). The life-centred approach was situated within a catechetical context and assumed that students belonged to and practised the Catholic faith tradition (Catholic Education Office, Melbourne, 1973; 1984; 1995). This approach received much criticism for this assumption as well as its emphasis on the lived experiences of students (Ryan, 1997). Some considered that this over emphasis was counter productive to students understanding the traditions and teachings of the Church (Constable, 1992). Another criticism of this catechetical approach with its emphasis on catechesis was that it excluded students who were not Catholic and not inculcated into the faith life of the Catholic Church (Engebretson, 2002; Liddy;

2002; Lovat, 2002; Rossiter, 1988). The ability of the religious education programs in Catholic schools to cater for all students was a concern (Engebretson, 2002).

Another factor influencing the move towards an outcomes based text-based curriculum was the state accredited religious education courses. The objective approach adopted in these two state accredited courses generated much interest in student learning reflected in the large numbers of students enrolling in them each year (Engebretson, 2000; 1991). The courses were more academically demanding (Engebretson, 2002) than school based courses that were underpinned by the life-centred catechetical model. However these courses exposed gaps in students' knowledge about the Catholic faith and Tradition. Parents and teachers were concerned that the life-centred approach had not effectively enabled students to learn about the Catholic faith and traditions (Constable, 1991). Discussions about an education in religious education with an emphasis on learning knowledge about a religious tradition were raised (Crotty & Crotty, 2000; Rossiter, 2000; Thomas; 2000).

An influential response to the questions raised about the shortcomings of the life-centred approach came from Cardinal Pell, the former Archbishop of Melbourne, who in 1997 called for curriculum reform in religious education and set up structures to establish a knowledge centred outcomes based approach to religious education throughout the Archdiocese (Pell, 2001; see also Engebretson, 2000, p. 30). It is probable that this decision was influenced by the Victorian government's well established outcomes based curriculum in Victoria (VCAA, 2001). Against this background it would seem a sensible move to adopt an outcomes based educational approach to religious education. The adoption of such an approach would address the concern about providing a religious education curriculum that was accessible to all students as well as provide a more accurate and consistent way of measuring a student's level of academic achievement. A knowledge centred outcomes based focus in religious education could also help to better prepare students with an appropriate preliminary background beneficial to undertaking stated accredited course in religious education.

## *Theoretical Position Underpinning the Text-based Curriculum in the Archdiocese of Melbourne*

Cardinal Pell believed that a more focussed approach to religious education could be achieved throughout the Archdiocese by establishing a text-based curriculum (Pell, 2001, p. 5).[4] As outlined in the Introduction section of this book, Cardinal Pell established an Episcopal Vicariate for Religious Education in the Archdiocese with the responsibility for producing a textbook series for use in Catholic schools and parishes throughout the archdiocese. Academic staff from Australian Catholic University, Melbourne campus were employed to write the secondary textbooks in the *To Know Worship and Love* series. Engebretson and Rymarz, the writers of the secondary textbooks, adapted Habel and Moore's (1982) typological schema for the secondary textbooks in the series. This decision marked a shift from the catechetical model underpinning the life-centred approach to a knowledge-centred educational approach to religious education in the Archdiocese. Engebretson

---

[4] An explanation of the term text-based curriculum and its origin has been outlined in the Introduction section of this book.

(2000) argued that the adaptation of the typological schema was a useful way of grouping topics in the *To Know Worship and Love* textbook series because it provided some theoretical continuity between the Year 7-10 curriculum and the state accredited religious education courses offered at Years 11 and 12. The *To Know Worship and Love* textbook series adapted the eight aspects of the typological schema of the *Religion and Society Study Design* (1999): beliefs, myths and sacred literature, rituals, symbols, sacred text, ethics, social structure and individual experience. The adaptation resulted in the textbooks containing six categories as a way of grouping the topics: beliefs, worship and symbol, story and scripture, ethics and values, Church and religious experience. In addition to the typological schema positioning the text-based curriculum within a knowledge-centred paradigm, there was an emphasis on knowledge-centred, outcomes based learning and teaching.

This educational approach underpinning the text-based curriculum initiative was intended to overcome much of the criticism emanating from the life-centred approach (Engebretson, 2002). The text-based curriculum was also influenced by outcomes based learning which was influencing curriculum development in many educational institutions throughout the western world.

## Outcomes Based Learning

In Australia, as in other western countries, curriculum development in education has been driven by forces of both an economic and political nature (McInerney, 2004). Outcomes based approaches to school curriculum design have been trialled in Europe and North America as well as Australia. Supporters of this approach argue that outcomes based learning helps to raise the standard of student learning (Ryan, 1998). The *Victorian Curriculum Standards Framework II* (2001) emphasised an outcomes based approach to learning and teaching. However this document did not apply to or was not binding upon religious education in Catholic schools. In view of these trends, the teachers books supporting the *To Know Worship and Love* (Elliott, 2001a; 2001b; 2002a; 2002b) textbook series organised the learning and teaching process within the broad range of outcomes based learning.

The outcomes based learning associated with the text-based curriculum was centred within a knowledge centred educational paradigm. This was on par with outcomes based learning trends in other key learning areas (VCAA, 2001). Support for an educational approach to religious education can also be found within authoritative statements of the Church. For example, Cardinal Pell authorised the text-based curriculum acknowledging its "… distinctive emphasis on the cognitive dimension of learning, that is on knowing the content of Catholic teaching …" (Pell, 2001, p. 5). Another authoritative statement supporting an educational approach to religious education is located within the *General Directory for Catechesis* (CC, 1998).

> It is necessary, therefore that religious instruction in schools appear as a scholastic discipline with the same systematic demands and the same rigour as other disciplines. It must present the Christian message and the Christian event with the same seriousness and the same depth with which other disciplines present their knowledge. (CC, 1998, # 73).

## Cognitive and Affective Outcomes Associated with the Text-based Curriculum

The teachers' books supporting the text-based curriculum included both cognitive and affective outcomes. Cognitive outcomes focus on knowledge content and affective outcomes are achieved when students interact with the knowledge in a personal, applied way (de Souza, 2005; see also Engebretson et al., 2002).

It was suggested earlier in this chapter that each new approach to religious education is a successor of those that have gone before it (Grimmitt, 2000). The text-based curriculum initiative was also influenced by preceding approaches to religious education. It applied theories and adapted strategies from typology (Habel and Moore, 1982) and phenomenology (Smart, 1978) which have been located within an educational paradigm. In addition to this, attention to the affective dimension of learning, a feature of the life-centred catechetical approach promoted in *Guidelines* (Catholic Education Office, Archdiocese of Melbourne, 1995) was implied in the text-based curriculum. Perhaps this suggests an attempt to maintain a link with the catechetical tradition of learning and teaching in religious education in the Archdiocese.

The outcomes based educational approach to religious education emanating from the *To Know Worship and Love* textbook series emphasises the acquisition of knowledge within an overarching catechetical framework. The inclusion of affective outcomes for each content chapter in the textbook series suggests that within the affective domain students can interact with the knowledge which has been the starting point for teaching and learning in this approach. The combination of teaching towards the achievement of cognitive outcomes and the opportunity to explore the cognitive learning within the affective domain can "aid the Church to fulfil its catechetical mission" (CCE, 1977, # 52). Figure 4 provides examples of cognitive and affective learning outcomes from chapter nine of *To Know Worship and Love Teaching Companion -Year 10* (Elliott, 2002c). Note how the cognitive outcome focuses on the specific knowledge the student will gain by the end of the unit, and the affective outcome is concerned with providing an opportunity for the student to interact with the cognitive content in a personal or intuitive way.

---

**Chapter 9 -THE GOOD NEWS OF MARK**

**Cognitive outcome**

**By the end of this unit students will be able to:**
- Describe the structure of Mark's gospel, explaining the term 'chiastic'
- Describe the kind of kingship displayed by Jesus in contrast to that of Pilate.
- Describe the role of the centurion in Mark's account of Christ's crucifixion.

**Affective outcome**

**By the end of this unit students will have an opportunity to:**
- Reflect on their own feelings when reading about the events leading up to and including Jesus' death. (Elliot, 2002, pp. 81-83)

*Figure 4.* An example of a cognitive and affective outcome.

---

*Summary of the Theoretical Position Underpinning the Text-based*
*Curriculum*

Typology (Habel and Moore, 1982), phenomenology (Smart, 1978) and knowledge-centred outcomes based learning and teaching (Buchanan, 2004) have informed the theoretical position underpinning the text-based curriculum. These features situate the text-based curriculum within an educational paradigm that is primarily concerned with the acquisition of knowledge. Cardinal Pell, who instigated this curriculum initiative with an emphasis on the acquisition of knowledge, suggested that it was also consistent with the catechetical approaches that had preceded it in the Melbourne Archdiocese (Pell, 2001, p. 5).

The text-based curriculum initiative based on the *To Know Worship and Love* textbook series complements a knowledge-centred, outcomes-based educational approach to learning and teaching in religious education. The attention to affective outcomes suggests that while this educational approach is knowledge-centred, it does not ignore its catechetical potential to act as a vehicle for spiritual and personal faith formation in the Catholic tradition through attention to knowledge, understanding and critical inquiry (Engebretson et al., 2002, p. 19). Figure 5 locates on a continuum the various approaches to religious education, which have informed its development in the Archdiocese of Melbourne.

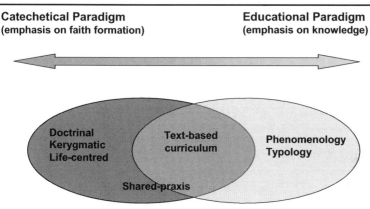

**Catechetical Paradigm**
**(emphasis on faith formation)**

**Educational Paradigm**
**(emphasis on knowledge)**

Doctrinal Kerygmatic Life-centred

Text-based curriculum

Phenomenology Typology

Shared-praxis

*Figure 5.* Approaches that inform(ed) the orientation of religious education within Catholic schools in the Archdiocese of Melbourne.

The distinctions drawn between the approaches suggest differences in the theoretical positions underpinning them. However the interlocking rings imply that each approach is not mutually exclusive. For example, the text-based curriculum can be viewed as a channel to spiritual development as well as personal and communal faith through attention to knowledge, understanding and critical inquiry (Engebretson et al., 2002, p. 19; see also Elliot and Rossiter, 1982; Rossiter, 1981a).

## Conclusion

This chapter has reported on the approaches which have informed learning and teaching in religious education in Catholic schools in the Archdiocese of Melbourne. The text-based curriculum initiative is situated within the context of other approaches and they have been presented chronologically as a means by which to understand the development and application of each approach.

Since the time of European settlement the trends in religious education in Australian Catholic schools have been influenced by worldwide developments. While religious education in Catholic schools has a significant relationship with catechesis and the evangelising mission of the Church, there has been an apparent shift in emphasis from catechesis to knowledge-centred approaches. The knowledge-centred approaches to religious education in Catholic schools gain credibility in the formal religious education classroom when understood not only as an academic discipline but also as a channel to personal and communal faith (Rossiter, 1981a; 1981b).

In the following chapter, literature is reviewed to demonstrate the immediate context of this study within research, as well as the broader areas of academic thinking which provided a frame out of which the research has arisen and in which the data will be analysed.

# CHAPTER TWO
# Research on Change and Leadership in Religious Education

The previous chapter of this book situated the text-based curriculum initiative within the context of approaches to teaching and learning in religious education, thus enabling the change to be understood in terms of its interrelatedness to pre-existing approaches. In order to investigate, discuss and analyse how RECs managed the change to a text-based curriculum in Catholic secondary schools in the Archdiocese of Melbourne, it is necessary to review a range of related literature. The purpose of this chapter and the following chapter is to review the areas of literature relevant to this current research, providing a framework in which the theory generated from this study can be discussed and analysed. Given that this study seeks to study the perspectives of RECs' in secondary schools in the Archdiocese of Melbourne regarding their management of a particular curriculum change, this chapter reviews literature about educational and curriculum change, as well as literature associated with the role of RECs in Australia. Chapter three subsequently reviews literature concerning textbooks in education and textbooks in religious education. The literature reviewed provides a context in which to situate the RECs' management of this change to a text-based curriculum.

## Educational and Curriculum Change

Fullan (1993) suggested that issues associated with curriculum change are not significantly different from those concerning educational change in general. This study is primarily concerned with the management of a particular curriculum change and therefore literature concerning educational change is drawn upon to the extent that it provides insights into understandings about curriculum change. This section of the chapter considers literature on change as it applies to curriculum in educational contexts. The following section of the chapter will: outline the origins by which change may be instigated; provide a summary of forces outside the school that influence change; present an overview of "top down" (Morris, 1995) change; and explore the significance of attitudes regarding change and the interplay between change and professional growth; and explore some factors that assist and impede change.

## *Origins by Which Change May Be Instigated*

The change to a text-based curriculum in religious education in Catholic schools in the Archdiocese of Melbourne can be positioned within the context of broader educational and curriculum change.

One way of viewing change is as a result of trying to improve shortcomings in student learning. In this context Smith and Lovat (2003) suggested that curriculum work such as planning, development, management, implementation and evaluation is concerned with change. There are two main origins by which change can be instigated (Marsh, 1997). Change can be a result of forces occurring from outside the school environment or from forces generated from within the school. The source from which the change initiative originates will determine whether a school will be responsible for adopting or inventing or adapting a particular change.

## Appropriation of Change: Adopted – Invented – Adapted

Schools adopt change in situations where the curriculum change originates from forces outside of the school, and change initiatives that originate from within the school are referred to as "inventing" (Marsh, 1997). Inventing curriculum change and strategies for curriculum change generally occur within the school context when teachers are focussed on improving shortcomings related to student learning. Brickell (1972) identified a third strategy known as adaptation. "Adaptation can be understood as the invention of modifications in what is being adopted" (p. 399). Adaptation of a curriculum innovation occurs as a result of the interplay between adoption and invention of a curriculum initiative. Brickell (1972) perceived adaptation as the superior alternative to both adoption and invention, especially in situations where those responsible for managing the curriculum initiative have a clear understanding of the principles and spirit underlying the innovation.

A pertinent question for this study concerns the extent to which the curriculum change, which was the subject of this research, was adopted or adapted. It is arguable that the Catholic authorities who mandated the curriculum change expected an adoption acquiescence. However much literature on teacher appropriation of curriculum change shows that the process of implementing a curriculum initiative is more complex than this (Cornbleth, 1990; Elliot, 1998; Johnson, 2000a; Marsh, 1997; Smith and Lovat, 2003). The research reported in this book adds to understandings about the process of change in the context of a highly specific, and mandated, "top down" (Morris, 1995) curriculum change.

Marsh (1997) suggested that forces outside of the school are able to influence the development of curriculum initiatives and change. Brady and Kennedy (2003) and Lee (2001) have commented on the ability of outside forces such as those discussed in the following paragraphs, to influence curriculum change.

## Forces Outside of the School Influencing Curriculum Change

Brady and Kennedy (2003) suggested that curriculum can be understood as something beyond a private transaction between teacher and student. Outside forces such as parent, government and business groups are noted in the literature as influencing school curriculum.

The role of parents in setting curriculum directions is acknowledged (Newport, 1992). In 1946 the Australian Council of State School Organisations (ACSSO) was established on behalf of the parents of students. It was made up of the eleven school/parent organisations that operated in various Australian states and territories. In 1962 the Australian Parents' Council (APC) was formed and brought together state and territory non-government school parent associations. Both school parent groups had been committed to the belief that parents have a role to play in the curriculum at all levels of education. The Victorian Curriculum Assessment Authority has a "parent member who has broad experience in local school groups and in parent groups that exert a State-wide influence" (Brady & Kennedy, 2003, p. 22). At the local level, opportunities for parents to be involved in setting the curriculum have been at the discretion of the school.

However the extent to which parents have been involved in setting the curriculum has been marginal. Most "parents work at the margins of either schools or school authorities, inserting themselves individually where they have a concern about their own children and collectively where there is sufficient agreement around a particular issue" (Brady & Kennedy, 2003, p. 22). In relation to this study there appears to be no evidence that consultation with a body representing the views of parents with regard to the text-based religious education curriculum was undertaken. The writers of the *To Know Worship and Love* textbook series and some other personnel involved in the textbook project were in fact parents. However, their responsibilities and involvement in the project were due to their expertise in other areas relevant to the project, rather than to reflect the views of a parent body. This researcher's interviews with RECs regarding their perspectives on the management of the change which is the focus of this study, did not reveal that consultation with a parent representative group was crucial to the management of this change.

Lee (2001) explored school reform initiatives in Japan, Korea, England and the United States, and indicated that curriculum in schools has gained much influential attention from governments. Brady and Kennedy (2003) suggested that governments have an interest in school curriculum because they understand its capacity to act as a mechanism of social and economic development. Other groups within the broader public domain also have an interest. The business community has an interest in school curriculum as a means of developing productive workers. It "is in no doubt that the curriculum is important and that it must be structured in a particular way to deliver outcomes that are relevant to employment opportunities and the economic needs of society" (Brady & Kennedy, 2003, p. 5).

Religious groups have also demonstrated an interest in school curriculum. In Australia some religious groups have sought to influence school curriculum by establishing their own schools. For instance, approximately one fifth of the student population in Victoria is educated in Catholic schools (Engebretson, 2002) and a religious bias underpins the delivery of curriculum in such schools.

The Catholic Church and particularly those who look to the future of the institution, such as bishops, show great interest in the religious education curriculum. Bishops are responsible for Catholic education within their respective dioceses. There is a sparsity of recent literature concerning the influence of bishops in relation to curriculum reform in Australian Catholic schools. In recent times two archbishops have been active in instigating a major curriculum reform in religious education and this initiative underpins this study. Cardinal Pell, the former Archbishop of Melbourne, and Archbishop Hart, the current Archbishop of Melbourne have been significant outside influences on curriculum reform in religious education within Catholic schools. The text-based curriculum initiative was a "top down" (Morris, 1995) curriculum reform instigated by

35

Cardinal Pell and each Catholic school in the Melbourne Archdiocese was required to implement this curriculum reform.

> As Archbishop of Melbourne, I decided that the time had come for a more focussed approach to religious education by way of a text-based          curriculum. This change is made in continuity with all the good work accomplished in the past. Carried out gradually, after much consultation,    the text-based curriculum builds on current "best practice" in our schools. It maintains a "call to faith" model of catechesis that my predecessors have consistently required. (Pell, 2001, p. 5)

Taking over from Pell, Hart also maintained this curriculum initiative. His comments stated below suggest that a bishop's ability to influence curriculum has social as well as educational implications.

> In particular the text-based curriculum program implemented by my predecessor, Archbishop George Pell, will continue. This will ensure that religious education in our schools gives young people a knowledge of the Catholic teaching on faith and morals and a realisation of its relevance to their lives and contemporary society. (Hart, 2002, p. 6)

His vested interest in the social implications of this "top down" (Morris, 1995) curriculum reform is unquestionably apparent in the following comment. "We want to offer our young people a religious education based on truth, able to withstand the secular onslaughts of our post-modern society and yet always related to the lives of children and youth" (Hart, 2002, p. 6).

Outside forces such as governments, the business community, and the Catholic Church can have an influence on how school curriculum is constructed in Catholic schools in Australia. The form that a curriculum takes represents a compromise between groups/individuals in society seeking to influence the education of young people. Curriculum therefore cannot be neutral as it represents the view(s) of various groups (Brady & Kennedy, 2003, p.11). The particular curriculum innovation, which is the focus of this study, has been influenced by outside forces. The discussion of this "top down" (Morris, 1995) curriculum reform instigated by the former Archbishop and supported by the current Archbishop will contribute to the limited body of current literature relating to the influence outside forces such as authorities within the Catholic Church may have on curriculum reform within the school.

## Top Down Curriculum Change

The term "top down" curriculum refers to curriculum innovation that is prescribed by a centralised body (Morris, 1995). Marsh and Bowan (1987) suggested that "top down" strategies are most effective when the content of the reform is targeted towards all students, when external pressures drive the curriculum innovation and when textbooks support the reform. The specific curriculum that was investigated in this review has had an impact on all primary and secondary students in the Archdiocese of Melbourne from preparatory level through to Year 10. The reform was supported by the use of a series of textbooks relevant to each specific year level and was driven by the Episcopal Vicariate for Religious Education under the direction of the Catholic Archbishop. These circumstances are consistent with the criteria described by Marsh and Bowman (1987). Among other things, the research reported in this book will provide insights into the extent to which these conditions make for effective curriculum change.

## *Adopting or Adapting Top Down Curriculum Initiatives*

"Top down" (Morris, 1995) approaches to curriculum innovation require schools to adopt or adapt the prescribed curriculum initiative. Morris (1995) revealed that there was a difference between the curriculum innovation prescribed by a centralised body and the real curriculum implemented in the classroom. The classroom teachers who put the innovation into practice ultimately decide what aspects of the curriculum innovation will be implemented. The role of the teacher in the management of a curriculum innovation has not been underestimated in the existing body of literature (Carr & Kemmis, 1983; Elliot, 1998; Fullan, 1993; Hargreaves, 1998; Johnson, 2000b; Marsh, 1997). Marsh (1997) indicated the crucial role teachers play in the implementation of a curriculum innovation in the following way:

> Curriculum starts as a plan. It only becomes a reality when teachers implement it with real students in a real classroom. Careful planning and development are obviously important, but they count for nothing unless teachers are aware of the product and have the skills to implement the curriculum in their classrooms. (p. 156)

The real curriculum translated into practice is one that is negotiated or adapted in the classroom between student and teacher. Boomer (1982) argued that the students have a role to play in decisions made about the curriculum. Brady and Kennedy (2003) suggested that despite all the stakeholders exercising influence over the curriculum it is the teachers and students who have the most influence over the curriculum.

> Thus, while policy makers plan the curriculum and seek to involve stakeholders in the planning process, it is at the local level that some of the most critical decisions are made: decisions by students and teachers. In the end it is teachers and students who exercise the ultimate control over the curriculum, although the boundaries are becoming more defined and accountability mechanisms more prominent. (Brady & Kennedy, 2003, p. 25)

Boomer (1982) suggested that what is negotiated between the teacher and the student will influence the way in which the curriculum is adapted in the classroom.

"Top down" (Morris, 1995) curriculum initiatives that originate from forces outside the school are dependent on personnel within the school to manage and implement the change initiative. The attitudes of those involved in managing and implementing change within the school is represented in an existing body of literature, which is now explored.

## *Significance of Attitudes Regarding Change*

According to Marsh (1997) there is a significant attitudinal element involved in implementing new curriculum and in determining what is actually implemented. Curriculum implementation is not about transmitting what has been agreed to or decided upon, but rather about bargaining with and transforming those responsible for putting the curriculum innovation into practice (p. 156). Literature concerning the influence of the attitudes, beliefs and capacities of teachers in the process

37

of implementation is plentiful (Cornbleth, 1990; Dalton, 1988; Hargreaves, 1998; Lewis, 1988; Marsh, 1997; McLaughlin, 1987; Werner, 1987). Hargreaves (1998) has indicated the importance of attending to the difficulties, constraints and tensions associated with curriculum change (pp. 558-575). Dalton (1988) confirmed that implementing curriculum change involved the representation of sub-cultures and interest groups, which have the capacity to pull the school in many directions (p. 7). These situational factors are one aspect of the tensions associated with curriculum change. Another aspect is the human characteristics particularly those of teachers involved in curriculum change.

A question for this research is the extent to which attitudes about the change to a text-based curriculum have had an impact on the management of the change. The significance of attitudes, particularly in terms of pedagogical implications, rationale and content relevant to the change is an area this study explores. According to Stenhouse (1975) "Most innovation changes both subject content and method. As innovators, teachers are asked to take on, initially at least, the burdens of incompetence" (p. 18). An important requirement of any teacher involved in change concerns developing proficiencies in order to master and use a curriculum innovation.

## *Interplay Between Change and Professional Growth*

While involvement in curriculum change can be challenging for the teacher it may also contribute to the professional growth of a teacher (Fullan, 1993; Hargreaves, 1997; Johnson, 1995; 1996; 2000a; Marsh, 1997; Stenhouse, 1975). Stenhouse (1975) considered the challenge curriculum innovation can have on a teacher's sense of professional competence particularly in situations where their skills and values are tested. Elliot (1998) argued that there can be no curriculum change without professional growth particularly for teachers as researchers of their own practice, in schools and classrooms (p. 17). The task of the teacher is to find out how to use the new curriculum innovation as effectively as possible. Marsh (1997) suggested that in these circumstances the dominant management questions for the teacher tends to be: How do I do it? Will I ever get it to work smoothly? To whom can I turn to get assistance? Am I doing what practice requires? and What is the effect on the learner?

For the teacher, change involves exploring unfamiliar pedagogical approaches, and forming new partnerships with colleagues, parents and other members of the educational community. Hargreaves (1997) described this as post-modern professionalism and emphasised the importance of teachers developing content knowledge and technical skill development, as well as competence to participate effectively in the face of continuous educational change (pp. 86, 99-108). Teachers are the major actors in the change process, and those who have the mindset to contend with the complexity of the change forces are well placed to shape learning and teaching environments that suit the needs of students (Johnson, 1996, p. 5). Fullan (1993) also acknowledged the teacher as the main participant in the change process, and suggested the importance of building learning societies that establish connections between internal and external environments that help to contend with complex change forces (p. 41). Johnson (1995) suggested that a new professionalism can emerge from a culture of change where teachers may explore new opportunities to take up new roles in

38

learning communities, which are characterised by the desire for improved learning and teaching environments which benefit the whole community (p. 3).

Literature relating to educational change has explored the quest for schools to take control and make sense of the change forces that have an impact on the school environment (Fullan, 1993; Fullan & Hargraves, 1992; Fullan & Steigelbauer, 1991; Hargreaves, 1994). Teachers who were open to continuous learning as well as demonstrating skills in working collaboratively, were more likely to bring about educational change (Fullan, 1993, p.46). For curriculum leaders such as RECs, a possible aim would be to provide a culture where changes are related to the needs within the community. Change can be effective if resources as well as the structure and relationships within the school culture support it. Educational change results in the professional growth of the teacher not only in the technical knowledge and skills of the teaching and learning process, but also in the attitudinal and behavioural aspects and the teachers' professional beliefs and understandings.

Teachers learn best when learning is focussed on their needs and their real work, when it involves reflective practice, when it provides the solution to a problem and when it contributes to the desired outcomes for the whole organisation (Johnson, 2000a). Teacher learning thus becomes integral to the work of the implementation and evaluation of the learning and teaching process.

However the pace of change can lead to resistance to change and professional growth (Hargreaves, 1994). Pressure on schools to keep up with the pace of change has contributed to a growth in the work of teachers. This can be identified in factors such as increased work demand, expectation, complexity and accountability. The intensification of demands on the teacher in the workplace has the potential to mitigate against professional growth in teachers (Hargreaves, 1994, pp. 14-16, 108). The genuine implementation of curriculum innovation does not occur unless teachers become personally committed to ensuring its success (Hoyle, 1972, p. 385). Resistance to change is a natural response experienced by many teachers and there is little benefit in forcing such change upon unwilling teachers (Hoyle, 1972, p. 394). To change the curriculum implies changing people and institutions (Taba, 1962, p. 391). Minimising resistance to change, according to some of the literature, requires the development of a culture of change within the school where professional growth can be fostered (Fullan, 2004; 2001; 1993; Hargreaves, 1998, Johnson, 2000a). Schools that take control of the forces for change and shape them to suit the needs of their students and the learning and teaching environment can contribute to the professional growth of teachers (Johnson, 1996, p. 86).

This study will contribute to the existing body of knowledge which has explored the complementarity between curriculum change and professional growth. This nexus can be viewed as one factor that is able to optimise the management of curriculum change.

To this point this chapter has explored literature about educational change as it applies to curriculum change. It has emphasised that change may be adopted, adapted or invented. It has also considered the potential influence forces from outside the school may have on influencing curriculum change. The significance of attitudes regarding change and the interplay between change and professional growth were also examined. The following section explores factors that assist change.

39

**Factors That Assist Change**

Certain literature explores the factors that contribute to effective change in school curriculum and the importance of the teacher and organizational structure in the process of change (Fullan, 2004; 1993; Scott, 1999; Smith & Lovat, 2003). Teachers who understand the nature of the change can assist by being involved in the planning process and by establishing support and feedback networks for staff. In addition an organisational climate that fosters an open supportive environment, and has appropriate staff who are committed and capable is also considered as assisting change. The extent to which the teachers are involved in implementing the change can also affect the efficacy of the change. The ability to communicate, negotiate and work cooperatively are characteristics that have been identified from research as factors that are important to successful change (Berman, 1980; Jackson, 1992; Fullan, 2004; 2001a). Change can be assisted by certain factors which are discussed in the following paragraph (Smith and Lovat, 2003).

*A School's Previous History of Change*

If a school staff has been successful in bringing about change in the past, according to Smith and Lovat (2003), then it is likely to be more willing to engage in a curriculum change than a school staff that has not. They also indicated that schools have less than a fifty percent chance of achieving a desired result from any change process. Furthermore, small changes are likely to be more successful than larger changes. However larger changes are likely to have a higher success rate if they are divided into sequential and achievable parts or phases (p. 209).

*Proposal for Change*

Teachers involved in change must have the capacity to bring about change (Durrant & Holden, 2006). If change is to be successful it is important that each person understand the change in the same way. School staff members need to have an explicit and shared understanding of the problem. If the problem is clearly and mutually understood by each person then the potential for ambiguity and abstract discussion can be minimized, and less emphasis placed on convincing people about the change. In addition, school staff members need to clearly identify and share reasons for the change. Furthermore appropriate time needs to be given for staff to negotiate and explore with one another proposed changes in collaborative ways (Smith and Lovat, 2003).

*Collaborative Cultures: A Means to Assist Curriculum Change*

Literature relating to curriculum and educational change suggests that collaborative cultures assist the process of effective change (Fullan, 1999; Hargraves, 1994; Fullan & Hargraves, 1991; Lieberman, 1990). The advantages of collaborative cultures are numerous and Brady and Kennedy (2003) have identified several. They have suggested that they promote opportunities for teachers to learn from each other. This can be achieved by observing each other's learning and teaching strategies. Another advantage is the sharing of knowledge and insights that are gained as a result of collegial work relating to a change initiative. The feedback from peers and the opportunity to share insights can help to establish a collective body of knowledge and expertise owned by the group rather than individual teachers (Frost & Durrant, 2002). Collaborative cultures can also help to reduce the workload of teachers and alleviate the stress and burden of change by making it a shared commitment (Fullan, 2001a). A collaborative culture can provide an opportunity for teachers to create clear boundaries within which the change may take place. This can help to reduce the level of anxiety and uncertainty associated with change (Brady & Kennedy, 2003, pp. 312-313).

These favourable aspects should be viewed in the context of the main criticisms of collaborative cultures. The individuality and creativity of the teacher has the potential to be compromised in situations where collaboration requires an emphasis on conformity (Hargreaves, 1994). There is also a possibility of contriving collaboration as an administrative mechanism. This could lead to the restraint of the desire for teachers to collaborate (Hargreaves, 1994).

## Support to Teachers Involved in Change

Schools change only because individuals themselves have changed (Fullan, 1999) and educational change challenges teachers' perceptions of themselves and their own competencies (Smith and Lovat, 2003, p. 210). Attention to the issues where people are most likely to be affected by change may help to assist the change process. According to Smith and Lovat (2003) attention to four significant issues can assist the change process. The first and most important issue concerns feelings and perceptions. Change challenges one's beliefs, perceptions and ways of working with established practices. Change concerns people more than things (Fullan, 1999; 1987; 1982; Stenhouse, 1975) and therefore strategies that promote change must heed people's feelings. The second key issue concerns conflict. People will not always perceive things the same way. Smith and Lovat (2003) suggested that if change does not involve some conflict then the change is not likely to be important or significant (p. 195). If those managing a curriculum change can expect that there will be conflict and accept conflict as a positive force for change then the change process can be assisted by planning ways to manage the conflict as part of a strategy for change (Smith and Lovat, 2003, p. 195). The third issue noted by Smith and Lovat (2003) refers to a change dynamic involving a phase where initial feelings and conflicts as well as the need for support can be intense. The change process may be assisted if strategies and resources are provided to support people during this potentially intense time. The fourth point Smith and Lovat (2003) made emphasised that change is concerned with process not product. Curriculum change can be assisted by establishing strategies that help to deal with the process and not just the change product. Smith and Lovat have indicated that "too many attempts towards change in education have not recognised these features nor provided ways to deal with them" (p. 195). The research reported in this book will make a contribution to the literature in this area.

## Commitment to Change

Effective change in curriculum requires commitment by all those involved in implementing the change. It is particularly important that the school principal and other leaders within the school actively support the change (Smith and Lovat, 2003). The chances of the change succeeding are limited if the school leaders are not committed to it, and are not seen to be supporting the change (Frost & Durrant, 2002). Ultimately teachers must also be committed to the change since they must implement it in the classroom (Durrant & Holden, 2006).

This section of the literature review has explored the notion that humans play an important role in assisting change. Those who understand the nature of the change are more likely to support it and provide feedback about the effectiveness of the change. As already stated a school's previous change history can be another factor that assists change (Smith & Lovat, 2003). In addition to these factors, enabling time to reflect on the change and to establish collaborative cultures committed to bringing about change have also been explored as factors that can assist change. The next section will outline some of the factors that impede curriculum change.

## Factors That Impede Change

### Diminishing Responsibilities of Teachers as Curriculum Leaders

During the 1970s greater importance was placed on the responsibility of the teacher to develop curriculum. Brady and Kennedy (2003) suggested that state intervention through statutory bodies such as the Victorian Curriculum and Assessment Authority and the Victorian Board of Studies, have considerably limited the role teachers exercise in curriculum development and change. The emerging responsibility of outside forces to develop curriculum has separated teachers from the responsibility of developing curriculum (Apple & Jungck, 1991). Instead they have been made responsible for implementing someone else's curriculum. Consequently "most teachers are at the end of a development process over which they [have] little control" (Brady and Kennedy, 2003, p. 24). The demarcation between curriculum development and implementation is considered to be one aspect of the de-professionalisation of teachers in Australia (Apple and Jungck, 1991). "Instead of professional teachers who care greatly about what they do and why they do it, we have alienated executors of someone else's plans" (Apple and Jungck, 1991, p. 3). A diminished responsibility for curriculum innovation can be regarded as a factor impeding change.

### Teacher Workload

Schools are generally part of a more centrally controlled system where outside forces and authorities continually make multiple demands upon schools. The pressure on schools to keep up with change is constant (Smith and Lovat, 2003, p. 208). Such demands often result in increased teacher workload and accountability. In some situations there is rarely any support given to teachers (Fullan, 1999) and this has led to a sense of teacher overload, which makes constant change seem unreasonable and difficult to keep up with.

### Working in Isolation

The organisation of a school can militate against effective communication and collaboration and contribute to teachers' sense of working in isolation. Schools are generally organised around individual classrooms, grades or subject departments. It is not uncommon for teachers to work alone in such an environment (Smith and Lovat, 2003). Working in isolation limits the potential for teachers to be informed as well as be part of the change initiatives and it can also limit the ability of a school to demonstrate change within the school (Brady & Kennedy, 2003, pp. 315-316). Separation and isolation are counter productive to facilitating change. The isolation of teachers in the workplace can contribute to the difficulties involved in using teacher expertise as well as initiating and implementing change. Effective change depends more upon communication and collaboration than upon individuals working in isolation (Smith and Lovat, 2003, p. 206).

While factors that impede curriculum change are widely known (Smith and Lovat, 2003; Marsh, 1997; Cornbleth, 1990; Elliot, 1998; Johnson, 2000a) the research reported in this study adds a new dimension to this knowledge, since it provides evidence of factors which impede change in a highly specialized curriculum innovation and one that was mandated from outside the school. In addition it provides information about curriculum change in a rarely researched dimension of curriculum, religious education.

The literature has explored the diminishing role of teachers as curriculum leaders as a key factor impeding change. The establishment of external statutory bodies with the authority to develop school curriculum has diminished the responsibilities of teachers as curriculum leaders. Greater demands and levels of accountability have been placed on teachers from outside forces as schools become more centralized to implement curriculum rather than develop it. The next section will investigate literature about RECs in Australia.

### The REC in Australia's Catholic Schools[5]

This section of the literature review surveys and analyses contemporary literature on the role of the REC in Australian Catholic schools in order to uncover the complexities, challenges, contradictions and possibilities that surround the role. In order to do this, the review summarises literature on the role of the REC from several Australian dioceses. In addition there is a review of more general literature on the leadership role of the REC, and finally, this section of the chapter explores contemporary Australian studies in some detail.

*How Has the Role of the REC Been Conceptualised?*

*The Archdiocese of Sydney*

The 1983 handbook entitled *The Religious Education Coordinator* published by the Catholic Education Office of Sydney (CEOS) indicated that the role of the REC was essentially concerned with curriculum development and planning, and with supporting and assisting in the professional development of religious education teachers (pp. 10-13). By 1988 the role began to emerge as a position of leadership where "the REC, as a delegate of the principal, has the responsibility of providing leadership in the development of the religious education program within the school (CEOS, 1988, p. 4). In 1989, the document, *Religious Education: Its Place In Catholic Secondary Education* (CEOS, 1989) broadened the role of the REC. In addition to leadership in religious education curriculum, the role was also perceived as one of witness to the mission of the Catholic Church in the school, as well as one responsible for promoting a school's Catholic ethos (L. Crotty, 1998, p. 10). By 1996 the role of the REC was regarded as a significant position of leadership in

---

[5] Parts of this section have been published in:
Buchanan, M. T. (2005b). The REC: Perspectives on a complex role within Catholic education. *Journal of Religious Education, 53* (4), 68-74.

both primary and secondary schools, particularly in the area of school policy and administration (CEOS, 1996).

The Catholic Education Office of Sydney argued that the role should be one of senior leadership, with representation on the school executive. "It is expected that the REC will have a very real part to play in formulating the total school policy and in the general administration of the school" (CEOS, 1996, p. 13). With the principal, the REC was required to develop an annual role description based on four areas outlined in a document titled, *Religious Education Coordinator: Conditions of Appointment and Employment* (CEOS, 1996). These areas were: leadership in the liturgical and faith life of the college; ensuring quality teaching and learning in the coordination of religious education programs; nurturing positive relationships in the school; and administering the organisational and record keeping aspects of the religious education program (CEOS, 1996). Section four of the document outlined selection criteria which applicants for the position of REC were required to meet.

In summary, the conceptualisation of the role of the REC as noted in key documents from the Catholic Education Office of Sydney includes: a) religious education curriculum development, planning, administration and implementation; b) the professional development of religious education teachers; c) leadership of and witness to the mission of the Church in the school; d) leadership in the development and maintenance of the Catholic ethos in the school; e) leadership in school policy and administration; f) leadership in the liturgical and faith life of the school; g) nurturing positive relationships in the school; and h) administering the organisational and record keeping aspects of the religious education program.

## *The Archdiocese of Hobart*

In 1978 the Catholic Education Office of the Archdiocese of Hobart (CEOH) recommended that each school appoint an REC. Subsequently, conceptions of the role were largely based on the 1984 document *The Religious Education Co-ordinator* (CEOH, 1984), which positioned the role within the concept of the Catholic school as a community in faith. The Religious Education Coordinator "shares the concern for the development and enrichment of the school, as a vital faith community" (CEOH, 1984, p. 4). The *Declaration on Christian Education (DOCE)* of the Second Vatican Council (1962-1965) had claimed that the role of the Catholic teacher was a vocation within the Church (1965, # 5), and the CEOH emphasised this, claiming that integral to the role of the REC was the responsibility to assist teachers in fulfilling their vocation. The role of the REC required not only professional competence, but also "a living commitment to the Catholic faith tradition [and] a living commitment to Catholic education" (CEOH, 1984, p. 7). The role involved "the development and implementation of a coordinated sequential program of religion..." (CEOH, 1984, p. 9), but also saw as essential to the work of the REC the planning of opportunities for reflection, prayer and liturgy which would "enable all to develop as people and to grow in their personal faith" (CEOH, 1984, p. 1). It also required attention to pastoral care and personal development programmes, retreat programs, staff development, development of the Catholic ethos of the school and resource management (CEOH, 1984, pp. 2 – 6). While the overall responsibility for religious education lay with the principal, the REC held a position of "responsible leadership within the school community working with, but always accountable to the principal" (CEOH, 1984, p. 2).

In summary, the dimensions of the role of the REC according to the CEOH were: a) assisting teachers to fulfil their vocation as Catholic educators; b) commitment to the Catholic tradition and to Catholic education; c) development and implementation of a sequential religious education curriculum; d) provision of a prayer, liturgy and retreat programme; d) provision of pastoral care and personal development programmes; e) development of the Catholic ethos of the school and e) management of religious education resources (CEOH, 1984, pp. 2 – 6).

## *Canberra/Goulburn, Darwin, Brisbane, Western Australia, Parramatta*

In 1979, the Catholic Education Office of the Archdiocese of Canberra and Goulbourn (CEOCG) published a document entitled *The Religious Education Coordinator in Catholic Schools.* This document emphasised the role of the REC as a position of leadership in "the Catholic school and the school's apostolic mission of the Church" (CEOCG, 1979, p. 1) and conveyed the following dimensions as integral to the role. Firstly the RECs were to be Catholic, committed to Catholic faith and moral values and able to be a witness to the life of the Church. They were required to promote the Catholic ethos in the school, inspire faith, share vision and build community, as well as offer spiritual leadership. Furthermore the REC was responsible for managing resources, enriching learning and developing excellence in the religious education curriculum (CEOCG, 1979, pp. 1 – 5).

In the diocese of Darwin (Catholic Education Office, Diocese of Darwin, [CEOD] 1998) an REC or an assistant principal (religious education) was expected to be an active member of the Catholic Church and demonstrate by deed and example a strong commitment to the work of the Church. They were seen as a role model for teachers, able to lead the prayer and liturgical life of the College and to develop the school as a faith community. The role also required the REC to have approved tertiary qualifications in religious education, be a member of the school executive and coordinate a religious education curriculum focussed on quality teaching and learning (CEOD, 1998, pp. 1 – 6).

The Archdiocese of Brisbane saw the role of the REC as one of leadership and management, and emphasised its educational dimension.

> The primary focus of the role is the enhancement of effective teaching and learning of students. The assistant principal religious education (APRE) has delegated responsibility for the leadership and coordination of the teaching of religion in the classroom. The APRE has shared responsibility for the religious life of the school community. (Catholic Education Office Brisbane, [CEOB] 1997)

In 1986, the Catholic Education Office of Western Australia produced a handbook entitled *The Religious Education Coordinator,* which emphasised the responsibility of the REC in implementing the religious education curriculum (pp. 9-12).

In the diocese of Parramatta the role was described as a position of central leadership, promoting the mission of the Church as well as undertaking specific responsibilities outlined as follows:

The Religious Education Coordinator has a specific responsibility for learning programs, resources and the professional development of staff in order to enhance the quality of teaching and learning in Religious Education. (Catholic Education Office Parramatta, 1997, p. 1)

## The Archdiocese of Melbourne

In 1995, the Catholic Education Office of Melbourne's (CEOM) curriculum document, *Guidelines for Religious Education for Students in the Archdiocese of Melbourne (Guidelines)* included a section concerning the role of the REC. *Guidelines* (1995) focussed on three areas: formation, curriculum and administration. *Guidelines* (1995) did not define the role of the REC but recommended that the role should be constructed by each individual school according to its particular needs.

Schools and parishes should clearly define the role of the religious education coordinator in the light of their needs, expectations and profile, and within the school provide sufficient release time so that a clear vision of the Catholic school as an integral part of the Church's mission is demonstrated. (CEOM, 1995, p. 21)

*Guidelines* (1995) conceptualised the role of the REC primarily in theological terms. The 1988 document *The Religious Dimension of Education in a Catholic School* (RDECS) by the Congregation for Catholic Education, framed the role of the teacher of religious education in terms of being a personal witness to the faith tradition. While the RDECS (CCE, 1988) referred to the importance of professional and pedagogical training in religious education, it emphasised that it was the personal witness of the teacher that brought the teaching to life (CCE, 1988, # 96). The essence of this understanding of the religious education teacher stemming from the RDECS (CCE, 1988) was enshrined in *Guidelines*.

Religious educators are called to be prophets and cooperate with parents in communicating the living mystery of God to their students. Ultimately, the school program depends on the staff who are both models and teachers of faith. (CEOM, 1995, p. 20)

The role of the REC was to provide for the formation of the religious education teacher, and to develop, implement and administer the religious education curriculum.

## Overview

The foregoing overview of approaches to the role of the REC in several Australian dioceses suggests that there is no uniform perception about the role. Liddy (1998) explored the role from the perspective of RECs across several Australian dioceses and found that : "There was a general consensus that the role as described in CEO [Catholic Education Office] documents from each diocese was too big for one person to manage..."(p. 27). The eighteen religious education coordinators whom Liddy (1998) interviewed claimed this because it involved many diverse aspects such as curriculum development, pastoral care of staff and students, professional development, managing resources, coordinating the liturgical programme, convening social justice activities, faith formation programs for staff, and maintaining communication with students, staff, parents, and their Catholic Education Office.

The various dimensions assigned to the REC role in the diocese studied are summarised in table 1 which indicates the nature of the key emphases in relation to the educational and the ministerial aspects of the role. It gives an overview of the many and varied tasks that are stated and implied in the role of the REC.

Table 1

*Emphases put on the role of the REC and its dimensions in eight Australian dioceses.*

| Place | Employment centralised | Emphasis | Educational tasks | Ministerial tasks. |
|---|---|---|---|---|
| Sydney | Yes | Educational | Implementation and administration of the RE curriculum; the professional development of religious education teachers | Mission of the Church; Catholic ethos; liturgical and faith life; positive relationships. |
| Hobart | Yes | Ministerial | Implementation and administration of the RE curriculum including resources. | Teacher formation; commitment to the Catholic tradition and Catholic education; prayer, liturgy and retreats; pastoral care and personal development; Catholic ethos. |
| Canberra Goulburn | Yes | Ministerial | Implementation and administration of the RE curriculum including resources | Mission of the Church; commitment to Catholic tradition and Catholic education; witness; Catholic ethos; inspire faith; share vision; build community; spiritual leadership. |
| Darwin | Yes | Ministerial | Approved tertiary qualifications in religious education; member of the school executive; coordination of religious education curriculum. | Active member of the Catholic Church; role model; prayer and liturgy; develop the school as a faith community. |
| Brisbane | Yes | Educational | Educational leadership of the religious education curriculum; member of the school executive. | Contributes to the Catholic ethos and the religious life of the school. |
| Western Australia | Yes | Educational | Religious Education curriculum leadership. | |
| Parramatta | Yes | Educational | Learning programs; resources; professional development; quality of teaching and learning. | Mission of the Church |
| Melbourne | No | Ministerial | RE curriculum leadership and administration. | Witness; models and teachers of faith. |

These indications of the diverse nature of the role of the REC provide a framework within which the REC as a manager of curriculum change may take place.

## Research on the Leadership of RECs

The diocesan policies referred to above have conceptualised the role of the REC as one of leadership. Integral to the leadership aspect of the role of the REC according to Rymarz (1998), is the ability to inspire and motivate students; teachers and the school executive (p. 29). Another important quality required of a leader is the ability to "articulate the purpose and mission of the school" (D'Orsa, 1998, p. 35). This is integral to building up a Catholic school's culture which is a responsibility that the REC shares with the Principal. Therefore RECs are challenged to be not only leaders in religious education but "integrated educational leaders" (D'Orsa, 1998, p. 36).

Linked with the need for visionary leadership is the literature that discusses aspects of the personality of the REC. Liddy (1998) has indicated that the personality of the REC shapes the job within the school (p. 27), and Rymarz (1998) has suggested that "RECs who can connect good professional knowledge and behaviour with strong human values are much more likely to inspire students and teachers" (p. 29). D' Orsa (1998) suggested that "in the human domain the REC is required to build up the quality and morale of teachers of religious education by providing support, and by listening and challenging" (p. 34).

## *Curriculum Leadership and Leadership for Change*

The literature concerning the leadership aspect of the role of the REC has discussed the responsibilities in terms of vision, mission, motivation, inspiration and reflection (Crotty, 2002; Fleming, 2002). Curriculum leadership is another important dimension of the role which, if neglected, has critical consequences for the quality of religious education in a school. Blahut and Bezzina (1998) have argued that the RECs' responsibility for the development, implementation and evaluation of religious education curriculum should be a primary concern. However, they claimed that more time and energy is often invested in meeting other responsibilities of the role (p. 6). Johnson's (1989) research into the role of RECs in the Archdiocese of Sydney revealed that, even in times where the classroom curriculum in religious education was in need of attention, RECs tended to focus on the ministerial aspects of the role. The research of Crotty (2005) also indicated the "tendencies for some RECs to make the liturgical and ecclesial dimensions the main focus of the position (p. 54).

Curriculum leadership in religious education is educationally and professionally demanding. It requires a "good deal of understanding about the theory of religious education" (Rymarz, 1998, p. 30), and necessitates that the REC keep up to date with curriculum and pedagogy not only in the area of religious education but also in all key learning areas (Mackenzie, 1998).

In a period where religious education is subject to significant change, for example the time after the Second Vatican Council (1962-1965), the articulation of the role of the REC as a leader of and for change is critical. According to Smith and Lovat (2003) change agents are generally people who have the following characteristics: empathy, or the ability to place themselves in the teachers' situation; homophily, or having the same experience and background as the teachers; credibility. While Credibility is strongly related to homophily it is also distinguished by the perception that the change agent is well informed about the change; and hard working and active in working collegially with teachers (p. 200).

The notion of RECs as curriculum change agents in a rapidly changing Church and social context may help to sharpen the concept of the role of the REC as a curriculum leader (Marsh, 1997, p. 189). The investigation of this research into the RECs' perspectives on the management of a major curriculum change will contribution to the literature in this area.

## RECs as Managers
The REC role comprises aspects of leadership and management (Engebretson, 1998). The management aspect of the role involves "carrying out plans, achieving outcomes efficiently, and working effectively with people" (Fleming, 2001, p. 23). In particular curriculum management in religious education requires informed understandings of educational theory and knowledge. "An important tool for the effective management of the curriculum is a comprehensive knowledge of a number of complex educational theory" (Rymarz, 1998 p. 29). Therefore a clear understanding of these aspects is imperative to those who lead, manage and coordinate religious education in Catholic schools (Paxton, 1998).

The importance that content knowledge and educational theory plays in the leadership and management aspect of the role of the REC is explored in this study.

## Leadership in Professional Development and Staff Support
The REC directly supports teachers in their work (Malone and Ryan, 1996). Several RECs across a number of Australian dioceses agreed that their role encompassed the professional development of religious education staff (Liddy, 1998, p. 27). Rymarz (1998) suggested that skilled RECs who have an understanding of the professional competencies and needs of the teachers in their faculty, could initiate appropriate professional development opportunities for religious education teachers (p. 30). The backgrounds of teachers of religious education in terms of theology and religious studies are often minimal and varied. "Just as students at Catholic schools now exhibit a wide diversity of backgrounds and expectations, the RE [religious education] staff can exhibit a variety of levels of knowledge and commitment to the faith and life of the Church" (Rymarz, 1998, p. 30). These levels can range from little knowledge about the Catholic tradition to extremely informed levels where teachers have tertiary qualifications in religious education and theology (Thomas, 2000). The diversity of backgrounds and expectations of religious education teachers can make it difficult for the REC to provide professional development experiences because there may be "lack of a clearly identifiable Catholic population and a sense of shared values" (Mackenzie, 1998, p. 39).

## Overview of the Research on the Leadership of the REC
Table 2 summarises the key concepts in the literature on the leadership of the REC, once again highlighting the complexity and challenge of the role.

Table 2

*Key concepts in the literature on the leadership of the REC*

| Visionary leadership | Personality leadership | Curriculum leadership | Leadership for curriculum change | Management | Leadership in professional development and staff support. |
|---|---|---|---|---|---|
| Inspiration; motivation; articulation of mission; leadership in Catholic culture; general educational leadership. | Support; listening; challenging; professional knowledge and behaviour; values. | Development, implementation and evaluation of religious education curricula; understanding the theory of religious education; general knowledge of curriculum and pedagogy. | Empathy; homophily; credibility; hard working; collegial. | Carrying out plans; achieving outcomes; working effectively with people; understanding educational theory. | Support for teachers; professional development for religious education teachers. |

## Challenges to the RECs' Role: Recent Australian Studies[6]

In view of the challenging and multi-faceted position outlined in the previous two sections of this literature review, it is not surprising that it is difficult to attract people to the role of REC. Some of the literature concerning RECs points to the rapid turnover of appointees (Blahut and Bezzina, 1998). Even in dioceses where criteria for the role are well documented, young and relatively inexperienced teachers tend to take it up (L. Crotty, 1998). Rymarz (1998) and Engebretson (1998) have indicated that the average employment of the REC in Victorian Catholic Schools is approximately two years. Blahut and Bezzina (1998) argue that the rapid turnover of appointees to the role hinders schools' ability to promote quality religious education. It is clear that for this trend of rapid turnover to be reversed, clear policy initiatives regarding the role of the REC need to be taken. The final section of this literature review provides some analysis and direction which may inform this policy development.

### Fleming's 2002 Study

As has been shown in Table 1, in Catholic schools in Melbourne, the role of the REC has predominantly been seen as one of Church ministry, with curriculum leadership elements introduced into this paradigm. Fleming (2002) gave an overview of the development of REC role statements from the first 1975 *Guidelines for Religious Education for Secondary Students in the*

---

[6] Parts of this section have been reported in
Buchanan, M. T. & Engebretson, K. (2006). *The religious education in Australian Catholic schools: A review of the literature.* Unpublished paper for the Primary RECs Project, Catholic Education Office, Melbourne. Australian Catholic University, Australia.

*Archdiocese of Melbourne*, through to the 1977, 1984 and then the 1995 editions of the *Guidelines,* revealing a strong emphasis on the ecclesial and ministerial aspects of the role. Against this background, Fleming sought to discover how RECs in the Catholic secondary schools of Melbourne perceived their role. Using in-depth interviews with 23 RECs, he provided the first study of this kind in Australia, a study that was notable for its concentration on the experiences and perceptions of the person in the role, rather than only on national and international Church documents that spell out its requirements.

A key finding was that perceptions of the role hinged on the theoretical position that the REC held in relation to the nature and purpose of religious education, and its role in the Catholic school. Particular views of the nature and purpose of religious education in the school (that is whether it is more concerned with providing specific opportunities for faith sharing, whether it is more concerned with teaching and learning in the discipline, or whether it is concerned with a judicious mixture of these) led to particular perceptions about the emphases that were to be taken by the REC in fulfilling the role. One of Fleming's conclusions was that the role of the REC would continue to be plagued by uncertainty and differing interpretations until the issue of the theoretical underpinnings of religious education in the Archdiocese was clearly articulated (Fleming, 2002; see also Buchanan & Engebretson, 2006; Engebretson, 2006).

## Crotty's 2002 Study

Crotty's study, undertaken in 2002 and published in 2005, was entitled: *The impact of the REC on education in the Sydney system of Catholic schools from the perception of principals and RECs.* In an earlier section of this literature review, a description of the role of the REC as articulated by the CEOS has been given, and Crotty's study needs to be considered against this background. Conducted through focus groups with six RECs and six principals in the Archdiocese of Sydney, Crotty's research found both support for and ambiguity about the REC position. Among much evidence of support for the leadership of the REC, and evidence that it has had a positive impact on the education offered by Sydney Catholic schools, Crotty identified (among several) the following ambiguities, which lessened this positive impact:

- there was lack of clarity about the priority the REC should give to the classroom curriculum and the Church ministry aspects of the curriculum;
- too often the REC felt a need to be the "conscience" of the school;
- the leadership of the REC always involved the education of students and the education of teachers;
- in the secondary school the REC had the largest faculty of teachers with the inherent challenge of most religious education teachers not being specialists in their area, and some not wishing to be teachers of religious education at all;
- approaches to classroom religious education have changed over the duration of the role, and secondary school RECs have needed to resource schools and teachers for state based religious studies courses;

- the role of the REC has assumed the pastoral activities originally carried out by the members of the religious orders who founded the school such as sex education, counselling, pastoral care, liturgies, and retreats; and

- often the REC is seen as almost solely the focus of all religious activity in the school.

When put together, this small sample of Crotty's findings about ambiguities in the role of the REC point to a job that is especially complex and demanding, most of all because it is seen by the Archdiocese, by the school and its community, and by the RECs themselves as belonging both to education and to Church ministry. The emphasis given to either of these dimensions by school leadership will determine the skills that are sought in an REC, and the weight that is given to the different aspects of the role. For example, Crotty found (2005, p. 54) that RECs will often give far greater weight to the Church ministry aspects of the role, even when the classroom religious education curriculum in the school is in urgent need of leadership, when it is poorly planned and under-resourced, when teachers are uncertain and confused and when, therefore, a poor religious education product is the result. She too called for a clearer articulation of the role that finds a workable balance between its educational and ministerial aspects (Crotty 2005; see also Buchanan & Engebretson, 2006; Engebretson, 2006).

## The role of the REC: Educational Leadership or Church Ministry?

The relationship between catechesis and religious education has been spelled out in Church documents, and this can guide Catholic Education Offices in the development of policies for the role of the REC. This relationship is one of distinction and complementarity (Engebretson, 2006) and both need to be acknowledged. "There is an absolute necessity to distinguish clearly between religious instruction and catechesis" (#. 73), argues *The General Directory for Catechesis* (CC, 1998). The Directory continues:

It is necessary, therefore, that religious instruction in schools appear as a scholastic discipline with the same systematic demands and the same rigour as other disciplines. It must present the Christian message and the Christian event with the same seriousness and the same depth with which other disciplines present their knowledge. (# 73)

The 1988 *Religious Dimension of Education in a Catholic School* had put it just as clearly:

The aim of catechesis, or handing on the Gospel message, is maturity: spiritual, liturgical, sacramental and apostolic; this happens most especially in a local Church community. The aim of the school however, is knowledge. While it uses the same elements of the Gospel message, it tries to convey a sense of the nature of Christianity, and of how Christians are trying to live their lives. It is evident, of course, that religious instruction cannot help but strengthen the faith of a believing student, just as catechesis cannot help but increase one's knowledge of the Christian message. (CCE, 1988, # 69)

The document also states that: "The distinction between religious instruction and catechesis does not change the fact that a school can and must play its specific role in the work of catechesis" (CCE, 1988, # 69). The advice given by these two Church documents is echoed by Moran (1991), who argued for a clear distinction to be made between the two processes of religious education, that is, understanding religion and being religious (Moran, 1991, p. 249).

Understanding religion is the work of the classroom. It is an intellectually vibrant, open, critical, and rational study of the Catholic tradition. The second process is learning to be religious in a Catholic way. Here the emphasis is on formation, for as Moran (1991) argued, while spirituality may not involve religion, one can only be religious through a religious tradition. So the purpose of learning to be religious is the development of religious commitment, and the centre for this is the worshipping community of the parish, and the faith community of the school. Both processes (understanding religion and learning to be religious) must be attended to in the whole religious education curriculum, and these two processes frame and demarcate the work of the REC.

The whole of religious education is not a terribly complex project. It requires that those of us who appropriate the term "teacher" know which of the two processes they are engaged in at a particular time and place. The tragedy would be that for lack of clarity about this distinction, institutions end up doing neither: their academic enquiry is not challenging enough and their formation is not particular enough. Endless talk about Christianity is not religious education. What deserved that title is teaching people religion with all the breadth and depth of intellectual excitement one is capable of -and teaching people to be religious with all the particularity of the verbal and non verbal symbols that place us on the way. (Moran, 1991, p. 249)

The REC takes part in two processes. In the educational work of the school they are informed and skilled teachers, masters of the content of religion, able to lead others by example in this, and able to teach the subject at some distance from the religious commitments of students. In the ministry of religious formation, they are co-travellers in faith with other staff and with students, witnessing to the Church and its life in the school community. It is difficult to do both tasks well, yet commitment to both, and a high standard of co-operation in both is required (Engebretson, 2006).

This section of Chapter two has reviewed literature concerning the role of the REC in Australia. It explored the way in which the role had been conceptualised according to several diocesan and archdiocesan policies. It provided an outline of the role in terms of leadership, management, and as leader in professional development and staff support. It presented insights about the role based on literature emanating from studies undertaken in Australia. Perspectives of the role in terms of its educational and ministerial dimensions were also explored.

Chapter two has considered existing research concerning educational change as it applies to curriculum change in the school context as well as research concerning the role of RECs in the Australian context. Chapter three explores research about textbooks in education and religious education.

# CHAPTER THREE
# Research on Textbooks in Education and Religious Education[7]

Chapter two of this book reviewed literature from two areas that provided a context for understanding the RECs' management of this particular change to a text-based curriculum. The first area focussed on change as it applies to curriculum in educational contexts. The second area focussed on literature relating to the REC in Australian Catholic schools. This chapter reviews literature referring to the part textbooks play in broader educational areas in an endeavour to gain insights for the application of textbook use in religious education (to the extent that the insights gained can be applied to the use of textbooks in religious education). In this chapter a broad overview of literature concerning textbook use in education is presented and this is followed by a summary of literature concerning textbook use in religious education.

Some literature about the use of textbooks is concerned with areas such as the position of textbooks in contemporary classrooms; teacher reliance on textbooks; assessment of the quality of textbooks; and selection criteria for choosing a textbook. The issues surrounding the part textbooks play in broader educational areas offers insights that can be applied to the use of textbooks in religious education.

## The Position of Textbooks in a Contemporary Classroom

Instructional innovations such as radio, television, programmed learning, multi-media packages, language laboratories and other information technologies have challenged the position of textbooks in education (Gopinathan, 1989, p. 62). However mass communication techniques including information technologies have not replaced textbooks (Ferning, McDougal & Ohlman, 1989). They have nevertheless, contributed to the redefining of the context in which textbooks are used: "The notion of the textbook as a single, stand alone tool for teaching and learning appears to be outmoded" (Ferning et al., 1989, p. 204). However, the textbook has remained the preferred teaching and learning option for most teachers (Kerin & Nixon, 2005; Britton & Woodard, 1993). Hirsch (1996) argued that a well-written textbook was the most effective resource to use for learning subject matter (p. 269). While textbooks remain the preferred option the literature suggests

---

[7] Parts of this chapter have been published in:
Buchanan, M. T. (2006d) Textbooks in religious education. In M. de Souza, K. Engerbretson, G. Durka, R. Jackson, & A. McGrady (Eds.). *International handbook of religious, moral and spiritual education* (pp. 747-760). Netherlands: Springer.

that teacher reliance on textbooks has not continued in a like manner (Britton & Woodard, 1993; Hirsch, 1996).

## Teacher Reliance on Textbooks

The degree to which teachers rely on textbooks varies and beginner teachers are likely to rely heavily on textbooks in comparison to experienced teachers (Britton &Woodard, 1993). According to Vespoor (1989) the actual use of, and interaction with, textbooks and teacher manuals can help teachers to develop confidence and mastery over a subject, and help to improve the quality of learning and teaching. Reliance on textbooks can be considered a vehicle to gain professional competencies in the learning and teaching process.

Textbooks appear to be a popular resource with teachers because they are non-threatening and are comparatively inexpensive and easy to maintain (Hatoss, 2004; Vespoor, 1989, p. 56). They continue to dominate the classroom despite the impact of other forms of media and learning resources (Watson, 2004; Woodard & Elliot, 1993) and 75% to 95% of classroom instruction is organised around textbooks (Tyson & Woodard, 1989, pp. 14-17). According to Vespoor (1989) textbooks contribute to the quality of education. However, it is also argued that a textbook itself has no significance until a teacher and student interact with it (Marsh, 1997, p. 84).

It has been argued that the achievement of high quality learning gained from textbook use depends on the skill and competence of the teacher (Crotty & Crotty, 2000; Finlay, 2000; Reilly; 1998). However, textbooks also have the potential to "compensate for the weakness of teachers" (Tyson-Bernstein, 1989, p. 74) and act as an "insurance policy against poor teaching" (Rossiter, 2000, p. 13). A well designed text-book can also accommodate atypical learners from both ends of the learning spectrum (Crawford & Carnine, 2000).

## Assessing the Quality of Textbooks

Issitt (2004) has indicated the difficulty in assessing the quality of textbooks is associated with the diverse range of uses. He suggested that there "is such a wide range of uses for the textbook, from garage manual to classroom aid, that a typology of uses offers little analytical consistency" (p. 685). However, textbooks should not be assessed in isolation from other factors that interact with the teaching program. "All elements of a program – teachers, texts and teaching methods – must be congruous and at the same developmental stage" (Vespoor, 1989, p. 53). For example, a good textbook used by a competent teacher can be a very effective teaching and learning resource. The same textbook in the hands of an unskilled teacher may not be used as effectively. Therefore an incorrect assessment about a textbook may arise if it is not considered in association with other elements of the learning and teaching program.

## Style of Textbook Language

A study by Garner and Biewer (1983) identified styles of language and writing in textbooks that had the potential to hinder the learning and teaching process. There were two main areas of concern. The first related to the vocabulary and language style exclusive to a particular subject. Their study revealed that teachers were concerned that the overuse of subject specific language did not assist students in the process of learning from textbooks. This unease was experienced across a number of subject areas. "Teachers of science, mathematics and other specialised areas of the curriculum expressed concern that textbooks often used language which is too difficult for students" (Garner & Biewer, 1983, p. 5). This problem could be alleviated if students were seen as the primary purpose for which the textbook was written, with language and style directed towards them and supported with examples that are aimed at "bridging the gap between the expert and the novice" (Pepper, 1981, p. 259). In addition teachers should not ignore their responsibility to help students become familiar with subject specific language presented in the textbook. "Teachers must draw to the attention of students the language of their own subject if textbooks are to be a realistic tool for the classroom (Garner & Biewer, 1983, p. 10).

The second area of concern identified by Garner and Biewer (1983) related to the writing style contained in textbooks. Some textbooks have the potential to inundate students with a great deal of content information leading to the likelihood of students becoming overwhelmed with the quantity of material to be learned (Crawford & Craine, 2000, p. 387). Kinder and Bursuck (1991) argued that "good students may come to view their task as one of learning many details … less able students may come to view their task as simply impossible" (p. 271). Understandings about writing styles can help students to interact effectively with a textbook. The style of writing generally found in textbooks for secondary school students can present difficulties for students in transition from primary school to secondary school.

The biggest "hidden" problem faced by students in the transition years is the change in writing style of textbook- whereas in the primary years students become accustomed to the story or narrative form, in the post-primary school they are expected to extract meaning from a descriptive or expository form of writing. (Garner & Biewer, 1983, p. 5)

The theory generated and reported in later chapters of this book suggest that some RECs involved in the curriculum change perceived that students and teachers were at times constrained by the content, vocabulary and stylistic structures of the textbook in use.

## Selection Criteria for Choosing a Textbook

The selection criteria teachers use for choosing a textbook, "exposes deep-seated assumptions about the relationship of the learner to the teacher, of the learner to the author, of the learner to structures of knowledge and of the learner to the power relations in society" (Issitt, 2004, pp. 684-685). The selection criteria for textbooks in France, Germany, the United Kingdom and the United States is applied at the production stage and publishers were required to adhere to it (Newman, 1989; see also Gopinathan, 1989, pp.66-67). There are other countries where the selection criteria are applied after the production stage and in some cases at the point of purchase. According to Marsh (1997, p. 86) principals, teachers, students and authors preferred to select textbooks according to criteria shown in Table 3

Table 3

*Preferred criteria of principals, teachers, students and authors for selecting textbooks*

| Principals | Teachers | Students | Authors |
|---|---|---|---|
| Up-to-date content; | A core of important learning; | Information that is easy to understand; | The presentation of information in an interesting way; |
| Material that is easy to understand; | Some new content or rearranged content; | Information that is an up-to-date summary of a particular topic; | The textbook is unique and special; |
| Relatively cheap to purchase. | New ideas about organising their teaching; | Material directly relevant to the syllabus and examinations; | The teachers and students will recognise its usefulness and use it in class. |
| | | Instruction on basic skills. | |
| | Up-dated resource lists; | | |
| | An up-to-date summary on a particular topic; | | |
| | Instruction on basic skills. | | |

While textbooks may be used and interacted with in many different ways, the expectations of a textbook are held constant across the key interest groups (Marsh, 1997, pp. 84-87). Textbook selection criteria may help authors to redesign textbooks to make them more effective and efficient teaching tools (Carnine, 1991).

## Summary of Main Points about Textbooks in Education

The literature explored to this point in the chapter about textbooks in the broader context of education also provides insights that are relevant to textbook use in religious education. The position of textbooks in education is strong and remains the preferred learning and teaching option (Britton & Woodard, 1993). However with the growth in, and access to, information communication technologies, teachers are less likely to rely on textbooks as the sole resource (Hirsch, 1996). The extent to which teachers rely on textbooks in the classroom varies. Inexperienced teachers have a greater dependency rate than experienced teachers (Britton & Woodard, 1993) and textbooks can compensate for poor teaching (Rossiter, 2000). A textbook can help a teacher to gain confidence and mastery as well as lead to improved learning and teaching especially in subject areas with which they are not familiar (Vespoor, 1989). Assessing the quality of a textbook is best done in context with other factors associated with the learning and teaching process such as, teachers, teaching methods and the curriculum. However because of the diverse range of uses associated with textbooks, difficulties arise in assessing their quality (Issitt, 2004). Consideration was given in this chapter to the selection criteria for choosing a textbook. In some countries authors of textbooks must write according to a set criteria in order to have their work published (Neumann, 1989). In other countries the criteria is determined by the purchaser of the textbook and Marsh (1997) indicated that principals, teachers, students and authors have varying criteria for determining a good textbook. In religious education in Australia there has been discussion about the position of textbooks, teacher reliance, textbook quality and selection criteria for textbooks in the discipline. The following section provides an overview of some of the literature concerning textbooks in religious education, which has emanated from the introduction of the Church-sponsored textbook series, *To Know, Worship and Love*.

## Overview of Literature Concerning Textbooks in Religious Education

### *Qualities of a Good Religious Education Textbook*

The quality of a textbook in religious education is sometimes compared to the quality of textbooks in other disciplines. In a secondary school, learners are generally enrolled in a range of subjects and in many cases interact with a variety of textbooks from various disciplines. Students in such situations are likely to consciously or unconsciously make comparisons between the qualities of various textbooks. According to Rossiter (2000) inferior quality textbooks in religious education can devalue attitudes towards the study of religion.

> If student texts in religion are not comparable in the quality of production, then they will immediately give students an impression of being deficient and this can reinforce negative views of religious education. (Rossiter, 2000, p. 14)

Teachers of religious education in Catholic schools teach across a range of disciplines, and therefore are also in a position to make comparisons and judgements between the quality of textbooks from various fields (Thomas, 2000).

While the layout and presentation style of a religious education textbook may influence the judgements made about the quality of the textbook, other factors can also be taken into consideration. Factors such as the philosophical and/or educational approach underpinning the textbook may also come into play when making judgements about the quality of the text. Rossiter (2000) has indicated that, "new student texts in humanities emphasise a critical inquiring approach to education" (p. 15). He argued that such an approach to teaching and learning is appropriate to teaching and learning in religious education, where areas of theology, scripture, world religions and contemporary spiritual and moral issues are covered in the curriculum. A good textbook can inform the learner as well as provide incentives "for inquiry and discussion and the threads of continuity in the study" (Rossiter, 2000, p. 16). Textbooks are less effective if their aim is to promote personal commitment, but Rossiter (2000) acknowledged that content focussed textbooks can stimulate opportunities for personal reflection and possible transformation.

The text is there to provide content for critical examination and reflection. If the content/issue is important enough it will naturally have components that are belief and value oriented, and personal. (Rossiter, 2000, p. 15)

The task of an effective textbook in religious education is to be informative, and the presentation of the textbook may help to provide the impetus for learner inquiry and critique or discussion (Rossiter, 2000, p. 16). A good textbook can help teachers and students to achieve excellence in religious education. Textbooks can offer a range of strategies and skills that can be used to engage students in the learning process. Reflecting on her expertise as a textbook writer, Engebretson (2000) suggested that through the use of textbooks students can gain or develop the following skills: comprehension, application, analysis, critique and evaluation, reflection, contemplation, intuition and creativity. Table 4 outlines the characteristics of a good religious education textbook according to Engebretson (2000).

Table 4

*Characteristics of good religious education textbooks*

| Characteristics: |
| --- |
| 1. A good textbook opens up historical, cultural, scriptural, liturgical and ethical riches in a way that respects the student's intellectual and psychological development. <br> 2. Students are given access to the best current developments in scriptural and theological scholarship, and this is done through either particular methodologies in the text, or, included as part of the information on a   given topic. <br> 3. Unless it is intended for use in only the narrowest of contexts, a good religious education text acknowledges diversity of religious commitment, ranging from unbelief to belief, and the many positions in between. <br> 4. A textbook attempts to engage the student at the intellectual and personal/reflective levels. <br> 5. A good religious education text provides highly specific information and gives more than enough information in any give topic. <br> 6. Numerous choices are given in the form of activities, research assignments, discussion topics, revision questions, quizzes, and activities,  which use  the  student's  creative capacities. <br> 7. A good religious education textbook is visually attractive. <br> 8. A good religious education textbook acknowledges the role played by information technology in education, and assists students to use this technology to find out more about topics under consideration.                                        (Engebretson, 2000, p. 29) |

A good religious education textbook has the potential to act not only as a sound educational tool but may also have the potential to transform the learner's view of the world in the religious realm.

## The Cognitive and Transformative Potential of Religious Education Textbooks

A good religious education textbook may promote cognitive intellectual learning as well as have the potential to appeal to the affective and transformative domain of the learner (Mudge, 2000; Dwyer, 2000; Ryan, 2000). Mudge (2000) has suggested that there has been a tendency for religious educators and textbook writers to place an over-emphasis on the cognitive or intellectual dimensions of textbooks at the expense of exploring the affective dimensions. He argued that to present the cognitive and affective dimensions of learning as an either/or choice could limit the potential of a good religious education textbook and that religious educators and text writers should incorporate both.

> A good RE text encourages aesthetic attitudes of both critical distance and immediate involvement; objective disinterest and close, passionate intimacy; transcendence and immanence; contemplation and concrete praxis. (Mudge, 2000, p. 3)

Good religious education textbooks do more than impart knowledge when the teacher and learner interact with them.

> The material has to be faithful to the teaching of the Church; it has to help the teacher achieve the aims of the local RE syllabus; it has to suit the students; and it has to bring some joy and enthusiasm into the work of the teachers and those who are learning with them. (Dwyer, 2000, pp. 17 – 18)

The transformative potential of a good religious education textbook can therefore be viewed from the perspective of the role the teacher plays in text-based learning.

## Religious Education Textbooks and the Teacher

Reilly (1998) argued that it was the teacher or the "teacher's heart that brings to life any RE textbook or programme" (p. 137) and that it was the "teacher who transforms the syllabus from a dead letter into a living experience of the faith" (p. 137). From the perspective of hermeneutics, Mudge (2000) argued that a textbook is not restricted to "cognitive critique and rote-learning" (p. 5) but a resource to be interacted with in the learning and teaching process. Textbooks should be regarded as tools that assist rather than define the teaching of religious education (Dwyer, 2000).

> The text can only come alive with its full power when it takes account of and wrestles with the whole social, historical, aesthetic, psychological and other 'worlds' surrounding the subject and the reader. (Mudge, 2000, p. 5)

Textbooks in religious education help the teacher to understand the "thinking about religious education and the theological understandings and nuances that were current when it was written" (Engebretson, 2000, p. 28). Good textbooks are able to help teachers identify a particular curriculum theory which teachers can convey to students through the teaching and learning activities in which they are able to engage students (Ryan, 2000, p. 20). The religious education textbook series used in the Melbourne Archdiocese was an "attempt to provide up-to-date religious education materials which spring from the renewal of the post conciliar period" (Rymarz, 2000, p. 43). Textbooks that are up-to-date also assimilate current thinking and approaches to religious education. A good textbook enables a teacher to interact with it and to use his/her authority as a

60

teacher to design a curriculum appropriate for his/her students. However the ability of the teacher to make such curriculum decisions can be compromised by his/her own background and/or expertise in religious education.

> Even when it is required that teachers of religious education are accredited and have completed a certain amount of professional development, many still feel that they teach religious education because the school expects it rather than because of their competence in the discipline. This makes the situation difficult for making curriculum choices. (Thomas, 2000, p. 5)

While textbooks are able to play an important role in assisting the teacher in the development of high quality curriculum design in religious education, they are not the only factor. Consideration should be given to the competencies of the teacher.

> Textbooks are not the only answer to the question of what sort of religious education is needed today. The quality of teachers is obviously still of prime importance. And religious education teachers need good grounding in scripture, theology and the theory of religious education/catechesis as well as an awareness of the culture and spirituality of children and young people. (Finlay, 2000, p.60)

The competencies of the teacher have a significant impact on how well a religious education textbook can be used. It is the teacher who controls the learning experience by deciding the content and methodology appropriate to a particular class. A textbook in this context can be viewed as a tool in the hands of the teacher (Engebretson, 2002, p. 44). If teachers have no understanding of the theoretical framework in which the textbook was written, then the chance of it being used out of context increases. Thus while textbooks can provide teachers with relevant content and activities they cannot correct uninformed views about religious education and its purpose.

## Religious Education Textbooks and the Student

While it is established that the use of religious education textbooks in teaching can have a significant impact on the curriculum, Crotty and Crotty (2000) have considered the possible educational influence of student interaction with religious education textbooks.

> Students may interact with textbooks in ways that extend beyond the intended purposes of the teacher and curriculum (Crotty & Crotty, 2000). Even in situations where the teacher may at first skilfully manipulate and mediate the content of the religious education textbook, it is possible for students to interact with textbook at a level that incorporates their own biographical, cultural and religious persuasion.

> What is transmitted as worthwhile knowledge for the student in the classroom is not necessarily what is in the curriculum. Nor is the knowledge in a textbook necessarily transmitted in the classroom. Even what a teacher interprets from a curriculum and textbook may not be transmitted since students are capable of effective resistance. (Crotty and Crotty, 2000, p. 24)

A good textbook in religious education could enable a student to learn despite poor quality teaching.

Even when religion teachers have little background in religious education, or where teachers may be unmotivated, the possibility of placing good materials in the hands of students ensures that they will have a better chance of learning effectively about the topic. (Rossiter, 2000, p. 13)

A good religious education textbook can give a student an informed understanding of the tradition within the religion under investigation, as well as help students to "gain skills in informed critical thinking about the tradition, about religious history and literature including the sacred texts associated with a particular religion" (Engebretson, 2000, p. 40).

Good textbooks in religious education provide opportunities for students to interact with the content of textbooks through comparison and inquiry (Ryan, 2000). Ryan also argued that good textbooks in religious education can promote an understanding that the curriculum in religious education has similar educational requirements which support it as a discipline as equally valid as other curriculum areas.

## Research on the *To Know Worship and Love* Textbook Series

Engebretson and Rymarz (2002 & 2004) have reported on the implementation and use of the Church-sponsored textbooks, *To Know, Worship and Love*. Their reports involved collecting data through a questionnaire from approximately 300 Year 7-10 teachers of religious education in Catholic schools. As noted earlier in this chapter, by 2002 the textbooks were introduced into all Catholic secondary schools in Melbourne after approximately three-decades of absence of uniform textbooks in religious education. The report suggested that textbooks in the hands of teachers of religious education were a welcomed resource. This was indicated by the high consistent level of usage in the teaching and learning process (Engebretson & Rymarz, 2002, p. 7).

### *Some Findings from Engebretson and Rymarz's Research*

The report indicated that the majority of teachers used the textbooks frequently in class. Frequent use of the textbook was understood to be at least one in every three lessons of religious education. There did not appear to be a significant discrepancy regarding the frequency of textbook use between experienced and inexperienced teachers (Engebretson & Rymarz, 2002, p. 7). The frequency of use of the textbook was not affected by the formal qualifications of the teachers. "Among those with no formal training, 61% used the textbooks every lesson or weekly, while among the more highly qualified this frequency of use was 67.3% (Engebretson & Rymarz, 2002, p. 7).

The inclusion of the textbooks in the Year 7-10 teaching and learning program in Catholic secondary schools led to an increased treatment of the depth of content and amount of content taught across the year levels (Engebretson & Rymarz, 2002, p. 8; Engebretson & Rymarz, 2004, p. 8). The use of textbooks had not added to teacher preparation time. The amount of teacher preparation time remained constant for experienced teachers, and slightly reduced the amount of preparation time for inexperienced teachers. Inexperienced teachers have a higher dependency on the textbook and the use of the textbook also reduced the amount of time used to prepare lessons (Engebretson and Rymarz, 2002, p. 14). The report also indicated an improvement in the teaching and learning of religious education and an improvement in the amount and quality of independent learning in the classroom. Furthermore their findings also suggested an improvement in the amount and quality of assessment given to students. The teachers on the whole indicated that there had been an improvement in their teaching of religious education and an improvement in the students' attitude towards religious education (Engebretson & Rymarz, 2002, p. 16).

In contrast to the teachers of religious education, the RECs who responded to the questionnaire claimed that the introduction and use of the textbooks had increased their workload significantly. Engebretson and Rymarz (2004) suggested, "this is to be expected because as curriculum leaders they would have had responsibility for the oversight of the implementation of the series" (p. 20).

## Implications of the Introduction of Textbooks

The introduction of Church-sponsored textbooks in religious education from preparatory level through to Year 10 in the Archdiocese of Melbourne, has led to the occurrence of "a drastic change in the content of the RE curriculum" (Crotty and Crotty, 2000, p. 23). Crotty and Crotty (2000) suggested that the content of the Melbourne Archdiocese textbooks "should entice RE educators to look once again at the question of what should be taught and why" (p. 23). Questions relating to what should be taught and why are underpinned by questions relating to "how"? Textbooks in religious education have an implied pedagogical approach and the Church-sponsored textbook series in the Archdiocese of Melbourne is no exception. The authors of the Year 7 – 10 textbooks presented the content of the textbooks within a typological framework (Engebretson, 2002, pp. 40-41) based on Habel and Moore's (1982) typological approach, which had been developed from Smart's (1998) phenomenological approach, as indicated in Chapter one of this book. The Archdiocese of Melbourne Church-sponsored religious education textbooks proposed a particular approach to teaching that was fundamentally educational and encouraged a critical inquiring approach (Engebretson, 2002, pp 40 – 44). The textbooks have the potential to change the approach to religious education in the Archdiocese of Melbourne (Rymarz, 2000, pp 42 – 43).

Textbooks in religious education can make significant contributions to curriculum development.

Good textbooks can convey an appropriate curriculum theory with clarity and consistency across a system; provide teachers with subject matter upon which to create imaginative learning activities; engage students with printed resources which encourage comparison and inquiry; and present to students an image of a curriculum area with similar requirements and validity as other curriculum areas. (Ryan, 2000, p. 22)

Textbooks in religious education can be viewed as tools that assist teachers in the development of course content and curriculum focus. For a teacher who is not familiar with the content of a religious education curriculum, a good textbook can be an aid to their curriculum development (Dwyer, 2000, p. 17).

Experts in the field generally design textbooks and a teacher can use them to design and modify the curriculum to suit his/her particular class (Thomas, 2000, p. 54). Textbooks have remained the preferred teaching option for classroom teaching regardless of the mass production of communication techniques and technologies (Gopinathan, 1989; Ferning et al., 1989, Hirsch, 1996, Woodard & Elliot, 1993). The introduction of uniform textbooks in the Archdiocese of Melbourne and other Catholic dioceses and in the eastern states of Australia suggest an emerging preference for textbooks in religious education.      Teachers tend to rely on textbooks to varying degrees (Britton & Woodard, 1993). However teacher use and interaction with textbooks contributes to teacher confidence and mastery over a subject, and can help to improve the quality of teaching and learning (Vespoor, 1989). The use of textbooks in religious education would be particularly beneficial in religious education where many teachers are likely to lack qualification and/or inexperience (Thomas, 2000).

While it is difficult to assess the quality of a textbook given the wide range of uses (Issitt, 2004), when a textbook is considered alongside other factors such as the students, the teachers, the programme, pedagogy, judgements can be made about its appropriateness (Vespoor, 1989). Suitability can be measured fittingly when key interest groups are in agreement regarding the quality or criteria of a particular textbook (Marsh, 1997).

## Summary of the Research

The quality of textbooks in religious education should be of a high standard and students and teachers sometimes compare their quality to that of textbooks from other disciplines (Rossiter, 2000; Thomas, 2002). Good quality religious education textbooks can be used to achieve excellence in the teaching and learning (Engebretson, 2000). Concerns were raised regarding the *To Know Worship and Love* textbook series and the extent to which a textbook can emphasise cognitive learning and simultaneously inculcate students within a particular faith tradition (Dwyer, 2000; Mudge, 2000; Ryan, 2000). It has been indicated that textbooks are not stand-alone learning instruments. The role of the teacher is integral to using knowledge-centred textbooks within a catechetical religious education model (Finlay, 2000; Reilly, 1998; Thomas, 2000). Religious education textbooks also help students to organise religious data and critique religious knowledge (Engebretson, 2000). Textbooks in religious education can be used to create a degree of independence from the teacher in the learning and teaching process (Ryan, 2000), as well as enable students to learn despite poor quality teaching (Rossiter, 2000).

Research indicates that good quality textbooks provide insights into current pedagogical approaches to religious education. They present a guide for the development of curriculum as well as impact on teacher preparation time (Engebretson & Rymarz 2002; 2004). Table 4 provides an overview of the main points of the literature reviewed in Chapters two and three of this book, and it indicates the significance of the literature in relation to the analysis of the RECs' management of a curriculum change, which is the focus of this study.

Table 5. *An outline of the key points in the literature review and their significance to this study.*

| Area of Literature Review | Key Points | Significance to this Study |
|---|---|---|
| EDUCATIONAL AND CURRICULUM CHANGE | **Appropriation of change: *Adopt, Invent, Adapt.*** <br>• Change can be *adopted* from outside forces (including "top down change"(Morris, 1995) where schools are required to adopt a change initiative organised by a centralised body) <br>• Change can be invented and originate from within the school in situations where the teachers are focussed on improving student learning. <br>• Change can be the result of adaptation which occurs as a result of the interplay between adaptation and invention. | Understandings about the appropriation of change and the origins of the change provided a context for understanding how RECs managed a "top down change" directed by the Archbishop of Melbourne. |
| | **Attitudes Regarding Change** <br>• Attitudes impact on determining what is actually implemented | The significance of attitudes towards change influenced the way some RECs managed the change to the text-based curriculum. It provided a framework by which to understand the challenges, constraints and tension which have the capacity to pull the change initiative in many directions. |
| | **Interplay between change and professional growth** <br>• Curriculum change can be challenging for a teacher but it can also contribute to professional growth. <br>• Curriculum change involves teachers developing content knowledge and technical skills. <br>• Professional learning cultures develop to skill teachers in the face of change. <br>• Professional growth through collaborative learning cultures minimises resistance to change. | This study explored how the RECs managed the curriculum change by focusing on the professional needs of the staff members in the religious education faculty. |
| | **Factors that Assist Change** <br>• The ability to communicate, negotiate and work cooperatively, contribute to successful change. <br>• Schools that have been successful in bringing about change in the past are more willing to engage in other change initiatives. <br>• Time needs to be given to those involved in the change to understand it and consider its implications. <br>• Collaborative cultures promote change and provide opportunities to establish the boundaries within which the change will take place thus reducing uncertainty associated with change. <br>• Commitment to change is more likely if school leaders (including the principal) support the change. | This study explores the RECs' perspectives on the factors that assisted the change to the text-based curriculum and the literature provided a context for analysing these in the highly specialised area of religious education in faith-based Catholic schools. |
| | **Factors that Impede Change** <br>• Development of centralised curriculum has caused a division between curriculum development and implementation and has diminished the role of teachers as curriculum writers. <br>• Centralised authorities place pressure on schools to keep up with change and this increases teacher workload. <br>• Support for increased teacher workload is rare. <br>• Teachers usually work in isolation and this is counter-productive to facilitating change which depends upon communication and collaboration. | This study explores the RECs' perspectives on the factors that impeded the change to the text-based curriculum and the literature provided a context for analysing these in the highly specialised area of religious education in faith-based Catholic schools. |

| Area of Literature Review | Key Points | Significance to this Study |
|---|---|---|
| **RECs IN AUSTRALIAN CATHOLIC SCHOOLS** | **Conceptualising the REC role**<br>• Various archdiocese and dioceses throughout Australia have attempted to explain the REC role. The complexities, challenges and possibilities that surround the role emanate from the literature.<br>• There is not a uniform perception of the role throughout Australia.<br>• The role is a very diverse one within Catholic education. | Understandings about the role of the REC provide a context for exploring their role as managers of curriculum change and analysing their perspectives on curriculum change management. |
| | **REC Leadership & Management**<br>• REC Leadership in terms of vision, mission, motivation, inspiration and reflection.<br>• Educational and professional demands and expertise involved in Curriculum leadership in religious education.<br>• REC leadership and management requires an understanding of curriculum theory and pedagogy in all other curriculum areas as well as religious education.<br>• REC leadership and management required the ability to fulfil a change agent role and bring about change.<br>• Management also involves carrying out plans, achieving outcomes efficiently and working effectively with people.<br>• RECs leadership involves providing professional development and support for staff members. | The RECs in Catholic secondary schools were responsible for managing the text-based curriculum change. Literature about the leadership and management aspects of the role provide a context for analysis the RECs' management of this change. |
| | **Challenges facing the REC role**<br>• Rapid turnover of appointees to the role of REC hinders the ability to promote quality religious education.<br>• Bi-dimensional role in terms of it being a role within the Church and/or within education.<br>• An added responsibility for the REC involves the education of teachers as well as students.<br>• REC are perceived as almost the sole focus of all religious activity within the school. | Literature about the bi-dimensional nature of the REC role provided a broader context for understanding the RECs' management of the curriculum change as one aspect of their varied responsibilities. |
| **TEXTBOOKS IN EDUCATION & RELIGIOUS EDUCATION** | **Textbooks in Education**<br>• Textbooks are the preferred teaching and learning option in contemporary classrooms.<br>• Teacher reliance on textbooks varies according to experience and expertise of the teacher.<br>• The preferred quality and style of a textbook varies from country to country.<br>• Principals, teachers, students and authors have varying reasons for choosing textbooks. | Literature about textbooks in education and religious education provided a context for analysing the use and perceptions of RECs about textbooks and managing the implementation of a text-based curriculum in religious education. |
| | **Textbooks in Religious Education**<br>• The quality of good religious education textbooks is compared to the quality of textbooks in other disciplines.<br>• Religious education textbooks can promote intellectual learning as well as have the potential to appeal to the affective and transformative dimensions of learning.<br>• It is the teacher who brings the textbook to life and a good textbook in the hands of a good teacher assists in the development of high quality teaching and learning.<br>• Teachers skilfully manipulate the content to be taught but students also interact with the textbook at a level that incorporates his/her own biographical, cultural and religious persuasion.<br>• Research into *To Know Worship and Love* textbooks explored teacher use and dependency, and improvement in learning and teaching in religious education. | Literature about textbooks and textbook use in religious education provided a context for understanding and analysing the RECs' perspectives on the management of a change to a text-based curriculum. |

# CHAPTER FOUR
# An Approach for Understanding the Management of Curriculum Change

This chapter establishes the framework of the empirical research component of the study. It explains and justifies the epistemological position adopted in the research, and the theoretical perspective, methodology and methods that flow from this. It describes in detail how the research was conducted, and why, and it discusses the process by which data was generated and analysed.

RECs in the Archdiocese of Melbourne have been responsible for managing a major curriculum change and this curriculum change involved the transition from a life-centred experiential approach, to a text-based knowledge-centred approach to learning and teaching in religious education. RECs in Catholic secondary schools were responsible for managing this "top down" (Morris, 1995) curriculum initiative in their respective schools. The aim of the research reported in this book was to develop theories from the data provided by the RECs, as they discussed their management of this change.

M. Crotty (1998) has suggested that the research question and the purpose of the research leads the researcher to the methods and methodology employed in a study. The purpose of this research was to gain insights into how RECs in Catholic secondary schools managed a particular curriculum change. Table 5 presents an overview of the path taken in this research and this path is discussed in detail in the following sections of the chapter.

Table 5

*Overview of the Research Design*

| Epistemology | Theoretical Perspective | Methodology | Method |
|---|---|---|---|
| Constructivism Knowledge is individually constructed based on socially contextualised↑ learning ↓ <br><br> Constructionism Reality is socially constructed through human interaction, in which meanings are shared in dialogue and new knowledge developed. <br> ↓ <br> Social constructionism <br><br> Beings construct meaning as they encounter the world they are interpreting, and share their interpretations in the community. | Interpretivism ↓ Symbolic interactionism Reality is experienced individually and meaning results from interaction with 'objects' of that experience. | Grounded theory A methodology that enables the researcher to move from the systematic collection of data to the generation of multivariate conceptual theory. Theory emerges from data through a process of constant comparison. | Unstructured in-depth interviews <br><br> Attempts to see the participant's worldview and allows the participant's voice to be heard. |

## Epistemological Foundations

Everitt and Fisher (1995) have drawn a distinction between empirical knowledge and *a priori* knowledge. "Empirical knowledge is knowledge derivable only from experience, and priori knowledge is gained by reason alone" (p. 2). The research undertaken in this study was concerned primarily with empirical knowledge. The aim was to develop theories based on the RECs' perspectives on their experience of managing a particular curriculum change.

The epistemological assumptions underpinning this research placed the study within a qualitative paradigm. A qualitative study has been defined as "an inquiry process of understanding a social or human problem, based on building a complex, holistic picture, formed with words, reporting detailed views of informants, and conducted in a natural setting" (Creswell, 1994, pp. 1-2). Qualitative research generally consists of the collection of thoughts, perceptions and experiences (Everitt & Fisher, 1995, p. 7) and holds that reality is subjective and dimensional as seen by participants in a study (Creswell, 1994, p. 5).

There are three main epistemological paradigms, which embody specific understandings about how we know what we know (M. Crotty, 1998, pp. 3-8). Objectivist epistemology (positivism) is common in quantitative research and "holds that meaning, and therefore meaningful reality, exists as such apart from the operation of any consciousness" (M. Crotty, 1998, p. 8). Constructionism, another epistemological view, stands in opposition to objectivism, and derives from a subjectivist ontology. Constructionism begins from the view that meaning is not discovered but constructed (M. Crotty, 1998, p. 42).

What then is Constructionism? *It is the view that all knowledge, and therefore all meaningful reality as such, is contingent upon human practices, being constructed in and out of interaction between human beings and their world, and developed and transmitted within an essentially social context.* (M. Crotty, 1998, p. 42)

This qualitative study exists within the epistemological paradigm of constructionism. It begins from a constructivist assumption which asserts that individuals construct meaning within their milieu, and then moves to a constructionist paradigm where these shared meanings, including those of the researcher, are put into dialogue, so that new meanings are developed and held in common. In contrast with a positivist epistemology where the researcher remains distant and independent of that being researched, the constructivist researcher aims to interact with those involved in the study, and minimises the distance between the researcher and those being researched (Burns, 1997).

For the qualitative researcher, the only reality is that constructed by the individuals involved in the research situation. Thus multiple realities exist in any given situation: the researcher, those individuals being investigated, and the reader or audience interpreting the study. The qualitative researcher needs to report faithfully these realities and to rely on voices and interpretations of informants. (Creswell, 1994, pp. 5-6)

Nevertheless the value-laden nature of the study must be acknowledged, and values and biases reported on (Creswell, 1994, p. 6). To this end a detailed outline of the researcher's background is provided later in this chapter when the voice of the researcher is discussed. Given that qualitative research is interpretative research, it is important that "such biases, values, and judgement of the researcher become stated explicitly in the research report" (Creswell, 1994, p. 147).

## Constructivism and Social Constructionism

Constructivism is concerned with the ways in which individuals make meaning. It accepts that each individual's way of making sense of the world is valid and worthy of respect (M. Crotty, 1998, p. 58) and that each individual can develop and share perceptions about the world. This research was concerned with discovering the reality of managing a curriculum change from the perspective of the RECs.

While constructivism is concerned with the ways in which individuals make meaning in their own contexts, according to M. Crotty (1998) constructionism is concerned with "the collective generation [and transmission] of meaning" (p. 58). A constructionist view of the world suggests that meaning is not discovered, it is constructed, and moreover it is constructed in human interaction. "Before there were consciousness on earth capable of interpreting the world, the world held no meaning at all" (M. Crotty, 1998, p. 43). According to a constructionist view, meaning does not exist outside of shared consciousness. Within a constructionist paradigm M. Crotty (1998) identified the concept of *social constructionism* to explain that beings construct meaning as they encounter the world they are interpreting, and they share these interpretations in the community.

Social constructionism suggests that all meaningful reality is socially constructed and that the social world and the real world are not to be seen as separate worlds. "They are one human world. We are born, each of us, into an already interpreted world and it is at once natural and social" (M Crotty, 1998, p. 57). Therefore, the data collection described in this study acknowledged the constructivist world of the participants, and the researcher, upon entering into the known world of the respondents, was also a socially constructionist learner. Social constructionism therefore was the underlying epistemology in this study.

The diagram in figure 6 demonstrates the interplay between constructivism and constructionism which underlies the epistemological foundations of this study: social constructionism (Bryman, 2001).

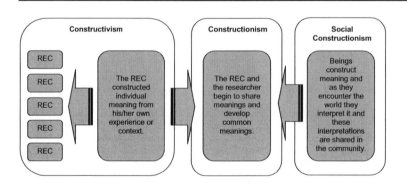

*Figure 6.* Mapping the epistemological focus.

## Theoretical Perspective

Constructionism stands in opposition to positivism, which holds that meaning exists in objects independently of any consciousness of those objects. The theoretical perspective that flows from constructionism is interpretivism. Interpretivist approaches include: (i) hermeneutics, where all experienced phenomena are interpreted through the action of the one who experienced them; (ii) phenomenology, which is the descriptive study of the individual conscious experience from the perspective of that individual; and (iii) symbolic interactionism, where reality is experienced individually, and meaning results from interaction with the objects of that experience (M. Crotty, 1998, p. 71).

The theories that have been developed from the data gathered in this study were drawn from the perspectives of RECs who have been responsible for managing a particular curriculum change. The RECs' reflections concerning their experiences relating to managing the curriculum change provided the empirical data that underpins the theories that have emerged from this study.

Symbolic interactionism is concerned with "the social world, the world as interpreted or experienced, rather than to the physical world" (Bowers, 1989, p. 38). The theoretical perspective of symbolic interactionism describes the perspective which underlies the gathering and analysis of the data, because "interactionists begin in the empirical world and build theories from there" (Bowers, 1989, p. 36). The "object" of the research, that is the management of curriculum change as the RECs perceive it, was first interpreted by them and this interpretation was then shared with the researcher using multiple symbols, but especially the symbols of words which subsequently became the means by which interaction occurred between the RECs and the researcher.

## Symbolic Interactionism

Symbolic interactionism emerged in response to functionalism. Functionalism has been described by Gouldner (1970), as "an unshakable metaphysical conviction: that the world is one" (p. 99). According to Bowers (1989), functionalism espouses the view that the (social) world is a singular system or unit made up of many parts that exist to fulfil the needs of a larger system. Consequently functionalist analysis focuses on the system as a whole and subsequent concern about parts that make up the unit are only of interest as they relate to the functioning of the whole system (Bowers, 1989, p. 33). Therefore parts only have meaning to the extent to which they are related to the whole.

An important feature of functionalist theory is that analysis of the parts (social groups, organisations, and individual roles) is significant only in relation to their consequences for the larger whole ... since the social system is perceived as a singular unit whose parts exist to fulfil the particular needs of the larger system, existing social institutions, organisations, groups and roles are by definition functional for society. (Bowers, 1989, p. 34)

Bowers (1989) suggested that functionalism was a logically derived theory rather than an empirically derived theory (p. 36). Symbolic interactionism is in contrast to functionalism and stems from the work of George Herbert Mead, a pragmatist philosopher and social psychologist (Mead, 1934) from the University of Chicago (M. Crotty, 1998, p. 72). Blumer, a student responsible for compiling Mead's papers and lecture notes summarised three premises as the starting points of symbolic interactionism.

The first premise is that human beings act toward things on the basis of the meanings that the things have for them... The second premise is that the meaning that such things have is derived from, or arises out of, the social interaction that one has with one's fellows. The third premise is that these meanings are handled in, and modified through, an interpretative process used by the person in dealing with the things he encounters. (Blumer, 1969, p. 2)

71

Symbolic interactionism therefore departs from functionalism, in that it holds that notions about society are not ordered, unified, and naturally evolving in whole (Bowers, 1989, p.35). Mead (1934) suggested that for the symbolic interactionist, the self is comprised of two key components, the "I" and the "Me". Bowers (1989) emphasised that "the Me component is conceptualised as the object of self-reflection, while the I component is the reflector" (pp. 36-37). Bowers (1989) also suggested that the "Me" is the part of self that can be identified and talked about, and according to the theory of symbolic interactionism each individual is comprised of multiple selves or multiple Me's. Individuals consist of multiple selves, which can exist individually or simultaneously as well as change over time. "Who I am depends on which Me is experienced as most salient at the time." (Bowers, 1989, p. 37)

When interviewing a REC about how he or she managed curriculum change, it was arguable that the informant's most salient Me was the REC. This assumption was supported by Bowers, (1989): "Who I am, therefore, depends on the Me that is called forth by the social context" (p. 37).

The functionalist notion of self can be viewed as an act of conforming to a predetermined or predefined role, whereas the self from an interactionist point of view is fundamentally social and created through the internalisation of social cues.

The functionalist sees role as primarily the consequence of complete or incomplete internalisation of norms, a unidirectional process from the larger system down to the individual. The interactionist views role as the consequence of a dynamic, interactive process between the self and the social context. (Bowers, 1989, p. 38)

This study was concerned with the thoughts and actions of the individual (in this case the RECs involved in this study). Symbolic interactionism is focussed on the actions and the meanings of the individuals who, in this study, are the starting point for understanding the phenomenon of the management of this particular curriculum change. The study commenced with the experiences of the RECs. The researcher entered into their world and theories were developed regarding how they had managed a particular curriculum change. This approach was consistent with symbolic interactionism and "begins in the empirical world and builds their theories from there" (Bowers, 1989, p. 36).

## Methodology

Methodology is concerned with the strategy or plan of action underpinning the use of the selected research methods (M. Crotty, 1998, p. 7). This study focussed on the management of a particular curriculum change in a highly specialised curriculum area. It relied on the perspectives of those responsible for managing the change.

Very little research has been undertaken about RECs as managers of curriculum change. According to Goulding (2002) grounded theory is a methodology that is commonly used to generate theory where little is known about a phenomenon being studied (Sarantakos, 1998). This methodology enables the generation of theory from the thoughts and perspectives of the RECs involved in the management of this change. This section of Chapter four provides an outline of the methodology of grounded theory and its application to this study.

*Grounded Theory*

According to Bowers (1989) the intellectual roots of grounded theory can be traced back to the Chicago school of sociology. Grounded theory was first developed by Glaser and Strauss (1967) and since that time it has received increasing attention and credibility as a methodology which can be used to generate theory in new areas of research (Sarantakos, 1998, p. 206). Glaser (1978) indicated that grounded theory involved a systematic generation of theory from social research data that have been obtained in a particular way. It is a theory that was discovered, developed, and provisionally verified through systematic data collection and analysis of data pertaining to a particular phenomenon (Strauss & Corbin, 1990). As a research method it is applicable to qualitative research where theory can emerge from the analysis of data. The task of the researcher is to gather data, analyse it and conceptualise theory from it.

Grounded theory involves a calculated and continual effort on the part of the social researcher, while at the same time allowing the theory to emerge from the data. Through constant crosschecking and immersion in the data, open coded and written memos are generated, and these grow in conceptual complexity, density, clarity and accuracy (Glaser, 1998). It is an inductive process leading to an integrated theory which emerges through sensitive and constant comparison and verification of codes from the data. As well as sensitivity, patience is required, for the naming of the categories and sub-categories is constantly adjusted or refined until the final phase where the force of the data leads to a point of saturation or certainty (Goulding, 2002).

Practical details about the methodology can vary. Glaser (1998) and Strauss and Corbin (1990) have disagreed on the issue of coding data. Miles and Huberman (1994) supported the use of coding when collecting data. They argued that "coding is not something one does to get data ready for analysis but something that drives ongoing data collection" (Miles & Huberman, 1994, p. 63). However the application of coding has met with some significant opposition since the development of grounded theory in the 1960s. In fact it marked a point of departure in the development of this methodology by Glaser and Strauss. In order to situate the application of grounded theory relevant to this study a brief outline of the developments in the methodology follow.

Glaser (1978; 1992) has continued to emphasise the essence of the nature of grounded theory, as a method where the theory must emerge from the data. Strauss and Corbin (1990) took grounded theory in another direction by focussing on the mechanics of the methodology. They developed multiple coding procedures such as open, axial and selective coding, as well as techniques of comparison. These procedures and techniques are now used to advance analysis through the intentional manipulation of data (Kools, McCarthy, Durham, Robrecht, 1996, pp. 312 – 330). Glaser (1992) opposed Strauss and Corbin's (1990) application of grounded theory and this marked a clear split in the use of the methodology. Glaser (1992) contended that Strauss and Corbin (1990) had over-emphasised the mechanics of the research and diminished the degree of theoretical sensitivity required for the theory to emerge from the data. Stern (1994) provided a succinct explanation of the differing views of Strauss and Corbin to those of Glaser. He argued that as Strauss and Corbin examined data they stopped at each word and asked 'what if?' Glaser kept his attention focussed on the data and would ask the question, 'what do we have here?' (pp. 601–615).

Goulding (2002) emphasised that "Strauss brings to bear every possible contingency that could relate to the data whether it appears or not, while Glaser lets the data tell their own story" (p. 47).

Glaser's (1978; 1992; 1998) understanding of theoretical sensitivity was applied to the collection of data in this instance suggesting that the theory should emerge from the categories arising out of the data. In this study the research methodology followed the original principles of data collection and analysis expressed by Strauss and Glaser (1967) and further emphasised by Glaser (1998).

*Emergence of Categories*

Grounded theory with theoretical sampling enables comparison, analysis and the systematic conceptualisation of data (Miles and Huberman, 1994). It is through this process that categories emerge and the main issues of the participants can be discovered. The systematic gathering of data and the interplay between the collection of data and analysis allows theory to evolve.

> ... one gets data in an area of substantive interest, and then tries to analyse what is going on and how to conceptualise it while suspending one's own knowledge for the time being. The researcher starts finding out what is going on, conceptualises it and generates hypotheses as relations between concepts. (Glaser, 1998, p. 95)

The process may not necessarily be straightforward and the researcher may experience a lack of clarity in the course of allowing the theories to emerge (Glaser, 1998). However the construction of a table, which identifies the categories according to the dominant organising data, can help to achieve a sufficient degree of clarity. As the categories emerged they were given a code, for example, category 1, 2, 3 etc. Within each category, sub-categories were identified and named (Glaser & Strauss, 1967, pp. 36-37). Glaser advised the researcher to note any concerns that may bias the research and record them during the memoing process (1998, pp. 98 –101). In the light of this the researcher remained conscious not to force the data but allow the categories and sub-categories to emerge from the data (Goulding, 2002). Figure 7 provides an example of a dominant organising category (category 7) and the associated sub-categories emanating from the data provided by the informants.

Category 7

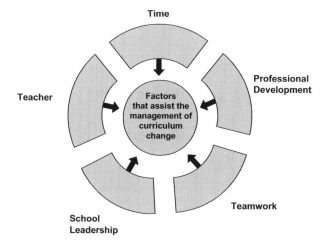

*Figure 7.* An example of a category and sub-categories emanating from the data

It was necessary to stay in the field only until no further evidence emerged. This process is referred to as category saturation (Goulding, 2002). During the process of data collection the researcher can begin to analyse the data through constant comparison, note taking, memoing and categorising.

When the categories have emerged and are saturated and no new data can be added, the sorting process begins, followed by the writing procedure. Rennie (1998) argued that this process provided grounded theory with an in-built mechanism for validating data and Goulding (2002) suggested that category saturation builds into grounded theory a mechanism that leans towards verification of the data. However, Glaser (1992) argued that verification belongs to quantitative researchers, not qualitative. Others have also argued that issues such as reliability, verification and validity are less relevant to evaluating the quality of a study within a constructivist paradigm (Bryman, 2001; Glaser, 1992; Goulding, 2002; Lincoln & Guda, 1985). However, according to Denzin and Lincoln (1998), Lincoln and Guba, (1985) and Guba and Lincoln, (1994) establishing the trustworthiness of a study determines the plausibility of a study in constructivist and naturalistic paradigms. The trustworthiness of this study is explored at length later in this chapter.

## Research Method

Keats (1993) suggested that interviews as a research method may be used as the sole source of data collection, or they could be used alongside other methods of obtaining data, and when trying to reveal a subject's reasoning, or trying to elicit opinions, attitudes or perceptions, interviews were best used as the sole source of data. Interviews were adopted as the sole method of collecting data because this study was concerned with the perspectives of RECs. "The in-depth interview is used to gain access to, and an understanding of activities and events which cannot be observed directly by the researcher" (Minichiello et al., 1995, p. 70).

## Unstructured Interview

This empirical research relied on understanding the experiences of RECs who had managed a particular curriculum change. According to Kvale (1996): "If you want to know how people understand their world and their life, why not talk with them?" (p. 1). The data collected for this study emanated from the interviews between the researcher and RECs. "The qualitative research interview is a construction site of knowledge. An interview is literally an *inter view,* an interchange of views between two persons conversing about a theme of mutual interest" (Kvale, 1996, p. 2). The aim of the interview was to understand from the RECs' perspective the management of the curriculum change. Taylor and Bogdan (1984) indicated that unstructured interviews enabled in-depth interviewing which allowed the researcher to understand the informants' perspective in their own words.

In an interview conversation, the researcher listens to what people themselves tell about their lived world, hears them express their view and opinions in their own words, learns about their views on their work situation and family life, their dreams and hopes. The qualitative research interview attempts to understand the world from the subjects, to uncover their lived world prior to scientific explanation. (Kvale, 1996, p. 1)

Unstructured interviews with the RECs provided the data used to develop theory regarding how RECs managed the change to a text-based curriculum.

The term unstructured interview implies that each individual interview "is allowed to determine the way in which the interview proceeds" (Keats, 1993, p. 30). The researcher adopted the method of unstructured interviews because it was an appropriate way of enabling each informant to share her/his perceptions in her/his own particular way. Unstructured interviews take on the appearance of everyday conversation (Minichiello et al., 1995, p. 47). However, Burgess (1982) suggested that unstructured interviews need to be controlled to the extent that they are geared towards the interests of the research. In order to minimise inappropriate intervention by the researcher a checklist was developed (and refined after each interview). This checklist enabled the researcher to keep track of the extent to which the informant was sharing insights relevant to the researcher's interest while at the same time minimising obstruction to the flow of the informant's discourse, thus maximising the opportunity for the informant to tell her/his story in her/his own way. The use and relevance of a checklist within this study is explored further in a later section of this chapter that describes how the research was conducted.

## In-depth Interviews

Unstructured in-depth interviews "rely in the social interaction between interviewer and informant to elicit information" (Minichiello et al., 1995, p. 65). According to Keats (1993, pp. 32-33), "all interviews progress through a temporal order." This order consists of three broad stages. The first stage of the interview allows for the mutual exploration of the demands of the task as well as the development of favourable attitudes. This stage is beneficial for rapport enhancement between the interviewer and the respondent and may allow for a greater understanding to flow from the increased social interaction arising out of an in-depth interview (Minichiello et al., 1995, p. 68). There is no specific method that can guarantee good rapport between researcher and informant. However, it is assumed that if there is good rapport the respondent will talk more freely with the researcher (Minichiello et al., 1995, p. 79). The second stage is where the content is elaborated and "probed" (Keats, 1993, pp. 32-33). This stage involves an encounter between the interviewer and the respondent and "implies an egalitarian concept of roles within the interview" (Minichiello et al., 1995, p. 68). The third stage of the interview is referred to as the "stage of release which brings the interview to its conclusion" (Keats, 1993, pp. 32-33).

The in-depth interview attempts to gain the informant's perspective in a language that is natural to them. This is particularly valuable because of the concern with the RECs' "experience of social reality through their routinely constructed interpretations of it" (Minichiello et al., 1995, p. 69).

## How the Research Was Conducted

### Determining the Participants

The aim of this study was to know and understand from the perspectives of the RECs, how they managed a particular curriculum change. Therefore it was important to interview RECs who were committed from the beginning to the management of this change. Much has been written about resistance to educational change and its application to curriculum change (Dalton, 1988; Elliot, 1998; Fullan, 1999; 1993; 1982; Fullan and Hargreaves, 1992; Hoyle, 1972; Jackson, 1992; Johnson, 2000a; 2000b; Leiberman, 1990; Lewis, 1988; Marsh, 1997; Scott, 1999; Smith and Lovat, 2003).

A major Australian study regarding the role of the REC identified considerable resistance to curriculum development and change in the highly specialised area of classroom religious education curriculum (Crotty, 2002). Crotty (2005) revealed that RECs tended to give greater attention to Church ministry aspects of the role even when classroom religious education curriculum was in urgent need of development and leadership (see also Engebretson, 2006). In order to gain an insight into the perspectives of RECs concerning their management of curriculum change and in the face of considerable resistance to this "top down" (Morris, 1995) curriculum initiative, the challenge for this research was to find and interview RECs who had demonstrated an active interest in successfully managing the change to a text-based curriculum.

Attempts to alleviate resistance to this curriculum change came in the form of financial incentives from the Catholic Education Office, Melbourne. Every school in the Melbourne Archdiocese was invited to apply for financial incentives to encourage initiatives to support the management of change to a text-based curriculum. Five RECs from Catholic secondary schools applied for the financial incentives offered by the Catholic Education Office, Melbourne, and all five schools were successful. The perspectives of the RECs from these five successful schools were of interest to this research because of the opportunity to gather rich data from those who had demonstrated an active commitment to the management of the curriculum change.

Against a general background of resistance to curriculum change, particularly in religious education (Crotty, 2005), it is arguable that the RECs who had applied for financial incentives to assist in the management of this curriculum change were an appropriate and accessible group to obtain rich data relevant to this study. Therefore with the intention of interviewing these RECs, permission was sought from the Director of Catholic Education, Melbourne, to invite RECs to participate in the study.

## Seeking Permission to Interview the Participants

A letter was sent to the Director of Catholic Education, Melbourne, seeking approval to write to school principals for permission to approach their RECs and invite them to participate in the study (see appendix A). The Director of Catholic Education consented to the request (see appendix B) and letters were sent to the principals (see appendix C). A letter was then sent to the RECs at each of the schools where the principal had subsequently granted permission. The letter outlined the purposes of this study as well as an invitation to participate in the study (see appendix D). Approval was granted at all levels and all five RECs who had received funding for curriculum change initiatives were willing to participate in the study and agreed to an in-depth interview.

## Conducting the Interviews

Prior to conducting the in-depth interview with each of the RECs a practice interview was organised with another REC who had experience in managing curriculum change in religious education. The aim of the practice interview was to provide an opportunity to fine-tune skills relevant to conducting unstructured in-depth interviews as well as to develop a checklist oriented towards the research interest.

Patton (1987) suggested that the researcher should develop a basic checklist in order to ensure that relevant research interest areas are covered in an interview. The practice interview assisted this researcher in preparing an interview checklist. The checklist was designed to enable each interview to flow in an unstructured manner while at the same time provide a mechanism to check whether the research interests were being explored (Burgess, 1982). The checklist also enabled the interviewer to explore, and probe further. Table 6 outlines the focus of the checklist which was constantly refined during the process of memoing, comparing and coding of the data collected after each interview (Mile and Huberman, 1984).

Table 7

*Checklist designed to help confirm that each unstructured in-depth interview explore issues relating to the research interest.*

Researcher's Checklist

- Preparing for the change.
- Attitudes and perceptions regarding the change.
- Managing staff involved in the change.
- Perceptions of religious education as a curriculum area.
- Role school leadership team and principal concerning the curriculum change.
- Factors that assisted the process of managing the curriculum change.
- Factors that impeded the process of managing the curriculum change.

Reference to a checklist enabled adherence to the unstructured interview method thus enabling the interview to shape its own course. At the same time the checklist was an invaluable tool to ascertain the extent to which the research interests were being explored. As discussed earlier in this chapter, an unstructured interview according to Keats (1993) has been defined as one where the procedure of the interview is not pre-determined, and when the manner in which the interview proceeds is determined by the interview itself. The unstructured interview enabled the participants to tell their story in their own manner from their own perspective. It required the adoption of an open and flexible approach thus enabling the interview itself to determine the way it would proceed, as well as allowing for checks to ensure that the research interests were being explored.

## Inviting the RECs to Participate in an Unstructured In-depth Interview

Each of the RECs who had applied for and received financial grants from the Catholic Education Office, Melbourne, agreed to be interviewed. Each REC was informed about the study and the purpose of the interviews prior to participating in an interview. Initially each REC received a letter which invited them to participate in the study. The letter also outlined the nature and purpose of the study (see Appendix D). At a later stage each REC was telephoned and the purpose of the interview and its relevance to the study was re-iterated. This also provided an opportunity for each REC to discuss any concerns they might have, as well as to arrange the interview time and location. Prior to the commencement of each interview there was a brief orientation for each REC regarding the purpose of the study and the relevance of the interview.

## The Actual Interviews and Locations

Barker (1968) suggested that the environmental context in which the interview takes place can affect behaviour, and it was the intention of the researcher to gain insights into the perceptions of the participants in their behavioural role as RECs. According to Bowers (1989), as discussed earlier in this chapter, there are multiple components of self that make up "Me" and the most salient "Me" at any given time is influenced by the "Me" that is called forth by one's social context. Therefore each interview took place at the participant's work-place, where she/he was employed in the REC role. The duration of each unstructured in-depth interview was approximately one hour and each participant was invited to share their perspectives on how they managed the change to a text-based curriculum. In order to minimise the disruption to the flow of the unstructured interview, permission was sought from each REC to audio-tape record the interview, as well as to note in writing any words and phrases spoken during the course of the interview. This strategy, together with reference to the interview checklist, enabled explorative and probing questions to be asked allowing the participant to elaborate on points they had raised during the flow of the interview. This process contributed to the gathering of rich data from each participant.

### After Each Interview

After each interview had concluded, extensive notes were written. Transcripts of the audio-tape recordings of each interview were used as a means of checking that the notes taken were a plausible account of what the informant had said. This checking process was designed to limit researcher bias, as well as providing a means to verify that any outside knowledge had been suspended. This procedure provided an assurance that the principles of grounded theory were respected in order to enable the issues to emerge from the data gained from the unstructured in-depth interviews with the RECs (Glaser, 1998, p. 95).

The categories emanating from the data began to emerge during note-taking, memoing, sorting, constant comparison and coding which was undertaken after each interview (Miles & Huberman, 1994). By the time all the RECs who had applied for funding to implement this curriculum change had been interviewed, several key categories had emerged and become saturated according to the principles of grounded theory (Glaser & Strauss, 1967, pp. 36-37).

Unlike quantitative studies, this qualitative study was not concerned with the quantity or number of participants involved in the study but rather with the collection of rich data. For the grounded theorist the number of informants does not contribute to establishing the plausibility of the study (Glaser, 1998). Category saturation is a more important factor that contributes to the plausibility of the study. In fact the researcher is required to stay in the field only until the categories are saturated (Glaser & Strauss, 1967). Saturation occurred when no new information or categories emerged from the informants.

### Cross-checking the Data from the Unstructured In-depth Interviews

Cross-checking data is a means to assist the qualitative researcher to scrutinise evidence of researcher bias. There are several strategies that the researcher can employ to cross-check data emanating from in-depth interviews. Minichiello et al. (1995) warned of a tendency for some researchers to hold the informant's view as paramount without employing strategies to cross-check the data as a means for assessing its accuracy. One technique used by this researcher to cross-check the accuracy of the data emanating from the interviews with the RECs was to interview other RECs who were actively responsible for managing the change.

All the RECs who had received funding and demonstrated an active commitment to successfully managing the change had been interviewed. Any cross-checking had to rely on other RECs who had not applied for funding. Permission was sought via a letter that was sent to each of the principals in the remaining sixty Catholic secondary schools. The letter sent to each principal sought permission to invite the REC from her/his respective school to participate in this study.

The researcher expected a reply from each principal within a month of the postage date. Six weeks after the letters were sent ten positive replies were received. Only nine principals had consented to the invitation for the REC from her/his school to participate in the study. RECs were contacted one by one and, in order to eliminate any bias in terms of the order of interviews, the name of each of the nine schools was placed in a small box. Each name was drawn, one by one, from the box by a colleague of the researcher. Each name was placed on a list in the order from which it was drawn from the box. The first name drawn was the first to be contacted. The next interviewee was contacted only after the previous interview was completed.

The researcher phoned the REC according to the list and outlined the nature and purpose of the study. Some RECs had indicated that they had not actively undertaken their responsibility to manage the mandated change. Since it was the intention of the researcher to discover how RECs managed the change it was deemed inappropriate to invite those who had not actively attempted to manage the change to participate in the study. They would not be able to share their perspectives on the change they had not actively undertaken or managed. The interview followed the same process used with the RECs who had received funding, as described earlier in this chapter. At the conclusion of each interview, memoing and ongoing coding of data was attended to and then the next REC on the list would be contacted and so forth. Figure 7 illustrates the participation suitability of RECs.

Table 8

*Participation suitability of RECs*

| Order Contacted | Suitability to participate in this study | Invited to participate in the study | Agreed to participate in an in-depth unstructured interview |
|---|---|---|---|
| 1 | Suitable | Yes | Yes |
| 2 | Not suitable | No | |
| 3 | Not suitable | No | |
| 4 | Suitable | Yes | Yes |
| 5 | Not suitable | No | |
| 6 | Not suitable | No | |
| 7 | Not suitable | No | |
| 8 | Suitable | Yes | Yes |
| 9 | Not Suitable | No | |

Three of the nine RECs were actively managing the change to a text-based curriculum in their respective school. The data emanating from their in-depth unstructured interviews provided an adequate cross-check that attested to the plausibility of the categories emanating from the data provided by the RECs who had applied for and received funding. After each interview with the RECs involved in the cross-check, the researcher continued the process of memoing, note taking, constant comparison and categorising the data (Glaser & Strauss, 1967). The data from these RECs supported the categories which had already been saturated from the interviews with the first five RECs who had received funding. No other categories emanated from the data of the RECs involved in the cross-check.

*Combining the Data*

The groups of participants are typically small in qualitative research and it is difficult to specify an exact number at the beginning of the research (Wiersma, 2005). Dick (2002) suggested that further data, for example as that obtained from the cross-check interviews, can be added even in situations where the categories are already saturated. Grounded theory is not obtained by means of an inflexible formula. It is empirical and according to Glaser (1998) "all is data which seeks to find out what is going on" (p. 91). Therefore the data obtained from the cross-check interviews served two important purposes. Firstly; it provided a means to cross-check the accuracy of the categories emerging from the data generated from RECs who had received funding, as well as to minimise concerns about researcher bias influencing the categories and properties. Secondly, the data from all the informants was combined and analysed and led to the development of theory concerning the RECs' management of a particular curriculum change.

Table 8 provides some information about the schools and RECs involved in this study who provided the data from which the categories emerged.

Table 9

*RECs who were interviewed for this research.*

| REC | Type of School: Catholic Year 7-12 | Years of experience as a REC | RECs Gender |
|-----|-----|-----|-----|
| *1* | *Boys* | *6* | *Male* |
| *2* | *Girls* | *7* | *Female* |
| *3* | *Co-education* | *6* | *Female* |
| *4* | *Girls* | *9* | *Female* |
| 5 | **Boys** | 12 | **Male** |
| *6* | *Girls* | *8* | *Female* |
| 7 | *Girls* | *15* | *Male* |
| *8* | *Girls* | *13* | *Female* |

(Italics indicate those RECs from schools that had not applied for funding)

## The Voice of the Researcher

Empirical research is concerned with the perceptions of those being studied (Creswell, 1998, p. 274). In this case those being studied were the RECs who managed a particular curriculum change. Every attempt was made to ascertain the perspectives of the RECs during the interview process. This involved the employment of techniques to delineate between the perspectives of the informants and the voice of the researcher. Clandinin and Connelly (1994) suggested that the distinction between the perceptions of the participants and those of the researchers are not always clear.

> … it is unclear … whether we, as researchers, are mere voyeurs of a life drama that we have been privileged to record or whether the drama takes place within the context of our own story, whether as researchers who have created a research setting in which the text is generated or whether the story takes place within the context of our own larger life story, in which case we, as researchers, are observing ourselves in participation with participants. (Clandinin & Connelly, 1994, p. 414)

83

This researcher employed several techniques to provide a plausible distinction between the informants' perspectives and the voice of the researcher. As discussed earlier in this chapter, field notes were checked against transcripts of the audio tape-recordings of each interview to verify the accuracy of the data provided by the informants. In addition, other RECs were interviewed in order to cross-check the plausibility of the categories that emerge from the interviews with the RECs who had received funding.

However several scholars have argued that the researcher's context cannot be totally excluded from the interview process, for researchers are also interpreters (Burns, 1997; Charles and Mertler, 2002; Denzin and Lincoln, 2003). According to Richardson (2003) the life experience of the researcher is not separate from the research undertaken by the researcher. "The research self is not separable from the lived self. Who we are and what we can be, what we can study, and how we can write about what we study are all tied" (Richardson, 2003, p. 197). Jansick (2003) suggested, "there is no value-free or bias-free design" (p. 53; see also Denzin & Lincoln, 1998, p. 23). Settelmainer and Taylor (2002) suggested that the researcher should take into consideration their life history and experiences and think about how such experiences will affect the research and their attitude towards what is heard from the participants. The life context of the researcher would impact in some way and according to Creswell (1998) "the researcher needs to decide how and in what way his or her own personal experiences will be introduced into the study" (p. 55).

In this research the voice of the researcher was not presumed absent in the collection and analysis of the data. An insight into the background from which the researcher's voice emanates provides readers with a contextual frame for research interpretation. The challenge for the researcher is to reach a balance between involvement and engagement on the one hand, and the detachment and objectivity necessary on the other hand to generate research without romanticising the topic so it loses credibility (Woods, 1992, p. 374).

Ellis and Berger (2003) suggested that, "researcher involvement can help subjects feel more comfortable sharing information and close the hierarchical gap between researchers and respondents" (p. 159). This researcher was known to the RECs in the Catholic secondary schools in the Melbourne Archdiocese and this prior knowledge did help to close the hierarchical gap between the researcher and the respondents. This researcher's context cannot be totally excluded from the collection and analysis of data and therefore it is appropriate to outline his professional background.

## Professional Background of the Researcher

This researcher's professional background involved approximately twelve years experience as a REC in Catholic secondary schools in the Melbourne Archdiocese and seven years experience as a member of the RECs' professional development committee for the Archdiocese. This researcher was also responsible for leading and facilitating professional development programs for teachers and RECs in the area of curriculum management and leadership for the Catholic Education Office, Melbourne. The researcher also reviewed, at the invitation of the writer, the year seven and year eight textbooks in the *To Know Worship and Love* textbooks series, and was a member of the expert consulting team for the senior textbook in the series. The researcher is also a lecturer in religious education in a tertiary education setting. Lincoln (1997) has commented on the carefully disguised presence of the researcher and Clandinin and Connelly (1994) have suggested that conventional research methods tended to silence the voice of the researcher. However, they argued that the voice of the researcher is a recognised factor in personal experience methods: "Without a sense of voice, a researcher is bound to the ever-refined writing and rewriting of field texts at a time that calls for research texts" (Clandinin & Connelly, 1994, p. 423). In this research an ☐nterpretivist role was adopted, a role justifiable given the researcher's knowledge of and experience in the field that was the focus of the study. In addition to the contributions of the researcher's voice to the analysis of data, consultation with four experts in religious education also provided for a deepening of the level of analysis.

## Religious Education Experts

Four experts in the field of religious education were asked for their responses to the categories and theory generated from the data. The professional background and expertise of each expert is outlined in detail in Chapter seven of this book. Consultation with the experts in religious education served two important purposes. Firstly, they confirmed the plausibility of the categories that emerged from the data. Secondly, their knowledge and experience provided insights into the categories and theory generated and contributed to a deeper level of analysis.

## Consultation Process

Each of the four experts in religious education agreed to be interviewed and each interview lasted approximately one hour. The already established professional relationship enabled the interviews to flow in a focussed and relaxed manner. Each expert consented to the audio tape-recoding of their interview. The recordings were later transcribed and used to check for the accuracy of the data collected from each informant.

Each interview commenced by outlining the nature and purpose of the study and showing each participant a copy of the theory generated and categories that emerged from the data generated from the earlier interviews with RECs. The process for each interview involved the experts being offered the opportunity to read about the categories and theory generated, and this was followed by a semi-structured conversation where insights were shared and discussed about the categories and theory generated. The insights shared by each of the experts attested to the plausibility of the theory generated and contributed the further analysis provided in Chapter seven. Figure 8 illustrates the process by which the final construction of the categories eventuated.

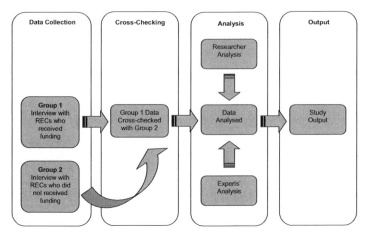

*Figure 8.* Process by which the final categories and sub-categories were constructed from the research data.

## Trustworthiness of the Study

According to Lincoln and Guba (1985) trustworthiness contributes to the plausibility of the study. They argued that trustworthiness asks, "how can the inquirer persuade his or her audience (including self) that the findings of an inquiry are worth paying attention to, worth taking account of?" (p. 290). Within a constructivist and constructionist paradigm the criteria for establishing trustworthiness, according to Denzin (1998), consists of four components: credibility, transferability, dependability and confirmability. The components of trustworthiness were addressed in this research and contributed to establishing the plausibility of the study.

### *Credibility*

Credibility is concerned with techniques that contribute to trustworthy findings and interpretations being produced within a constructivist paradigm. This study employed the practice of prolonged engagement and referential adequacy to address the contribution credibility brings to trustworthiness (Lincoln & Guda, 1985).

Prolonged engagement refers to spending sufficient time to become oriented in the research situation. Familiarity with the context or research site, as well as focussing on the importance of building trust with the participants are characteristics of prolonged engagement. Lincoln and Guba (1985) have indicated that building trust with the participants is time-consuming yet essential. Establishing trust was aided by the fact that the researcher was known to the participants as a former REC in the Melbourne Archdiocese. This association helped to minimise possible distortions that are sometimes difficult to overcome when trust has not been established between the researcher and the participants (Jackson, 1968).

Another procedure used by the researcher, which helped to establish credibility, was the technique of referential adequacy. Electronically recording data allowed the researcher the opportunity to establish a standard by which later data analyses and interpretations were checked for adequacy (Eisner, 1975, pp. 447-542).

Testing for misinformation was an important consideration particularly in light of the pre-existing relationship and rapport between the participants and the researcher. To minimise the possibility of introducing misinformation by distortion (Bilmes, 1975), recorded in-depth interviews on audio-tape and transcriptions of the interviews were compared against the researcher's notes taken during and after each interview. This allowed the opportunity to constantly check the data analyses and interpretations with the original source in order to minimise the chances of inadequate interpretations of the data. During this process of checking and constant comparison, care was taken to explore possible contradictions and misinterpretations.

## Transferability

Within a constructivist and constructionist paradigm the notion of transferability is different from that understood within a positivist paradigm which relies on external validity. Within a constructivist paradigm the researcher develops theory or sets out hypotheses and description relevant to the time and context in which they were found. Transferability within a constructivist paradigm depends on context (Lincoln and Guba, 1985).

> Whether they hold in some other context, or even in the same context at some other time, is an empirical issue, the resolution of which depends upon the degree of similarity between sending and receiving (or earlier and later) contexts. (Linclon & Guba, 1985, p. 316)

The researcher's task was to analyse the data concerning the RECs' management of a particular curriculum change. Within a constructivist and constructionist paradigm, it is the provision of a database "that makes transferability judgements possible on the part of potential appliers" (Lincoln & Guba, 1985, p. 316).

Transferability therefore applies to whether the categories and properties would appear in other contexts. As discussed earlier in this chapter, the data from the RECs who had applied for funding was cross-checked with the data from RECs who had not applied for funding. In this case the same categories and properties emerged.

## Dependability

Dependability is tested by the capacity of the reader to determine from the written account the point at which the various stages of analysis have occurred. An inquiry audit is one technique used to consider the dependability of a study. This technique can be used to authenticate the data analyses and interpretations. The intention of an inquiry audit is to establish fair representation of the trustworthiness of the stages of analysis (Lincoln & Guba, 1985, pp. 317-318).

> The auditor should see him or herself as acting on behalf of the general readership of the inquiry report, a readership that may not have the time or inclination (or accessibility to the data) to undertake a detailed assessment of trustworthiness. (Lincoln & Guba, 1985, p. 326)

According to Lincoln and Guba, (1985) the inquiry auditor must be sufficiently sophisticated to act in the role. Sophistication can be determined by a substantiative understanding of the methodological area as well as substantiative knowledge in the area of inquiry. The transcripts of the interviews were presented to two academics who were very familiar with both the methodology of grounded theory and the role of RECs in Catholic schools. They were able to identify, from the data, categories that were virtually identical to those identified by the researcher.

*Confirmability*

An inquiry audit can be used to simultaneously determine dependability and confirmability (Lincoln and Guba, 1985). In this study experts in the field of religious education were consulted. In addition to acknowledging the dependability of the study they also confirmed the accuracy and fairness of the data analyses and interpretations. While absolute objectivity is impossible in any research (Bryman, 2001), the process of constant comparison, and journaling such as the memoing process that is integral to grounded theory were undertaken throughout the data collection phase and assisted in avoiding personal values and judgements, or theoretical inclinations to overtly influence the research data.

The ultimate test of trustworthiness rests with the readers. In particular it will rest with those who participated in the study and other RECs in Melbourne Catholic secondary schools as well as those in leadership in the Catholic Education Office, Melbourne, who are responsible for religious education curriculum and the way it is managed by RECs.

**Conclusion**

This chapter has detailed the epistemology and theoretical perspective which underpinned this qualitative study into the RECs' perspectives on their management of a text-based curriculum change. The empirical component of this research has its foundation in qualitative research in the field of social science. It examined how RECs managed a particular curriculum change by obtaining their perspectives. The philosophical assumption of the methodological design is that meaning is a social construction. In order to enter into the world of the RECs and to understand their construction of how this text-based curriculum change was managed, unstructured in-depth interviewing was used. Analysis of the interviews used inductive principles in order for theories and understandings to emerge from the data.

In the following chapters the analysis of the data collected through the research design outlined in this chapter is discussed in relation to the literature reviewed in Chapters two and three.

# CHAPTER FIVE
# Managing Curriculum Change in Religious Education

This and the following chapter present the theory generated and an analysis of the empirical research on the RECs' perspectives on their management of a particular curriculum change in religious education. As shown in the previous chapter, a grounded theory approach was employed to determine the RECs' perspectives on how they managed the curriculum change in question. Seven categories emerged, each with associated sub-categories, which were significant in understanding how the RECs perceived the management of this curriculum initiative.

The theory generated presented in this chapter and in Chapter six have been presented to academics and educators at various forums. The forums include; the *Australian Association of Religious Education Conference* (September, 2004); the *Australian Association for Research in Education: International Education Research Conference* (November, 2004); the *Fourth National Symposium: Religious Education and Ministry* (March, 2005); and the *Australian Association of Religious Education Conference* (October, 2006). At these forums the responses from the participants attested to the trustworthiness of this research, provided further insights pertaining to the interview texts, and explored connections and meanings relevant to the theory generated and their analysis. Table 11 shown at the end of this chapter orients the reader to the theory generated relevant to the first five categories and their associated sub-categories. The final two categories or explored in Chapter six.

This chapter presents the theory generated and analysis of five key categories and associated sub-categories that emerged. They are:

- Category 1: Preparation for change
- Category 2: School outlook
- Category 3: Staff development
- Category 4: Attitudes and perspectives
- Category 5: Leadership in curriculum change.

The following chapter (Chapter six) presents the theory generated and analyses of the additional two categories and associated sub-categories. They are:

- Category 6:   Factors that impeded the curriculum change
- Category 7:   Factors that assisted the curriculum change.

This chapter contains a discussion and analysis of the theory generated from the RECs' perspectives on the management of a "top-down" (Morris, 1995) knowledge-centred text-based curriculum initiative. The presentation of the theory generated incorporates direct quotations from the participants to support the arguments being proposed. The use of quotations provided a means of presenting the opinions and the descriptions of the RECs. To maintain their anonymity, a letter code (A, B, etc) was allocated and references to the names of individuals and schools were removed from the text.

### Preparation for Change

The "top down" (Morris, 1995) curriculum initiative that was the focus of this study was directed by the Archbishop of Melbourne who is ultimately responsible for religious education within the archdiocese. The RECs stated strongly the importance of taking responsibility for preparing for the curriculum change. An analysis of the theory generated revealed that religious education coordinators had drawn from a range of sources in order to prepare for the curriculum change.

Preparation for change involved several initiatives that are identified as sub-categories in Figure 9.

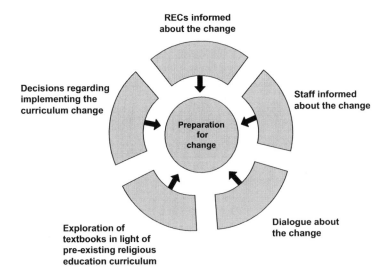

*Figure 9.* Category 1: Preparation for change and sub categories.

### *RECs Informed About the Change*

The RECs described what they did in order to become informed about the intended curriculum change. Most RECs commented on the lack of communication and information concerning the planning and implementation of the text-based curriculum initiative from the Episcopal Vicar's Office and the Catholic Education Office, Melbourne.

I was not sure where the idea for a textbook had come from. I recall attending an RE [religious education] network meeting in 1998 and the CEO [Catholic Education Office] staff representative mentioned that Archbishop Pell had set up an Episcopal Vicariate for Religious Education. She said that the Vicariate would be responsible for writing textbooks and every student from P-12 would be required to have a copy. I don't recall ever getting any information or letter outlining what was going on or what was to happen. It was all a bit vague to me. (O)

Information concerning the curriculum change, the context and rationale for the change was limited and not easily accessible. In the absence of informative written correspondence from the Episcopal Vicar's Office and the Catholic Education Office, the RECs interviewed for this study took responsibility for discovering information about the intended changes.

When we were informed about the changes that were going to be introduced, I thought it was first of all important for me to be aware and involved in learning about the change. I phoned anyone I knew from the CEO and in other schools who I thought might know something. I also attended various forums where I had hoped the implications of those changes would be outlined. However those forums tended to be about the content of the textbooks. (J)

The RECs explored several ways of becoming informed about the change. Opportunities to attend information sessions organised by the Archdiocese and facilitated by the authors of the textbooks were well attended. Some contacted the authors of the textbooks and agreed to read and trial draft chapters and try them out with their students. This process provided the RECs with an opportunity to become familiar with the content of the textbooks as well as provide feedback to the authors. Some RECs developed informal networks such as maintaining regular contact with other RECs and sharing any information they had discovered about the textbooks. Some RECs who were employed in Catholic schools owned by religious congregations held meetings and wrote letters to the Archdiocese in an attempt to become informed about the intended changes.

The religious education coordinators from schools belonging to the same religious congregation as my school, met to discuss the suggested changes. We put in a submission responding to the changes and made recommendations concerning those changes. We did not get a direct response to the recommendations contained within the submission, but were asked to trial the draft chapters of the textbooks. (A)

Some RECs tried to gather information about the intended changes from congregational leaders of religious orders. In the latter part of 1999, the researcher, as a former REC in a Catholic school owned by a religious congregation and another REC who was interviewed as a part of this study, were invited to attend a meeting of the Conference of Religious Congregational Leaders. The leaders of religious congregations who owned or sponsored schools in the Archdiocese were in attendance. The purpose of the meeting was to discuss how the schools owned by religious congregations would prepare for the changes to the religious education curriculum. During the course of the meeting it became apparent that the congregational leaders were equally ill-informed about the intention, status and context in which the textbooks would be situated in Catholic education and it was agreed that a letter would be drafted and sent to the Archbishop in order to ascertain information about the changes.

Several RECs sought information about the intended changes from their school principal. The overall responsibility for religious education in a Catholic school rests with the principal who delegates responsibilities to the REC (Catholic Education Office, Melbourne, 2005, p. 1). The RECs involved in this study revealed that school principals were equally ill-informed about the intended changes and in most situations relied on the REC in their respective school to keep them informed.

The principal was always asking me about the textbooks and the staff also questioned me. I did not know what to say, I had no answers to give them   and I did not know where to find the answers. I would talk to other RECs and they did not know much either. It was as if we were all kept in the dark. I did not find the CEO particularly helpful or informative. (B)

## Approaches Undertaken by RECs to Become Informed About the Change

The Archdiocese had directed the change but failed to provide adequate information to those responsible in schools for the management and implementation of this curriculum change. There appeared to be no one directly responsible for informing the RECs about the curriculum change and the implications of that change. Subsequently the RECs explored several avenues in order to become informed about the text-based curriculum change. The approaches taken by the RECs included: a) direct contact with personnel from the CEO, Melbourne; b) attendance at information forums facilitated by Catholic Education Office staff; c) reading and trailing draft chapters of the textbooks and providing feedback to the authors of the books; d) contact with authors of the textbooks; e) informal networks with RECs from other schools; f) discussions with leaders of religious congregations; and g) discussions with school principals.

As stated in Chapter two of this book, Marsh (1997) and Brickell (1972) have argued that the adoption of a "top down" (Morris, 1995) curriculum initiative requires a clear understanding of the intended curriculum innovation. The interviews with the RECs suggested that those authorities responsible for communicating the rationale and details of the intended curriculum change failed to provide adequate documentation or information about the change to RECs, principals or congregational leaders of religious schools in the Archdiocese.

As discussed in Chapter two, Rymarz (1998) argued that curriculum management required informed understandings of educational theory and knowledge. This study revealed that, in the absence of adequate information about the intended changes, the RECs explored various avenues in order to become informed about the intended changes. As curriculum leaders, most RECs perceived it to be their responsibility to know and understand the intended change and the implications of the change for the delivery of religious education curriculum in their particular school.

I had to find out all I could about the change because if I did not nobody else in the school would take responsibility for it and we would end up not knowing what we were required to do. (G)

This "top down" (Morris, 1995) curriculum initiative directed by the Archbishop of Melbourne, provides an example of the influence outside forces may have in affecting curriculum change in schools (Brady & Kennedy, 2003). According to Marsh and Bowman (1987) "top down" curriculum change can be effective when a textbook is used to support the initiative. The approaches undertaken by the RECs in order to become informed about the curriculum change suggested that a textbook in the hands of those responsible for managing the change is less effective without a clear understanding of the intention and rationale underpinning the change.

## Staff Informed About the Change

Regardless of how difficult it was for RECs to access information about the purpose and intention of the change, they believed that for them to manage the change they needed to keep their own staff informed. The RECs initiated several strategies to ensure that their staff had access to the available information. These strategies included: a) reports to the faculty by the REC; b) information dissemination; c) reading and trialling draft chapters of the textbooks; and d) professional development seminars.

The RECs made presentations at faculty meetings updating and informing staff about any new information they had received related to the curriculum change.

We had an RE staff meeting four times a term and I factored into the agenda a section concerning up-dates regarding the textbooks. Any information I had I would report to the RE faculty. (I)

The faculty meetings enabled members of their religious education faculty to ask any questions arising out of the curriculum up dates.

Another strategy commonly used by the RECs involved the dissemination of relevant literature and correspondence to members of the religious education faculty. According to the RECs most of the literature came from the Archdiocese and authors of the textbooks. It consisted mainly of information concerning timelines about the publication of the textbooks and when they would be available for purchase, overviews of chapter topics relevant to each year level, and draft copies of the chapters produced by the authors. A willingness to read literature concerning the curriculum change by members of the religious education faculty was sometimes compromised by other demands facing many religious education teachers.

As indicated in Chapter two of this book, many teachers of religious education in Catholic schools were not qualified or specialists in religious education (Thomas, 2000). For many teachers, religious education was a second or third teaching area and was given less priority in terms of lesson preparation and professional reading time (Fleming, 2002). The following comment by one REC expressed a view commonly held by most RECs who were interviewed.

Any correspondence that came my way I would photocopy and pass on to the teachers. It was a way of trying to keep them informed. Not many had time to read it but we would try to discuss the contents at RE meetings. I

Another strategy used by many RECs involved encouraging members of their religious education faculty to read and/or trial draft copies of the chapters intended for the textbooks with their religious education class. RECs had access to the draft chapters of the textbooks. The Episcopal Vicar's Office invited some schools to trial the draft chapters. All RECs in the Archdiocese were welcome to contact the authors of the textbooks and receive draft copies of the chapters. Most RECs encouraged members of the religious education faculty to read the draft chapters and become familiar with the contents.

Encouraging members of the religious education faculty to attend professional development seminars was highly favoured amongst the RECs. The professional development seminars for religious education teachers focussed mainly on the contents of the textbooks and possible strategies for teaching the contents of the textbooks. All the RECs involved in this study negotiated as many opportunities as possible for members of their religious education faculty to attend the professional development seminars. As discussed in Chapter two, many of the teaching staff the Catholic schools have only one religious education class as part of their teaching allotment (Thomas, 2000). This has accounted for very large religious education faculties in many Catholic schools throughout the Archdiocese. Schools with large religious education faculties found it was impossible to send all religious education teachers to the professional development seminars. The following comment was representative of most RECs involved in this study.

> We sent staff off to the various professional development in-services. I could not send all staff to each in-service. I sent one representative to each of the Year 7, 8, 9 and 10 in-services. They brought back a wealth of information regarding ideas about how they could use the textbooks in RE. (G)

The RECs believed that ensuring that their staff members were informed was integral to the management of this particular curriculum change. The information available about the change was limited to issues concerning publication timelines, overviews of the topics covered in the textbooks and draft copies of the chapters contained in the textbooks.

Textbooks have a wide range of uses (Issitt, 2004) and a good textbook can provide insights into current pedagogical approaches (Engebretson & Rymarz, 2002; 2004). However, the draft chapters did very little to inform staff about the nature and purpose of the change and the rationale and theoretical position underpinning the change. This is perhaps because textbooks are not stand alone instruments (Finlay, 2000) and they need to be understood along side other factors such as curriculum and pedagogy (Vespoor, 1989).

*Dialogue about the Change*

In order to prepare for the change most RECs provided opportunities for religious education teachers to discuss the intended changes. There were a variety of ways in which dialogue about the curriculum change occurred. They were: a) informal discussions about the intended change; b) forums to discuss concerns and feelings about the change; c) record keeping; and d) meetings to discuss strategies for implementing the change.

Most RECs commented on the importance of being available for members of the teaching staff who sought them out to discuss and to pose questions or concerns they had about the intended changes.

> Teachers would seek me out from time to time. They would come to my office and ask me questions about the textbooks and the intended changes. I felt it was important to stop whatever I was doing and just listen to their concerns and in some way reassure them that as a faculty we would work it out. (O)

It was also common for RECs to provide forums where staff could meet and discuss their concerns and feelings regarding the proposed change.

> We gathered as a faculty and discussed more broadly how people felt about the changes. We spent a bit of time exploring the level of feeling amongst the staff. As issues were raised and feelings expressed, we tried to come to some consensus about how we would approach these changes and the time frame it would take. (J)

The opportunity to discuss feelings enabled individual staff members to be heard by their colleagues. It provided opportunities for them to explore their concerns. Some RECs suggested that this process enabled the faculty to move forward and consider strategies for implementing the curriculum.

When the textbooks became available for use in schools some RECs suggested that religious education teachers keep a journal to record their experiences. As they trialled different sections of the textbooks they were encouraged to record notes after each lesson as well as write down their evaluations. It was intended that these reflections would be shared later in religious education meetings.

> At the end of the term the teachers at each year level would meet with me and share their insights which they had recorded in their journals. We shared these experiences from those records keeping notes that the teachers had been asked to do. And then I would base further discussion and further implementation of the process on their input. So in this regard keeping records was a more formalised requirement in terms of feedback and accountability, but it helped to determine how we should proceed as a faculty. (A)

Some religious education coordinators spent a minimum of time discussing feelings and reactions to the proposed changes. They adopted a task-focused approach to managing and implementing the curriculum change. The following comment from one REC was similar to the view held by others who were primarily task focused.

> Because of all the negative hype about the textbooks, I knew that some teachers would want to discuss whether we should or shouldn't have the textbooks. I wasn't going to go down that path. I knew that the textbooks were mandatory, and we had to use them. I wasn't going to waste my time discussing whether we should have them or not. I was the REC and my task was to implement the textbooks and once I sorted that out in my head I was clear on what had to be done. I got people on board by discussing how we would go about implementing the books. We met regularly to discuss the chapters we should teach and at what stage in the semester or year. (B)

Dialogue about the changes provided a way for religious education faculties in schools to move towards implementing the text-based curriculum. Several RECs commented on the opportunity for members of the faculty to talk about the intended changes and discuss any concerns. It was an opportunity for staff members to come together under the leadership of the REC, and explore ways of implementing the text-based curriculum.

Dialogue about the changes enabled teachers to express their feelings about the intended change. The opportunity brought to the fore feelings about the Church, religion and the ministry of Christian formation.

My unease is that an emphasis on doctrine without an adequate attention to personal experience and critical analysis isn't really authentic in terms of the process of Christian formation. We have members of staff that haven't had the opportunities for engaging in ongoing Christian formation and we are concerned that their own formation will be stifled if they perceive the textbooks as taking religious education back to the pre-Vatican II era. (A)

## *Approaches Taken to Dialogue about the Change*

Dialogue amongst members of the religious education faculty in each school about the change to a text-based curriculum was perceived as valuable in determining how the school-based curriculum would take form. This was particularly important since Catholic schools in the Archdiocese had a long tradition of developing school-based curriculum in religious education. Prior to the introduction of the *To Know Worship and Love* textbook series, *Guidelines* (1975; 1977; 1984; 1995) had established a tradition of school-based religious education curriculum. Under the direction of the REC each school was responsible for developing its own curriculum in religious education based on *Guidelines* (1995). This trend continued with the introduction of the textbooks into religious education in Catholic schools. It was assumed that each school would use the textbook as the main source for teaching and learning in religious education and would develop a school-based curriculum from the content contained within the textbooks (Pell, 2001).

Conflict is an integral part of change (Smith and Lovat, 2003). This study revealed that conflict issues were not limited to professional concerns but also personal concerns. Some teachers of religious education used the time to discuss issues of conflict related to their perception of the Church and their own Christian formation. Dialogue on these issues attested to the notion that change was perceived to be more about people than the curriculum initiative (Fullan, 1999; Stenhouse, 1975).

The RECs encouraged opportunities to engage in dialogue about the curriculum change in order to promote the change. Because this "top down" (Morris, 1995) change was mandatory, one REC set particular boundaries. This REC would not allow the time allocated for dialogue about the change to be consumed by concerns about the appropriateness of this curriculum change. As stated earlier, "I knew that the textbooks were mandatory, and we had to use them. I wasn't going to waste my time discussing whether we should have them or not" (B).

Curriculum change can be assisted by establishing boundaries that help to deal with the process of change not just the change product. Smith and Lovat (2003) have indicated that "too many attempts towards change in education have not recognised these features nor provided ways to deal with them" (p. 195). Other boundaries set by RECs involved encouraging teachers to keep a journal of their experiences and thoughts about the change. Time was set aside during faculty meetings for staff members to reflect on and discuss their journal entries.

Change challenges teachers' perceptions of themselves and their own competencies (Smith and Lovat, 2003). The opportunities provided by the RECs to dialogue about the change enabled staff members to contemplate how the changes would affect and influence them. According to Fullan (1999), change occurs because individuals themselves change. The opportunity to dialogue provided an opportunity for staff members to contemplate their own changing personal and professional views.

The opportunity to listen to and discuss feelings about the change and express concerns (both educational and religious) was considered an appropriate means to determine how to approach the text-based curriculum change at school level. Some RECs encouraged dialogue about the change in a more formalised manner and required teachers of religion to maintain written records when using the textbooks. Others set clear parameters around what would be discussed during curriculum planning meetings. Some RECs encouraged teachers to talk about their experiences and concerns. From the perspective of the RECs, opportunities for staff to talk about the intended changes assisted in determining the way forward in terms of implementing a curriculum based on the textbooks.

## *Exploration of the Textbooks in Light of Pre-existing Religious Education Curriculum*

In the process of preparing for the change to a text-based curriculum, most RECs explored the textbooks in the light of the pre-existing religious education curriculum, which had been developed from *Guidelines* (1995). This was done by a) auditing the existing curriculum; b) identifying key learning outcomes from the *To Know Worship and Love Teaching Companions*; and c) incorporating textbooks into classroom teaching.

Some RECs attempted to audit the existing curriculum in their school against the content of the text books. For some RECs the process involved matching the topics and units taught in the pre-existing curriculum with similar topics contained within the textbooks.

When I looked at Year 7 and 9 there were a lot of topics that we were already teaching. When the Year 8 text came along, there was a number of overlaps: Caring for creation, Sacraments, History and St Paul. The Year 10 text was also virtually what we were doing at our school anyway, World Religions, Mark's Gospel, Conscience, Morality. In preparing the curriculum from the content of the textbooks, I didn't feel that we were really doing anything new. I

This approach provided little impetus to explore content in the textbooks that was not relevant to the pre-existing curriculum.

One REC prepared for the change by identifying the key learning outcomes for each topic or chapter in the textbooks. The key learning outcomes were obtained from the *To Know Worship and Love Teacher Companions* (Elliott, 2001; 2002) supporting the textbooks.

I typed up all the outcomes for all of the topics in Years 7, 8, 9, 10. This helped me to understand the contents in the textbooks. After doing that I created a folder for each of the topics and identified the outcomes relevant to the topics. In each folder I would list strategies and other resources. We had used most of the resources included in each folder in the past. So gradually I built up and transferred from our old topics resources and strategies that still had relevance and could help achieve the outcomes that were set for a particular topic in the textbooks. (L)

In this situation the approach taken in order to prepare for, and implement the change provided more scope for identifying a sequence and range of topics emanating from the textbooks. The pre-existing courses were used to resource and provide further strategies for teaching the topics contained within the textbooks. Thus the content of the curriculum remained the nexus between the pre-existing course and the textbooks.

Another approach taken to prepare for the change involved encouraging teachers to interact with the textbooks in the classroom. This approach provided opportunities for teachers and students to encounter the textbooks and become familiar with the content contained within the textbooks.

It was really a matter of introducing the texts and saying: here are the texts; use them to teach RE. And there wasn't really any rewriting of the courses in accordance with what the textbooks were about. I think the courses are unsatisfactory because of this. You have teachers who are teaching different chapters from the texts. There isn't any uniformity and the courses weren't written in a comprehensive way when we introduced the texts. It has been a bit of a 'mish mash' but we are working on it now. (O)

This approach provided opportunities for teachers to incorporate the textbooks into a pre-existing curriculum it also provided more flexibility for each teacher to teach different content areas in the classroom learning and teaching process. This approach to preparing for the implementation of the text-based curriculum did not emphasise a uniform approach for each class at the same year level.

In many situations the content of the textbooks was used as an additional resource to be incorporated into an existing school-based curriculum. In some situations the use of the textbooks exposed deficits and overlaps in the existing curriculum thus allowing for further consideration of the relevance of content covered in the pre-existing curriculum.

They [the RE teachers] use the texts as a basis. There was no way you could d    o everything in the textbook anyway. There was too much content. So we took our curriculum, and we tweaked it, we moved it. We changed content from one particular year level to another. We made the content fit better and we are teaching stuff [content] that is in the textbooks that we hadn't been teaching in our curriculum. I found that at Year 7, 8, 9 and 10 level the textbooks have helped to structure the course a bit more as well as iron out any overlaps. (G)

## *Approaches to Textbooks in Light of Pre-existing Religious Education Curriculum*

The RECs believed that the management of the text-based curriculum primarily involved the integration of the content of the textbooks into a school's pre-existing school-based curriculum that was underpinned by *Guidelines* (1995). This approach undertaken by most RECs suggested an inadequate understanding of the theoretical underpinnings of both approaches.

Chapter one of this book demonstrated that the previous and present approaches to religious education in the Archdiocese of Melbourne have emanated from two distinctive theoretical paradigms. The life-centred approach adopted in *Guidelines* (1995) was based on theological principles (Engebretson, 1997, pp. 25-29). The approach assumed in the *To Know Worship and Love* textbook series was based on a knowledge-centred outcomes based educational approach

(Pell, 2001, p. 5; see also Buchanan, 2004). The integration of content between the pre-existing curriculum and the content contained within the textbooks suggested that the RECs did not account for the varying theories underpinning the current and pre-exiting curriculum approaches.

According to Ryan (2000), textbooks can assist teachers in identifying the particular curriculum theory that underpins them. However this study revealed that in most situations the RECs were primarily focussed on integrating the content of the textbooks into similar content areas associated with a school's pre-existing curriculum based on *Guidelines* (1995). They did not take into account the varying theories underpinning the current and pre-existing curriculum.

## *Decisions Regarding Implementing the Curriculum Change*

As discussed earlier in this chapter, discussion about the changes amongst faculty members was encouraged. Opportunities for dialogue provided occasions for religious education teachers to gain understanding about the change. However the management of this change required RECs to employ various decision making strategies. Three broad approaches to decision making were used by the RECs. They were: a) cooperative decision making; b) expert decision making; and c) informed decision making.

One REC, a leader of a religious education faculty of predominantly qualified and experienced teachers of religious education, adopted a cooperative approach to decision making and implementation. This involved religious education teachers making key decisions about what resources would be used and what strategies would be incorporated[8]. In such situations the RECs encouraged all teachers of religious education to be involved in the planning and implementation of the curriculum change.

> Most of our RE teachers are qualified, so what I did as the REC was set up at each year level a team leader who would divide up the topics to be taught at that particular year level and each teacher would develop a teaching unit incorporating the textbooks and other resources and strategies relevant to that particular topic. I

Most RECs were responsible for leading faculties where the teaching staff taught one class of religious education. In such schools the teachers taught mainly in other faculties for which they were qualified to teach. The limited involvement in religious education generally meant that preparation time for religious education curriculum was compromised.

> Most of our RE staff are not qualified to teach religious education and they teach mainly in two or sometimes three other faculties. Their time and energy goes into teaching in the faculty areas for which they are qualified. They find RE really difficult to teach and it doesn't help that each year they get an RE class at a different year level so they can't even consolidate their practical skills at a year level over a period of time. (I)

In situations where RECs perceived religious education teachers as having limited preparation time and knowledge in religious education, it was primarily the expertise of the RECs that underpinned the curriculum decisions.

---

[8] Despite the competencies of this particular religious education faculty, in terms of qualifications and experience, the REC made the decisions about which topics would be taught at each year level. This issue is addressed later in this chapter.

Limited time and the lack of expertise were factors that I think in the end meant that the staff pretty much left it up to me to complete the write up of the new curriculum. I looked at the content in the textbooks and what we had done in the previous years and I decided the way to go. The texts were enormous and impossible to cover in one year so I decided the topics and prepared the units of work. (J)

In some situations the process for preparing for the curriculum change ultimately involved a decision by the REC, but it was sometimes informed by the insights and issues raised by members of the religious education faculty. This measure of informed decision making was an approach that enabled RECs to gain insights and understandings about how members of the faculty perceived the changes. However, ultimately the final decision rested with the REC.

It takes a lot of energy. I think what you need is a core group of people who are committed to teaching the subject and to working in RE, rather than having teachers who have a class of RE tagged onto their teaching allotment just to fill up their timetable. You know, we are very lucky because we are moving away from that now. There are a lot of people who have three or four classes of RE and it makes a great deal of difference. People have time and are willing to work on curriculum issues. We now have twenty-six teachers in the faculty instead of forty-one. We discussed ways of implementing the curriculum but in the end I had to make the decisions. (B)

## Approaches to Making Decisions Regarding Implementing the Curriculum Change

According to Johnson (1996) schools that shape and control a change initiative to suit their situation are suited to effect change. The decisions made by RECs demonstrated initiatives to shape and control the change initiative by taking into account the composition, competencies and expertise of their teachers of religious education. These factors influenced their decision about how to manage the change. The role of the REC is diverse, challenging and demanding (Liddy, 1998) and well suited to a proficient operator. Fleming (2001) has indicated that RECs are effective in a management role when they have the ability to carry out plans and achieve outcomes efficiently. The RECs demonstrated an ability to involve other members of the religious education faculty in managing the change. In some cases the relationship between the RECs and members of their faculty could be interpreted as contriving collaboration as an administrative mechanism (Hargeaves, 1994) where the REC simply directs the faculty to achieve certain outcomes in order to bring about the curriculum change. Viewed in another light the parameters set by the RECs were based on decisions based on their perspectives on the skills and competencies of the members of their religious education faculty members. Subsequently a collaborative culture emerged where RECs provided an opportunity for change to take place by creating boundaries and so determining how the change would be managed. This approach has the potential to reduce the level of anxiety and uncertainty associated with change (Brady and Kennedy, 2003).

## Summary of the Key Points from Preparation for Change

While Archdiocesan documents have promoted the ecclesial and ministerial nature of the role of the REC, the management of change has required RECs to exercise "educational leadership" skills in managing the curriculum change. Certain challenges arose for some RECs because of this, and RECs undertook various initiatives in order to prepare for the change.

To become informed the RECs explored several avenues open to them suggesting a high degree of motivation. The RECs were aware of the Archdiocese's mandate that all classroom religious education curricula in Catholic schools in the Archdiocese of Melbourne be based on the *To Know Worship and Love* textbook series. However details about how this would take place were not clearly explained to those who were ultimately responsible for managing the curriculum change. This research has indicated that when RECs as curriculum leaders were not adequately informed about the change they endeavoured to explore various avenues in order to understand the change.

The RECs provided opportunities for teachers of religious education within the schools to become informed about the intended changes. It was necessary that classroom teachers of religious education understand the intended changes. This research has revealed that both RECs and religious education teachers saw the changes relating primarily to issues concerning curriculum content. This perspectives on the change indicated that the focus was on the practical application of the curriculum content. Concerns and understandings about the theory, and rationale relating to the change were not at the fore of this implementation process. However the scope of this change suggested a major paradigm shift in terms of how religious education would be taught in the Archdiocese. For this reason communication about the change with the RECs who were ultimately responsible for managing the curriculum change could have been more effective. The Archdiocese could have assisted the RECs by providing documentation and forums for RECs not only to understand the content contained within the textbooks but also to understand the pedagogy, rationale and theory behind the change.

## School Outlook

School outlook refers to the attitudes and perceptions that reflect the priority given to religious education within the school context[9]. In the process of managing the change some factors influencing a school's outlook are viewed from three broad areas. These areas of influence emerged from the interviews with the REC's. Figure 10 identifies the three areas as: appointment of religious education teachers; school leadership/executive; and curriculum credibility.

---

[9] Parts of this section have been published in:
Buchanan. M. T. (2006b). Curriculum management: Influencing school outlook towards religious education. *Journal of Religious Education, 54* (2), pp. 71-78.

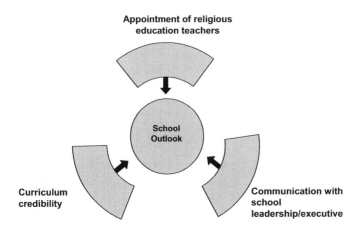

*Figure 10.* Category 2: School outlook and sub categories.

## *Appointment of Religious Education Teachers*

The appointment of religious education teachers was one factor that had an influence on school outlook towards classroom religious education. The range of involvement by the RECs in the appointment of religious education teachers varied and consisted of: a) direct involvement; b) negotiated involvement; and c) no involvement.

In some schools the principal involved the REC directly in the selection and appointment of religious education teachers. RECs who were involved in the short listing of applicants for interviews, the interview and the appointment process were perceived as having direct involvement in the appointment of religious education teachers. RECs who were directly involved were more likely to generate a cohesive perspective amongst their religious education faculty regarding the nature of religious education and the role of the religious education teacher. The following comment from one REC suggested that the degree of influence an REC may have is related to their involvement in the appointment process.

> The tradition at my school was that the REC was always involved in the appointment of staff. So I would actually have some input into the decisions about who would be teaching RE. I favoured an education in religion approach and selected staff who had RE qualifications and also favoured an education in religion approach. I

In situations where the REC had direct involvement in the selection and appointment of religious education teachers, there existed an opportunity to build a school outlook of shared views about learning and teaching in religious education, with faculty members. As early as the 1980s, Rossiter (1981a, 1981b) had distinguished between an education in religion approach and an education in faith approach to classroom religious education. The REC quoted above made the same distinction preferring "an education in religion approach". This person's direct involvement in the selection and appointment of religious education teachers contributed to fostering an educational focus on classroom religious education curriculum within the school.

In some situations the RECs were not involved in the selection and appointment of religious education teachers. However they were able to advise the principal as to the qualities and/or competencies they considered beneficial in appointments. In this book the term "negotiated involvement" is used to describe situations where the principal acted on the information received from the REC. The following is an example of how negotiated involvement influenced school outlook towards religious education. Recognising the emphasis on the acquisition of knowledge associated with the text-based curriculum, one REC foresaw the benefits of attracting qualified religious education teachers to the faculty. The REC had never been involved in the selection and appointment process of any staff member, but was able to negotiate with the principal the possibility of advertising for qualified teachers of religious education.

> Instead of advertising for a Maths teacher with a willingness to teach RE, the principal will now advertise for an experienced and qualified teacher of Religious Education and Maths. It has made a difference. We get some applicants who have a degree or diploma in RE. These staff members have a made a big difference to the RE faculty. The staff began to realise the importance of religious education in the school rather than just paying lip service to it. (L)

The transition to a knowledge-centred text-based religious education program highlighted the significant contribution qualified teachers of religious education make to classroom teaching as well as curriculum development and implementation. Advertising for, and appointing, qualified religious education teachers has influenced school outlook towards classroom religious education. This has promoted the importance of religious education curriculum among staff members.

Another example of negotiated involvement involved RECs negotiating continuity for teachers with the principal. Continuity was negotiated to enable a teacher to teach classroom religious education at the same year level in succeeding years. In this particular school (but not exclusive to this school) teachers were generally given one class in religious education as a means to meet their teaching allotment quota for the year. There was no guarantee from one year to the next that a teacher would be given a class in religious education. Nor was there any guarantee that a teacher would be given the same year level to teach religious education in succeeding years. The implementation of a knowledge-centred text-based curriculum provided the impetus for this REC to negotiate some continuity for teachers' teaching allotment with their principal.

> I was able to negotiate with the principal about staffing for the following year. I wanted to keep teachers at particular year levels because they had been teaching at that year level and they could consolidate what they had learned. I wanted some teachers to take more than one RE class at the same year level so they could develop the course and I wanted more qualified teachers. I think it was difficult for the principal to do all that, but a lot of the time, in most cases he was actually able to assist in that way. (B)

RECs who were able to successfully negotiate staffing issues with the principal who was ultimately responsible for the appointment and teaching allotments of all teachers, saw this as an opportunity to profile religious education as a subject of equal importance as other key learning areas within the school curriculum. Negotiated involvement also provided an opportunity for teachers to teach more than one religious education class at the same year level. Some RECs considered that if a teacher taught more than one class at the same year level, then there was a greater chance that the teacher would put more time and effort into planning religious education lessons, promoting a school outlook that lesson preparation for religious education was important in achieving the educational goals of the curriculum.

In situations where the REC indicated that they had no involvement in the selection and appointment of religious education teachers, a less favourable outlook towards religious education was expressed. Some RECs commented on the difficulty of promoting a uniform school outlook concerning the role of religious education and the religious education teacher. One REC alluded to the consequence of such circumstances and suggested that as a result it was difficult to achieve cohesion in the management and implementation of the text-based curriculum.

> In many cases teachers are given RE to fill up their teaching load and it is difficult to know who will be teaching RE from one year to the next. I think the courses are unsatisfactory because of that. You have teachers at the same year level who are teaching different things and don't follow any set course. There isn't any uniformity. For many it is their second or third teaching area and they only have one class in RE and don't make the time to prepare lessons. Some make it very clear that they do not want to be teaching RE and are not willing to put effort into the planning of the units of work. (I)

The experience quoted above suggested that staffing issues relating to religious education were regarded as peripheral. In a school environment where no opportunity was created for the principal and the REC to discuss staffing issues for the faculty, there appeared to be no vision of the role of classroom religious education shared between the REC and the principal, nor within the school community. In such situations the school's outlook or attitude towards religious education appeared unclear. An ability to achieve a uniform and cohesive approach to the management of the text-based curriculum posed many challenges as alluded to in the comments quoted above.

One REC suggested that the REC has to work with whoever has been appointed to their faculty. The statement quoted below indicates the difficulties associated with curriculum leadership in situations where the religious education faculty does not have a cohesive perspective.

> Any REC has got to work with the staff they are given. Sometimes you have a team who are all on side. Sometimes you have got to cajole teachers and other times you even have to push a little. Sometimes there are factions where some are extremely conservative and others quite radical and then there are those who are indifferent. Some have no qualifications in RE; others have done some RE subjects in their teacher training. On top of that many RE teachers are only teaching one class and they are committed to two, sometimes three, other faculties. (O)

School outlook towards religious education was influenced by the involvement of the REC in the appointment of religious education teachers to the faculty. Direct involvement in the appointment process provided significant opportunities for shared perspectives about the nature of religious education and the role of the religious education teacher. In situations where the REC had negotiated involvement in the staffing process, perceptions about religious education and the role of the religious education teacher were more cohesive than those in which the REC had no involvement at all. In other situations where no negotiation took place between the REC and the principal concerning staffing issues, it was not likely that a cohesive approach to learning and teaching in classroom religious education could be achieved.

According to Crotty (2005) when the principal and the REC share a common vision and relate well then the leadership of the REC is perceived to be more productive. Where the common vision is shared by the principal and the REC the potential to establish a faculty of religious educators which also shares a common vision is likely to be increased.

## Communication with School Leadership/Executive

Some RECs perceived that communication with the school leadership/executive team was influential in their management of the change. Formal and informal means of communication were employed by the RECs in order to inform members of the leadership/executive team about the intended curriculum change and the implications of that change for the school. Formal means of communication included presentations and reports at leadership/executive team meetings. Informal communication involved discussions with individual members of the leadership/executive team. Communication with the leadership/executive team helped to generate a school outlook conducive to managing the curriculum change. Communication with school leadership/executive had an influence on school outlook towards the change and management of the change in the following ways: a) it promoted good working relationships; b) it encouraged strategic planning; c) it encouraged staff development; and d) it encouraged a network of support.

In most situations the leadership/executive teams relied on the REC to be informed about the intended change. Most RECs commented on the importance of keeping members of the leadership/executive team informed. In some schools, members of the team offered support by offering to help the REC in any possible way to manage the implementation of the text-based curriculum.

> I did my best to keep the principal and other members of the leadership team informed about the changes. They really did not know very much and relied mainly on the information I could present to them. They were always very interested in learning anything they could about the change. Communication about the intended changes helped to clarify many of the issues that we needed to consider in order to effectively implement a text-based curriculum.
> (J)

Communication between the REC and the leadership/executive team generated support for the REC in their curriculum change management role. Good working relationships between the REC and other members of the leadership team were fostered and were typified by a willingness of other team members to support the REC.

The REC's ability to plan effectively for the curriculum change required the support of other members of the leadership/executive team. One REC suggested that keeping the leadership team informed about the curriculum change assisted in the process of developing a strategic plan.

> At leadership meetings there was a genuine interest in the curriculum and how I was managing the change. If I wanted staff to go on in-services, or if I needed time release, or if I wanted to run a professional development session or organise a guest speaker, we would

discuss it as a team and develop a plan so that it could happen without too much disruption to the school. (G)

The management of the text-based curriculum change highlighted the need for religious education teachers to have proficient religious knowledge and pedagogical competencies relevant to the new curriculum innovation. For many religious education teachers in the Archdiocese, professional development provided a way to achieve the required competencies. Most RECs commented on the support given to them by the principal and leadership/executive team when they were told of the need for professional development for religious education teachers in order to prepare them to understand the content in the textbooks.

I feel the principal and the leadership team are supportive of the new endeavours. Financial support is given to professional development initiatives. Financial support is give to any staff member who wants to do an RE or theology course. The leadership team is always very supportive of what is being done in RE and this has a positive impact on how RE is perceived in the school. (O)

RECs who communicated with members of the leadership/executive team commented on the level of support they received from other members of the team and how this assisted with the management of the curriculum change.

Most of the time, I feel alone in the REC role. Planning the curriculum change required me to communicate more with others especially with other members of the leadership team. I don't think I could have managed the change without their support. From this experience I have gained a really good support network and I can get things done. (I)

The RECs' initiatives to communicate issues concerning the curriculum change with the leadership/executive team helped to foster a school outlook supportive of the RECs' initiatives to manage the curriculum change. A supportive school outlook concerning the implementation of the text-based curriculum led to good working relationships, strategic planning, staff development opportunities and a confirmed network of support for the REC. This process was perceived as instrumental in promoting a positive school outlook towards religious education.

Communication with other members of the leadership/executive team enabled the REC to utilize and develop her/his educational leadership capacity and foster a school outlook that positioned classroom religious education within an educational paradigm. Fleming's (2002) research concerning the role of the REC suggested that when school principals appointed teachers to the position of REC, their decisions were mainly influenced by the ability of the teacher to fulfil a ministerial role rather than an educational role. Perceptions of the REC as a leader in Christian ministry implied a bias towards the importance of the role within the Church rather than within education (Crotty, 2005; Ryan, Brennan & Willmet, 1996). There was a tendency to appoint RECs who could fulfil ministerial tasks such as leading school liturgies, retreats, social justice groups and prayer groups.

Issues concerning educational leadership skills were seldom discussed in the appointment of an REC and this perhaps accounted for the fact that the position of REC was not perceived as a credible position of senior leadership in every Catholic secondary school (Fleming, 2002). Managing the curriculum change with the support of the leadership/executive team provided RECs with an opportunity to develop educational leadership skills, thus supporting the promotion of an educational outlook towards classroom religious education.

## Curriculum Credibility

Some RECs managed the curriculum change aware of its potential to endorse a school outlook that promoted religious education as a subject comparable with other curriculum areas. In some schools where broader curriculum change initiatives were occurring across the curriculum the RECs aligned aspects of the religious education curriculum with similar features associated with change initiatives in the wider school context. The main areas where the RECs made religious education consistent with other curriculum areas were: a) equal time allocation for each subject; b) outcomes based assessment; c) documentation of the religious education curriculum; and d) use of textbooks.

Most RECs considered that the textbooks contained too much information for a one year course. In most schools in the Archdiocese the time allocated to religious education had been considerably less than the time allocated to other subjects. One REC involved in implementing the text-based curriculum suggested that the school gave the same time allocation to religious education as other subjects.

> We were reorganising the time allocation for each subject within the whole curriculum and I thought we could achieve the same status for RE as any other subject. I had fought for Year 7, 8, 9 and 10 to have the same length of teaching time as the other subjects. We got six lessons per cycle whereas before we only had four. So now RE had the same power as any other subject. (G)

Equal time allocation was perceived as a means of encouraging a school outlook that religious education had the same credibility as other subjects.

In another school there was a whole school curriculum approach to developing an outcomes based assessment model for each unit of work taught in every faculty. The REC leading the curriculum change in this school incorporated the outcomes based assessment model into the religious education curriculum.

> The school was already moving in an outcomes direction in all other K.L.A.s [key learning areas]. The RE teachers thought it was good to actually have outcomes in RE. It gave us an opportunity to raise the standard so RE was considered equivalent to every other subject. The students' RE report form will look like other subjects and assess students according to their achievement of academic outcomes. (B)

This REC believed that adopting the school's outcomes based assessment model would promote a school outlook that perceived religious education as being of equal to other subjects within the curriculum.

In an attempt to help raise the standard of religious education in another school the REC encouraged the documentation of the text-based curriculum in a way that was consistent with the way curriculum was documented in other faculties.

> When I came to the school they were still using *Guidelines* and they did not have much of a curriculum, just a few handouts here and there. At that time we were preparing our courses for inspection by the Registered Schools Board. I thought if the other faculties were

documenting their courses then this would be a good opportunity for them to write the courses based on the textbooks. It was a good idea because the teachers were used to writing courses in their other subjects so they did the same in RE. It made a big difference. Teachers felt more confident and made demands on students and the students took RE more seriously as well. (J)

Another REC belonged to a school where a textbook had been prescribed for every subject taught in the school. In order to maintain a perceived equal status amongst the subjects, textbooks had been prescribed for religious education since the early 1990s. The Archdiocesan decision requiring all schools to implement a text-based curriculum was perceived as fostering a view that all subjects had equal status.

We were using textbooks in every other subject so having a textbook in religious education helped to promote the credibility of RE just like any other subject in the eyes of both teachers and students. I

The RECs who managed the curriculum change utilised opportunities to promote a school outlook that fostered classroom religious education as having the same curriculum credibility as other subjects. The RECs' management of this curriculum initiative was contrary to the findings of Johnson (1998) and Crotty (2005) who argued that RECs tended to ignore their responsibilities to fulfil the curriculum aspects of their diverse role. As discussed in Chapter two, Johnson (1989) and Crotty (2005) revealed that RECs had a bias towards fulfilling the ministerial demands of the role even in situations where the curriculum was in need of serious development. However the RECs involved in this study were also committed to addressing the curriculum aspects and challenges of their role.

The absence of clear directives as to the implementation of the text-based curriculum from the Archdiocese provided the impetus for RECs to make decisions regarding how to manage the curriculum change. It could be argued that the life-centred approach that was outlined in Chapter one of this book did not emphasise the educational dimension of the subject and attention to the experiential aspects precluded classroom religious education from being viewed with the same credibility as other subjects. In an effort to gain curriculum credibility for religious education, some RECs took into account features associated with broader educational curriculum change. These features involved equal class time allocation for religious education, adopting uniform assessment procedures, documenting the curriculum and promoting the use of textbooks in the curriculum. The RECs who were able to negotiate these strategies anticipated that doing so would promote a school outlook that regarded religious education as an equally credible subject within the school curriculum.

## Staff Development

In the process of implementing a curriculum in religious education based on the *To Know Worship and Love* textbook series, the RECs noted some deficits in the abilities of many religious education teachers. In particular the RECs observed that many religious education teachers lacked depth of understanding in terms of knowledge about the Catholic faith tradition. In response to this perception the RECs encouraged staff development programs as a means to help religious education teachers build up competencies in the discipline of RE. Figure 11 identifies the sub-categories associated with the forms of staff development employed by the RECs in the process of managing the change. They include: a) "faith formation"; b) professional development; and c) professional learning experiences.

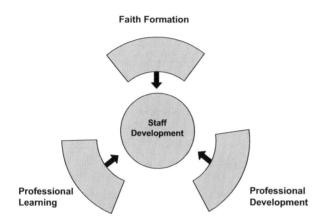

*Figure 11.* Category 3: Staff development and sub categories.

## Faith Formation

The term "faith formation" was used frequently by most RECs. It was difficult to determine exactly what the RECs meant by this term. The term "faith formation" when used by the RECs seemed to refer to issues such as Mass attendance, being actively involved in prayer, and speaking openly about personal religious faith. Some RECs suggested that many religious education teachers were "disconnected from the faith" and while this term was frequently used by the RECs it was never clearly defined by any of them. The term "disconnected from the faith" was used by the RECs to refer to situations where the religious education teachers were not attending Mass regularly, were not open to being actively involved in public prayer, were not speaking openly about their personal religious faith in the school setting. Some RECs commented on the benefits of religious education teachers being formed in the faith tradition and its relevance to managing and implementing the text-based curriculum. In situations where a REC perceived that the religious education teacher(s) were "disconnected from the faith" it was considered appropriate to offer staff development experiences that were concerned with "faith formation".

"Faith formation" opportunities for religious education teachers might seem misplaced within the process of trying to implement a knowledge-centred text-based curriculum. Furthermore the RECs criterion for determining whether or not a person was "formed in the faith" was problematic. There are many reasons why a person may not attend Mass regularly, or may not be actively involved in public prayer or may not openly talk about religious faith in a school setting. One cannot infer from non-involvement in one or all of these actions that a person is disconnected from the faith tradition. It is very difficult for any person to determine another person's level of faith; and the criteria put forward by the RECs focussed on actions such as: does one attend Mass regularly; does one pray in public; and does one openly talk about religious faith?

Johnson's (1998) study revealed that, in deciding to undertake the role, RECs were motivated by their own personal faith commitment and that they viewed their role as primarily ministerial rather than educational. As discussed in Chapter two, the role of the REC emerged approximately thirty years ago out of a theological and ministerial context (Crotty, 1998; Fleming, 2001; Engebretson, 1998). The *Renewal of the Education of Faith*, (Australian Episcopal Conference, [AEC], 1970) had a significant influence on religious education as education in faith.

> The school's fundamental preoccupation is the integral formation of man [*sic*] as citizen through contact with his culture. Religious education must be seen in this context as a duty and as a dutiful service which society renders to all. (AEC, 1970, # 154)

The emergence of the role of the REC was congruent with the publication of this document and its influence is noted in the ecclesial and ministerial focus of the role which was discussed earlier in this chapter as well as in Chapter two. It is against this background that some RECs organised and encouraged "faith formation" opportunities as an aspect of staff development assumed to be beneficial to the implementation of the text-based curriculum.

Some RECs commented on the dual focus of the curriculum change and suggested that opportunities for religious education teachers to be formed in the faith tradition of the Catholic Church had occurred in the process of managing the curriculum change. Staff development approaches to forming religious education teachers in the Catholic faith tradition involved: a) organising "faith formation" opportunities; and b) organising opportunities to develop knowledge content.

One REC did not consider competencies in religious knowledge and pedagogy to be the main focus when planning staff development initiatives to support teachers in teaching the text-based curriculum. In this case, staff development opportunities that favoured "faith formation" were the main focus for this REC. However in the process of implementing the text-based curriculum this REC held the view that having staff members formed in the faith tradition was paramount.

> We have a large number of staff who don't practice their faith in terms of Mass attendance and so forth. This has an enormous bearing on their ability to teach the subject. The primary gift of the RE teacher is to be a witness. I'd much rather have someone who was whole heartedly convinced of the Catholic faith, teaching RE, than someone who had a doctorate in theology. (I)

The main concern for this REC was to have teachers who were practising the faith teaching the religious education curriculum. This view ignored the emphasis placed on knowledge-centred learning associated with the text-based curriculum and suggested that only a teacher who practices their faith by attending Mass regularly will be suitable to teach the text-based curriculum. By this reasoning, tertiary training courses in religious education and theology seem not essential for teaching religious education in the Archdiocese of Melbourne. A REC who holds this view is likely to accept that those who are actively involved in parish life and attend Mass and other church services regularly would be suited to teaching religious education in Catholic secondary schools.

Such a view suggests a misguided understanding of the theoretical position underpinning this curriculum initiative.

Table 9 identifies the staff development opportunities organised by one REC to help form religious education teachers in the faith tradition of the Catholic Church.

Table 10

*Staff development opportunities organised by RECs regarding faith formation*

| Faith formation opportunities |
| --- |
| Exploring our prayer life |
| Keeping my faith alive |
| My personal spirituality |

*Note.* The opportunities presented here are not required to teach the text-based curriculum which is the subject of this study.

Some RECs suggested that the process of organising opportunities for religious education teachers to master the knowledge content about a specific area in the text-based curriculum, enabled some teachers to consider questions of faith in relation to their own life. Some RECs organised staff development programs that focussed on specific content areas relevant to the text-based curriculum. The following comment from a REC suggested that a focus on content specific staff development initiatives had the potential to help a teacher reflect on her/his own faith experience.

> I think *To Know Worship and Love*, is coming out of a different context, where we are being mandated to ensure that our students in schools know the Catholic faith, the Catholic traditions, the Catholic dogma and the doctrine. I think that's what they're ensuring that kids have an understanding of. Many of the staff don't have the knowledge background to teach the content in the texts, so I have been organising PD [professional development] opportunities to help give them that background. And I think the PD has not only helped them to understand religious content but many of them are asking questions about their own faith life and that is a good thing. (J)

This approach appears to parallel the context in which the textbooks were presented for use in the Archdiocese – that is with an emphasis on knowledge content as a means to help inculcate students into the faith tradition of the Catholic Church (Pell, 2001; Buchanan, 2003; 2004).

Several authors have argued that the acquisition of religious knowledge can act as a channel to personal faith formation (Engebretson et al, 2002; Elliot & Rossiter, 1982; Rossiter, 1981a; 1981b). The knowledge-centred text-based curriculum in religious education according to Pell (2001) has the potential to offer opportunities for formation in the faith tradition. However, within an educational paradigm which has an emphasis on the acquisition of knowledge, the primary focus on staff development should enable religious education teachers to develop competencies to teach the content of the curriculum rather than "faith formation" opportunities.

## *Professional Development*

The emphasis on knowledge acquisition associated with the text-based initiative encouraged RECs to provide professional development experiences that would enable teachers to have a better understanding about the content in the textbooks. The textbooks covered content that might have been lacking in the existing curricula within the schools, as well as within the teachers' understanding. For many RECs, the knowledge deficits provided the impetus and starting point for organising professional development seminars for members of the religious education faculty at their school. The various forms of professional development offered to the religious education teachers were: a) guest speakers; b) attendance at conferences and seminars; and c) participation in tertiary courses.

Guest speakers provided an opportunity for all religious education teachers at a particular school to receive the same information about a particular topic. Most RECs commented on this form of professional development as being the most preferred. It was less expensive than sending all the staff to seminars and conferences organised by organisations outside the school.

> I organised a guest speaker to come to the school and speak about Church history. It was really good. Church history is covered at most year levels and hardly any one knew much about the various events in the history of the Church. It was much cheaper and easier to organise than trying to send the whole RE faculty to a seminar off campus. (B)

Guest speakers also provided opportunities for all religious education teachers in a faculty to receive and discuss the same content and determine how it applied to the new curriculum.

In the earlier stages when RECs were preparing for the change, many RECs encouraged their religious education teachers to attended Archdiocesan seminars and forums about the textbooks. Most seminars were held during school hours. The high cost of classroom teacher replacement meant that not all religious education teachers could attend. Some RECs considered it better to have one or two religious education teachers benefit from attending a conference or seminar than none at all. There was also a possibility that other religious education teachers could learn something from those who attended (this point is explored further in this chapter in the following section on professional learning).

The professional development areas arranged by the RECs predominantly explored the content areas covered in the textbook series. To a lesser extent some professional development was arranged relating to skills and methodology. Table 10 indicates the content areas within which the RECs organised professional development with guest speakers and seminars. The limited number of professional development experiences relating to areas of skill and methodology are also listed.

Table 11

*Professional development opportunities organised by RECs*

| Content Specific | Skills and Methodology |
|---|---|
| • Catholic Social Teaching <br> • Church History <br> • God in the Hebrew Scriptures <br> • Images of Jesus in the Gospels <br> • Covenant Relationship <br> • People a Community of God <br> • Spirituality and Art <br> • Sexuality and Dignity of the Human Person <br> • Vocations <br> • Sarah and Hagar in the Hebrew, Christian and Muslim Tradition <br> • Images of Mary | • How to write a teaching unit <br> • Sharing common approaches to teaching Scripture |

*Note.* There was greater emphasis on content specific professional development than skills and methodology.

Professional development opportunities for religious education teachers through guest speakers, seminars and conferences were intended to provide an opportunity for religious education teachers to become more proficient in their understanding of some of the content areas contained in the textbooks. For some religious education teachers these provided the impetus to explore the possibility of undertaking a tertiary course of study in religious education or theology. In most cases the advice of the REC was sought regarding what course would be appropriate to pursue. The following comment by one REC provided an insight into this relationship between the implementation of the curriculum change and the professional development of religious education teachers.

We looked at the books in relation to our existing curriculum which was based on *Guidelines* and then our aim was to pick and choose how the content of the books could complement what we were already doing. This process exposed some gaps in our courses. So we looked at including and implementing those areas into our existing courses. Then coming out of that was that the teachers recognised that there were some gaps in their own learning that they needed to explore more formally than the professional development that I had organised. So they started to discuss with me about what tertiary courses they might do. (G)

## Professional Learning

Professional learning has been discussed at some length in Chapter two. Johnson (2000) has emphasised that within a school context teachers have acquired competencies that can be shared and can contribute to the development of high standards in curriculum development. The interviews with the RECs revealed that staff development through professional learning took the forms of: a) structured professional learning teams; and b) professional learning presentations.

In the process of managing the curriculum change, one REC provided opportunities for staff development by organising professional learning teams at each year level. The REC appointed a team leader for each level. The team leader was responsible for organising opportunities for the team to meet and discuss their practice, as well as share ideas and strategies relating to teaching the text-based curriculum.

> What I did at each year level was appoint a team leader. The team leader would then divide the topics to be covered at each year level. A teacher from that team would be responsible for developing that topic into a teaching unit. The teachers would meet regularly and present their unit to the team. Each teacher would explain the content and suggest ideas and strategies about how to teach the unit. I

Against the background of developing and implementing the text-based curriculum, the professional learning teams had considerable opportunity to share ideas and concerns about their practice. Johnson (2000) has suggested that professional learning teams provide a comfortable environment where teachers may be willing to share successes and failures experienced in the classroom.

Professional learning opportunities were not confined to professional learning teams. Some RECs provided opportunities during faculty meetings for individual staff members to present ideas and strategies they had been working on. The individual presentations enabled other colleagues to adopt (Marsh, 1997) and/or adapt (Brickell, 1972) the ideas for their own teaching situation. The following comment from one REC illustrates a benefit from a professional learning experience.

> We were exploring ways of learning and teaching beyond the scope of the textbook. One teacher developed "the Useful Box for RE'. It included many creative resources and strategies for the teacher to use to encourage learning beyond the textbook. It was an excellent professional learning experience and teachers could see the benefits. We now have a 'useful box' in each classroom and RE teachers not only use it but also add resources to it. (G)

The process of implementing the text-based curriculum showed up deficits in the religious education teachers' religious knowledge. Staff development opportunities were organised by the RECs and identified as professional development, professional learning and faith formation experiences. In nearly all situations (except one) the staff development experiences focussed on enabling religious education teachers to develop competencies and understandings about the knowledge content of the text-based curriculum. One REC considered staff development opportunities for religious education teachers that focussed on "faith formation" in the Catholic tradition rather than the development of knowledge content competencies, and this questionable approach has been discussed. The emphasis on staff development opportunities directed at developing knowledge of content is understandable in light of the deficiencies exposed by the implementation of the text-based curriculum.

None of the RECs interviewed for this research organised staff development opportunities for the religious education teachers to learn or understand the paradigm shift from a life-centred approach to an outcomes based educational approach. The reason for this is likely to be found in the earlier discussion which indicated that the RECs themselves did not understand the process as it occurred. This issue is analysed further in Chapter seven.

An expectation in the management of a "top down" (Morris, 1995) curriculum change is that the change would be directed by the centralised authority. According to Brady and Kennedy (2003) many decisions affecting the change and the management of the change are made at the local level. In relation to this particular change the RECs ultimately decided that staff development opportunities were essential. They also decided upon the content focus of the various staff development opportunities. Johnson (1996) argued that the forces of change help to shape the professional development environments. In most situations the RECs considered that it was essential that their staff members experience staff development opportunities that would enable them to develop content knowledge. Hargreaves (1997) attests to the growing professionalism amongst teachers resulting in the emphasis on the development of content knowledge. According to Elliot (1998) there can be no change without professional growth, therefore the professional development opportunities assisted the management of this change. Most RECs focussed on staff development experiences that would help teachers to teach the content of the text-based curriculum. Johnson (2000a) suggested that teachers learn best when the learning is focussed on their needs in the work place.

## Attitudes and Perspectives

The attitudes and perspectives of the RECs concerning the change to a knowledge-centred text-based curriculum were limited by their understanding of the actual context and implications of the change. Ignorance about the full implications of the change was evident in certain perspectives about the change, perspectives about the textbooks, perspectives about religious education teachers and perspectives about the religious education curriculum. Figure 12 shows the fourth category and sub categories.

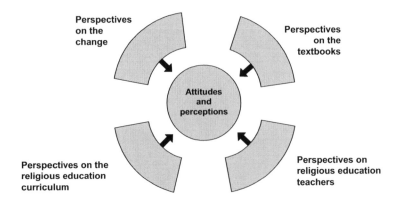

*Figure 12.* Category 4: Attitudes and perspectives and sub categories.

## Perspectives on the Change

The RECs' perspectives on the change influenced how they managed the change. Two factors which revealed the RECs' perspectives on the change were: a) an emphasis on incorporating the content of the textbooks into a school's existing curriculum; and b) an inability to grasp the implications of the paradigm shift.

The RECs considered that the change to a text-based curriculum could be achieved by incorporating the contents of the textbooks into the existing religious education curriculum which they had developed based on *Guidelines* (1995).

> When I was employed at the school in 1998 there wasn't much of a curriculum so I just had to spend the whole year writing one up based on the RE *Guidelines* which came out in 1995. Then all of a sudden we are told that things are going to be different. When we got the textbooks I realized that I could fit the textbooks into what we were already doing. There was too much information in the textbooks and we could not cover all that in one year. So I decided that we would use from the textbooks what was relevant to our existing course. (G)

Every REC involved in this study incorporated aspects of the old course with the new. In the absence of a centralised curriculum framework and/or clear directions regarding how to implement the mandated textbooks, most RECs perceived that editing their existing school curriculum was an effective way to manage the curriculum change.

Educational language and an emphasis on outcomes based learning marked a clear distinction between the pedagogical theories underpinning the textbooks and that of the previous life-centred approach (Engebretson, 2002). The emphasis RECs placed on incorporating the content of the textbooks into the existing curriculum ignored or failed to grasp the implications of the paradigm shift associated with the mandated textbooks.

The inability to perceive the paradigm shift was also evident in the RECs who focussed on ecclesial and ministerial issues concerning religious education in Catholic schools. When commenting on preparing teachers to implement the text-based curriculum one REC illustrated this point by emphasising the faith dimension rather than the educational context in which the textbooks are situated.

> I think ideally we have to expect and encourage and provide opportunities for RE staff to continue their own faith development and spiritual journey and the nourishing of those aspects of their lives if we are serious about teaching religious education in our schools. (A)

The RECs tended to trivialize the introduction of the text-based curriculum by: a) fitting the content of the textbooks within an existing curriculum based on *Guidelines* (1995); and b) focusing on providing professional opportunities for religious education teachers to explore their faith and spiritual journey. These approaches ignored the pedagogical context in which the textbooks were situated and revealed that the RECs had not been provided with adequate information about the implications of the change to a text-based curriculum. The inability of some RECs to articulate and comprehend the paradigm shift is explored further as a factor that impeded the curriculum change in Chapter six.

Where the management of a curriculum change was influenced by misunderstandings about the theory or pedagogy underpinning the curriculum, RECs managed the change based on their existing experience and knowledge of classroom religious education curriculum. Discrepancies between the curriculum change theory and the RECs' curriculum knowledge can trivialise the management of the change.

## Perspectives on the Textbooks

Chapter two of this book provided a lengthy discussion of the nature and purpose of textbooks in education and religious education. The perspectives and attitudes of some RECs concerning the *To Know Worship and Love* textbook series affected the implementation of the text-based curriculum. Some perspectives on the textbooks generated resistance to change. Two prominent perspectives on the change were identified as: a) historical perspectives; and b) perspectives about the intended audience.

From the 1970s through to the introduction of the *To Know Worship and Love* textbook series in 2001, the life-centred approach focussed on the sharing of life experience and it did not promote the use of uniform textbooks. Prior to the introduction of *To Know Worship and Love*, the only experience of uniform textbooks in religious education in the Archdiocese of Melbourne were doctrinal books in the 1960s. When considering the historical experiences regarding the use of doctrinal uniform textbooks it is not surprising that some RECs regarded the *To Know Worship and Love* textbook series as being doctrinal books. This generated a concern amongst RECs that, religious education teachers would be required to teach Church doctrine.

> I was hesitant about developing a curriculum based on the textbooks because I think that the textbooks are a consequence of the fact that students do not have an adequate understanding of Christian doctrine. My unease is that with an emphasis on doctrine, students run the risk

117

of receiving doctrine, Church history, and dogmatics, without adequate attention to personal experience and critical analysis. I think this is vital in the process of Christian formation. An emphasis on doctrine means we run the risk of teaching RE as it was taught before Vatican II. (A)

Some RECs did not consider the *To Know Worship and Love* textbooks as an adequate resource for student learning. One REC's approach to implementing the text-based curriculum was inhibited by a perspectives that the textbook was a teacher resource rather than a student resource.

I think they have confused the audience because I reckon they have written the books for the bishop first. Then they have written for parents so that they can be informed. Then they have written for the teachers so they can learn the content themselves. Then they have written for the students but I don't think the textbooks are student friendly. My view is that the textbooks are almost like an on-site resource book for the teacher rather than a textbook. (L)

The RECs' previous experiences of textbooks in religious education can influence their perspective and attitude towards the books associated with the text-based curriculum.

## Perspectives on Religious Education Teachers

REC's perspectives on the religious education teachers also influenced the way RECs implemented the curriculum change. The main perspectives emanating from the interviews with the RECs related to the professional and ministerial capabilities and experience of religious education teachers. The RECs' perspectives on the religious education teachers' role can be categorised in three areas: a) expertise; b) time commitment; and c) ecclesial and ministerial experience.

The RECs commented on the lack of qualified religious education staff members. It was not uncommon for RECs to adopt an attitude of sympathy for unqualified religious education teachers. This was reflected in the RECs' willingness to take responsibility for designing curriculum and writing the learning and teaching units for teachers in their faculty.

Now, very few of the teachers here have qualifications in RE so they don't come to RE with the same spontaneity and creativity that they bring for example to maths or history or any other subject they have studied at tertiary level. I am not putting them down; I am just naming a problem that I have to act on. So I meet with the RE teachers in year level groups once a fortnight as part of their load and I try to develop strategies to prepare lessons from the textbooks. But without qualifications they find it really hard and I end up writing the units of work and we meet to discuss how they teach it in class. (L)

Concern for the vulnerability of unqualified religious education teachers provided the impetus for some RECs to make the curriculum decisions and write the units of work that were to be taught in the classroom. One REC saw this as one way of enabling students to be taught a curriculum based on the textbooks.

I was the REC and my task was to implement the curriculum. I wasn't going to waste time talking around in circles with teachers who really struggled with RE. Many of them do not have qualifications and really struggle teaching RE. So once I sorted it out in my head and was clear on what needed to be done, I did it. I wrote the course and then I met with the teachers and explained to them how to teach it. It was hard work but they really appreciated it and hopefully the students learned something. (B)

There is a high proportion of unqualified teachers of religious education in Catholic schools (Thomas, 2000) despite the fact that for approximately three decades Church documents have highlighted the importance of such qualifications (CC, 1998, # 73; CCE, 1982, # 65; CCE, 1977; # 52). The RECs identified this problem and adopted a sympathetic attitude to the perceived limitations in the religious education teachers' capabilities and experience. The response of some RECs meant a greater workload in developing and documenting the curriculum based on, or incorporating, the contents of the textbooks. In some situations the additional workload was completed during the RECs' annual leave.

*Perspectives on the Religious Education Curriculum*
In the absence of clear directives from the Archdiocese that had instigated this curriculum change, some RECs held distorted perceptions about the curriculum innovation. The perspectives on the textbooks were: a) a return to conservative doctrinal approaches to classroom religious education; and b) able to be situated in existing curriculum based on the life-centred approach.

This "top down" (Morris, 1995) curriculum initiative was literally decided and directed by Archbishop Pell. The Archbishop is responsible for religious education in an Archdiocese and he had instigated and authorised the transition to a text-based curriculum in the Archdiocese. Archbishop Pell had been portrayed as a conservative Catholic leader. He mandated the application of the new textbooks within the context of a text-based curriculum in all Catholic primary and secondary schools in the Archdiocese (Pell, 2001, p. 5). The perception of Archbishop Pell as an authoritarian conservative, as well as an absence of appropriate information about the intended changes, helped to generate distorted views of the intended text-based curriculum. A view held by some RECs is reflected in the following comment.

We thought the books were going to demand that we teach doctrine as they did in the 1950s. [Archbishop] Pell was a conservative and determined to bring all Catholics back to the Church. It created a lot of stress. (G)

The stress experienced by some RECs could have been alleviated if the Archdiocese had developed a systematic and informative way of communicating the rationale and context of the changes. Communication has been identified as a factor that is integral to successful change (Berman, 1980; Fullan, 1993; 1987; 1982; Jackson, 1992). In relation to this change more attention should have been given to ensuring that the RECs understood it. The lack of communication from those directing the change contributed to creating an environment where RECs were isolated. In situations where those managing the change in schools are not appropriately supported, change can be obstructed (Fullan, 1999). Isolation issues can limit a school's ability to bring about the desired change (Brady & Kennedy, 2003).

## Curriculum Leadership

The management of the text-based curriculum innovation revealed a broader role for the REC as a curriculum leader. Crotty (2005) identified the role of the REC as bi-dimensional: both a ministerial role within the Church and a role within education. The literature reviewed in Chapter two has explored the ecclesial and ministerial perspectives associated with the role of the REC. Category 5 provided insights into the role of the REC as a curriculum leader. Figure 13 shows the sub-categories associated with the curriculum leadership aspect of the role of the REC.

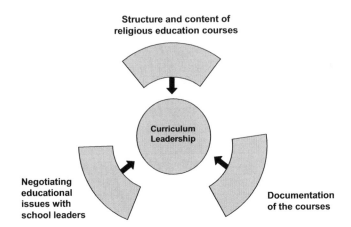

*Figure 13.* Category 5: Curriculum leadership and the sub categories.

### *Structure and Content of Religious Education Courses*

Decisions about the structure and content of the text-based religious education course demonstrated the educational expertise and competencies of the RECs in the following areas: a) sequential and cumulative learning; b) course content; and c) assessment in religious education.

Most RECs managed the change to a text-based curriculum by endeavouring to incorporate the content of the textbooks into their existing curriculum. Some RECs conducted a curriculum audit and discovered content areas in the textbooks that were not covered in the existing curriculum belonging to their respective schools. The typological framework in which the content of the textbooks was organised, as outlined in Chapter one, provided opportunities for RECs to implement a text-based curriculum where the content could be arranged within the context of sequential and accumulative learning structures. The following comment by one REC was indicative of most involved in this study.

> When I looked at the Year 7, 8, 9 and 10 textbooks I noticed that there were a lot of topics that were not addressed in our course. In the year 8 course we did not cover history and there is a lot of history in the year 8 book. I agree with that so I included it in the year 8 course. There were history topics in the year 7 course dealing with Moses and the Exodus and I included the history on the Early Church and St Paul in year 8. In year 9 we covered St

Ignatius and the Middle Ages through to Vatican II and in year 10 I included the unit on the history of the Catholic Church in Australia. So by the end of year 10 students should have a good grounding in Church history. (L)

The above example illustrates one way in which the typological framework underpinning the textbooks influenced the sequential and accumulative development of the text-based curriculum. In this example, Church history, a typological component of the study of religion was incorporated in the scope and sequence of the Year 7-10 classroom religious education curriculum.

The application of educational theory and practice concerning outcomes based assessment was also applied to the assessment process adopted by some RECs. Some RECs who belonged to a school where outcomes based assessment had been introduced across the curriculum also applied it to the text-based curriculum. This was indicated in the following comment from an REC:

We had outcomes based assessment in all other subjects since 2002. I thought why not in RE? The staff were used to it and it might help to raise the profile of RE as an academic subject. So I suggested it to the staff that had done some PD on outcomes based assessment and we went ahead with it. (O)

## Documentation of Courses

In general the RECs took responsibility for the actual writing and documentation of the text-based curriculum designed for their schools. This issue has been referred to earlier in this chapter, drawing attention to the lack of expertise and time religious education teachers had to commit to course writing. For some RECs undertaking the responsibility to write and document the course provided an opportunity to add credibility to religious education as a curriculum area.

All the faculties were writing up their courses for the Registered Schools Board. As you know documentation of the RE course is not required but I insisted we do so. If I wrote the course up the same as the other faculties did it would enable RE to be seen as important as any other academic subject. (J)

Some RECs held the view that writing and documenting the text-based curriculum according to the same design in other faculties would add credibility to how religious education was perceived as a subject within the curriculum. Perceiving the text-based curriculum as an academic subject, one REC emphasised that applying an educational format used in other faculties for course writing in religious education could also help religious education teachers to regard religious education as an educational subject with academic rigour.

People don't have time; they are too busy. They knew that the curriculum needed to be documented but they don't know how to do it. They don't want to make decisions about what should be included. There could be a whole lot of reasons why, but I think when they have no qualifications in RE and they only teach one class, then in many cases this means they don't understand it as an academic subject. So I wrote the course and used the criteria for course writing used at my school in the other subjects. I thought if the RE teachers see the course written in that way they would begin to realise the academic nature of the subject. (B)

*Negotiating Educational Issues with School Leaders*

Some RECs perceived the management of the text-based curriculum to be an opportunity to raise the profile of religious education within the school. They discussed educational issues relevant to the management of the text-based curriculum change with other school leaders in order to negotiate structures and strategies that could assist with its implementation. The main educational issues negotiated were: a) timetabling; b) curriculum; and c) staffing.

In addition to negotiations that enabled classroom religious education to be allocated the same classroom time as other subjects, other time issues were negotiated in order to assist with the management of the text-based curriculum change. For example, one REC was able to negotiate a time allocation of one class period per cycle for religious education teachers to meet and prepare for the change. During these meetings implementation strategies and staff proficiencies relevant to the text-based curriculum were developed. The time allocated for teachers to meet was regarded as a priority in a school with few qualified teachers of religious education. Several RECs were able to negotiate time release for religious education teachers to attend staff development opportunities related to religious education and implementation of the text-based curriculum. Other RECs were able to negotiate time release to attend information sessions as well as to document a curriculum based on the textbooks.

Documenting the text-based curriculum was an issue that some RECs aimed to achieve by ensuring the style and presentation was consistent with other disciplines within the school. This intention involved RECs negotiating and working with other curriculum leaders in order to ensure compatibility. It also enabled a teacher's skills in curriculum to be used in learning and teaching in religious education. The RECs' curriculum leadership drew upon the educational expertise and curriculum models commonly known to any classroom teacher and this enabled them to work more confidently with their schools' documented classroom religious education curriculum. In particular they were able to draw upon their skills in areas such as outcomes based learning and assessment and reporting.

As noted earlier in this chapter, some RECs were able to negotiate with principals and other members of the leadership team issues regarding staffing. RECs in some schools were able to encourage a trend towards qualified teachers of religious education. Some were able to negotiate a specialist religious education faculty where most teachers in the faculty would teach more than one religious education class. This was intended to encourage the teacher to invest more time into lesson preparation in religious education. Other religious education coordinators were able to negotiate a plan to enable a teacher to teach religious education at the same year level consistently over at least three years in order to develop some pedagogical competencies and experience in teaching religion at that particular year level.

According to Johnson (1995) a new professionalism can emerge from a culture of change where new opportunities are created and taken up. The management of this text-based curriculum initiative emphasised the curriculum leadership aspects of the role of the REC. This particular aspect of the role in the past has been ignored to some extent by both principals who, according to Fleming (2002), had a bias towards the employment of RECs as ministerial leaders, and also RECs who tended to ignore the curriculum demands of the role in preference for the ministerial aspects of the role (Crotty, 2005; Johnson, 1989). This "top down" (Morris, 1995) curriculum change also provided the impetus for RECs to focus on the curriculum leadership aspects of their role. The curriculum initiatives instigated by the RECs were in most situations inspired by change initiatives that had occurred or were occurring within the broader context of educational change. A school's previous history of change can assist the process of current change initiatives (Smith & Lovat, 2003). This research has indicated that the RECs drew upon experiences of previous change initiatives while in the process of managing the text-based curriculum change initiative.

## Conclusion

This chapter has presented and analysed the first five categories and their associated sub-categories which emerged from the data. Table 11 provides a summary of the theory generated relevant to these categories and their associated sub-categories. Chapter six presents the theory generated and an analysis of categories six and seven which report on the RECs' perspectives on the factors that impeded and assisted the change.

Table 12

*The theory generated relevant to the first five categories and associated sub-categories.*

| Category 1<br>Preparation for Change | Key Theory Generated |
|---|---|
| (i) RECs informed about the change | In situations where a comprehensive understanding about a "top down" (Morris, 1995) curriculum change is difficult to achieve from the centralised authority initiating the change, those responsible for managing the change in their local school context explored other avenues in order to become informed about the change. |
| (ii) Staff informed about the change | RECs who were responsible for managing the change perceived that it was necessary to ensure that teachers responsible for teaching the text-based curriculum were informed and up-dated about the change.<br><br>The RECs explored a variety of ways to enable religious education teachers to be informed about the change and its implications. |
| (iii) Dialogue about the change | Change affects people and RECs facilitated formal and informal opportunities for teachers involved in the change to dialogue about their feelings, concerns and possible strategies for managing the change. |
| (iv) Exploration of textbooks in light of pre-existing religious education curriculum. | In the absence of an informed understanding about the different theories underpinning various curriculum approaches, RECs managed a text-based curriculum change by blending the contents of the textbooks into a school's existing curriculum. |
| (v) Decisions regarding implementing the curriculum change. | Working in collaboration with religious education teachers, RECs as curriculum leaders ultimately managed the implementation of the change by making the key decisions about the structure and content of the new curriculum based on the textbooks. |
| Category 2<br>School Outlook | Key Theory Generated |
| (i) Appointment of religious education teachers. | Direct involvement: In situations where the REC has direct involvement in the employment of teachers of religious education the REC was more likely to establish a faculty where a shared philosophy about learning and teaching in religious education and the role of the teacher were compatible.<br><br>Negotiated involvement: In situations where the REC has "negotiated involvement" in the selection and appointment of religious education teachers, a biases towards the recruitment of qualified teachers as well as those committed to teaching more than one class was preferred. |

|  |  |
|---|---|
|  | No Involvement: In situations where the REC has no involvement in the selection and appointment of religious education teachers it was more difficult to promote a cohesive school outlook towards religious education and the role of the religious education teacher. |
|  | Employment of religious education teachers: The RECs' management of the text-based curriculum change has revealed a preference for qualified teachers of religious education and teachers who are willing to teach more than one class of religious education. |
| (ii) Communication with school leadership/executive. | Communication with the leadership/executive team about the management of the change to a text-based curriculum helped to emphasise an educational outlook towards classroom religious education, distinct from a ministerial outlook. |
| (iii) Curriculum credibility. | Through the management of a curriculum change RECs utilised other change processes happening within the school to promote classroom religious education as a discipline holding the same curriculum credibility as other subjects. |
| **Category 3 Staff Development** | **Key Theory Generated** |
| (i) Faith formation. | Some RECs managed the change to a knowledge-centred text-based curriculum by providing staff development experiences that focussed on the personal faith formation of religious education teachers. |
|  | Some RECs managed the change to a knowledge-centred text-based curriculum by providing staff development opportunities that focussed on developing knowledge content proficiencies while at the same time aware that the development of such proficiencies had the potential to probe personal faith issues for some teachers. |
| (ii) Professional development. | To prepare teachers for the change to a knowledge centred text-based curriculum RECs organised professional development experiences where teachers could develop proficiencies in content knowledge relevant to the curriculum. |
|  | The preferred professional development option was guest speakers with expertise in topics relevant to the content covered in the textbooks. Guest speakers were preferred because they were cost effective and provided an opportunity for all teachers to be involved in the professional development experience. |
|  | Teachers who became interested in pursuing tertiary qualifications in religious education sought the advice of the REC about which course to study. |
| (iii) Professional learning. | RECs organised professional learning teams and fostered professional learning presentations to enable teachers to learn from each other and develop their proficiencies in relation to the content knowledge associated with the text-based |

| | curriculum. |
|---|---|
| **Category 4**<br>**Attitudes & Perspectives** | **Key Theory Generated** |
| (i) Perspectives on the change. | Where the management of a curriculum change was influenced by misunderstandings about the theoretical position underpinning the curriculum, RECs managed the change based on their existing experience and knowledge of classroom religious education curriculum. Discrepancies between the theoretical position of the curriculum change and the REC's curriculum knowledge can trivialise the management of the change. |
| (ii) Perspectives on the textbooks. | RECs' previous experiences of textbooks in religious education can influence their perspective and attitude towards the books associated with the text-based curriculum. |
| (iii) Perspectives on religious education teachers. | RECs generally adopted a sympathetic attitude towards members of their faculty who are unqualified and RECs will undertake a greater workload in order to compensate for the limited capabilities of their staff members. |
| (iv) Perspectives on the religious education curriculum. | Perspectives on the text-based curriculum as an emphasis on teaching Church doctrine was sometimes influenced by the RECs' view of the Archbishop as an authoritarian, mandating a "top down" (Morris, 1995) change. |
| **Category 5**<br>**Curriculum Leadership** | **Key Theory Generated** |
| (i) Structure and content of religious education courses. | RECs successfully negotiated time within the school timetable to be allocated for teachers to meet and develop strategies and proficiencies to accommodate the management and implementation of the text-based curriculum. |
| (ii) Documentation of courses. | The RECs managed the curriculum change by documenting the text-based curriculum in a fashion similar to other curriculum areas. This enabled the classroom religious education curriculum to be more accessible to untrained religious education teacher because they were able to draw upon their general curriculum educational expertise. |
| (iii) Negotiating educational issues with school leaders. | RECs negotiated with school leaders the employment of qualified teachers of religious education in order to manage the implementation of the knowledge-centred educational focus of the text-based curriculum. |

# CHAPTER SIX
# Factors that Impeded and Assisted Curriculum Change

The previous chapter reported on and analysed the findings identified within categories 1 to 5. This chapter reports on and analyses the theory generated within categories 6 and 7, these being the RECs' perspectives on the factors that impeded and assisted the implementation of the text-based religious education curriculum in their respective schools. Prior to the conclusion of each interview, each REC was asked the following questions: What factors impeded the text-based curriculum change? What factors assisted the text-based curriculum change? Table 12 shown at the end of this chapter orientates the reader to the theory generated from categories 6 and 7 and their associated sub-categories.

## Factors That Impeded the Curriculum Change[10]

Figure 14 shows the five sub-categories associated with category six, factors that impeded the curriculum change.

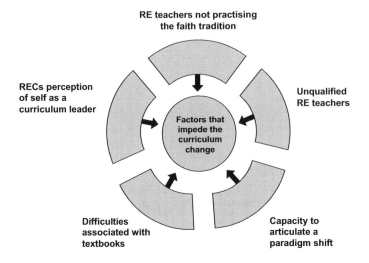

*Figure 14.* Category 6: Factors that impeded the curriculum change.

### *Teachers of Religious Education Not Practising the Catholic Faith Tradition*

A factor considered by the RECs as impeding the implementation of the new curriculum was their concern that some religious education teachers did not belong to or practise the Catholic faith tradition. It was their view that the curriculum change could not be successful if this personal faith commitment was missing. Some RECs considered that being a believing Catholic and being open about this was more important than having qualifications to teach religious education. Some RECs tried to offer experiences they described as "faith formation" for members of their religious education faculty (see Chapter five).

In the context of trying to manage the curriculum change in religious education, one REC suggested that if a choice needed to be made between a qualified teacher of religious education and one practising the faith, the preference appeared to be for the latter.

> We have large numbers of staff who don't practise their faith in terms of Mass attendance and so forth. I think this has an enormous bearing on their ability to teach RE. Philosophically my view is that the primary gift of the RE teacher is to be a witness to the Catholic faith. I'd much rather have someone who was whole heartedly convinced of the

---

10 Parts of this section of Chapter five have been published in:
Buchanan, M. T. (2006d). Factors that impede curriculum change: A preliminary report.
*British Journal of Religious Education, 28* (1), 51-63.

Catholic faith teaching RE, than someone who simply has a qualification. The kids see straight through it. If a teacher is teaching math, and feels that math is meaningless, the kids pick up on it, even if the teacher is teaching well. A large role of the RE teacher is to be an evangelist. (I)

While the Church-sponsored textbook innovation had an emphasis on knowledge acquisition, some RECs suggested that a teacher who taught knowledge content devoid of some form of personal witness to the Catholic faith tradition, compromised the intention of religious education in a Catholic school.

When teachers are not adequately engaged with a spiritual journey and personal faith formation… When that isn't happening for staff members that are in the classrooms using the texts, then I think they run the risk of the students receiving doctrine, church history, and dogmatics divorced from the life-giving source of personal engagement and faith formation. (A)

This view was consistent with Catholic Church teaching as reflected in Church documents, which suggested that it was the teachers' "witness" to the faith tradition "that brings the content of the lessons to life" (CCC, 1990, # 96).

Concern was expressed regarding how teachers of religious education who were not connected to the faith tradition could impede the delivery of a text-based curriculum in religious education. Some RECs suggested that it was the responsibility of the school to provide opportunities for staff to experience ongoing faith formation experiences.

We have to take responsibility in really significant ways for staff who haven't had the opportunities for engaging in ongoing formation, especially teachers who are disconnected from their tradition and who are not particularly aggressive or dismissive towards faith. For some teachers faith has failed to find a place to be nurtured. And I think we're responsible, especially if we're talking about ourselves as Church, then I think we have to take responsibility for that. (A)

The Congregation for Catholic Education (CCE) reflected a similar view:

Lay Catholic educators also have a right to expect that, within the ecclesial community, bishops, priests, and religious, especially those dedicated to the apostolate of education, and also various groups and associations of lay Catholic educators, will help to awaken them to their personal needs in the area of formation, and will find means to stimulate them so that they can give themselves more totally to the social commitment that such a formation requires (CCE, 1982, # 63).

Some RECs expressed concern about religious education teachers who were not practising the faith tradition and suggested that this impeded the curriculum change. It was argued by some RECs that the responsibility to form religious education teachers in the faith tradition was the responsibility of the school. This view is also reflected in Church documents (CCE, 1982, # 63). Schools may accept responsibility for the formation of someone in faith but this cannot occur without the agreement and personal commitment of the individual person or teacher.

This issue of the personal faith formation of the religious education teacher has long been debated in religious education literature, and there are many views that could be referred to here

(Groome, 1991; Hull, 1984; Lovat, 1995; 2002; Rossiter, 1981; Rummery, 1975; Ryan, 1997). However it is not the intention of this study to focus on this debate. In the context of reporting on and analysing the factors that the RECs perceived as impeding the management and implementation of the text-based curriculum, the RECs' concerns about the "faith formation" of religious education teachers will be further analysed later in this chapter and in Chapter seven.

A very broad understanding of the nature and purpose of religious education emanating from Church documents and other literature on religious education was explored in Chapter one and two of this book. Church documents (both international and national) have expressed the nature and purpose of religious education in terms of catechesis and in terms of religious education (in Church documents often referred to as religious instruction) (CCE, 1977; 1988). While catechesis is generally understood within a parish context, Church documents have also acknowledged the interplay between catechesis and religious education within a school context. The Congregation for Catholic Education which has authority for Catholic seminaries, universities and schools, addresses this issue in *The Religious Dimension of Education in a Catholic School* (CCE, 1988).

It is evident, of course, that religious instruction cannot help but strengthen the faith of a believing student, just as catechesis cannot help but increase one's knowledge of the Christian message. (# 69)

Both personally and professionally, the religious education teacher has been perceived as integral to the effectiveness of religious education. In particular it was perceived that "the effectiveness of religious instruction is closely tied to the personal witness given by the teacher" (CCE, 1988, # 96) However the Congregation for the Clergy offered a distinction between the roles of catechesis and religious education in *General Directory for Catechesis* (CC, 1998). It not only indicated that catechesis belonged to the whole life of the Church and that religious education was the responsibility of the Catholic school, but emphasised that there was "an absolute necessity to distinguish clearly between religious instruction and catechesis" (#. 73). Researchers have attested to the need for clarity in this area over three decades (Moran, 1991; Rossiter, 1983; Rummery, 1975).

The perspectives of the RECs suggested that no clear distinction regarding the nature and purpose of religious education and the role of the teacher has been uniformly agreed upon. One REC expressed a preference for religious education teachers who were practising Catholics over those who were qualified to teach religious education. Most preferred teachers who were both practising Catholics and qualified to teach religious education. One REC suggested that implementing and teaching a knowledge-centred text-based curriculum provided an opportunity to link the content of the religious education curriculum to the personal religious faith of the teacher.

The RECs were required to manage the implementation of the text-based curriculum with an educational emphasis on the acquisition of knowledge through outcomes based learning. Regardless of this context, the RECs perceived catechesis as integral to the religious education curriculum and teachers who were not practising Catholics would impede the catechetical dimension of the text-based curriculum. Fleming's (2002) research into the role of the REC suggested that they perceived the catechetical aspects of the role in terms of personal faith formation, prayer, liturgy and sacramental activities. The RECs involved in this study perceived that catechesis was also integral to the management and implementation of a knowledge-centred text-based curriculum. In contrast,

130

Rossiter (1982) has argued for a distinction between religious education and catechesis within an educational context. For the RECs the knowledge and educational elements of the curriculum were not to be separated from the faith dimension of the religious education curriculum. For this reason, a religious education teacher who is a practising Catholic assists the catechetical dimension of the text-based curriculum. For the RECs, implementing a text-based curriculum was not just about knowledge but also about faith. The RECs' perspective here was consistent with Church documents referred to above.

## *Unqualified Teachers of Religious Education*

The RECs involved in this study identified the employment of unqualified teachers of religious education as another factor impeding the management of this curriculum change. The emphasis on a knowledge-centred approach to religious education as a vehicle to faith formation (Elliot & Rossiter, 1982) exposed gaps in the religious knowledge of many teachers. One REC who expressed a preference for teachers practising the faith tradition over someone who was qualified to teach religious education, also acknowledged the benefit that training in religious education has for the teacher.

> So the reality is the majority of the staff aren't trained in RE. There are enormous gaps in their knowledge and understanding of the Catholic faith tradition and it is difficult for them to teach the content in the textbooks. (I)

When teachers expressed concerns about not understanding the content of the textbooks, the RECs tried to help them by offering professional learning experiences and suggesting sponsored opportunities to study for a tertiary qualification in religious education or theology. According to some RECs, professional learning experiences were preferred above undertaking tertiary studies in religious education or theology by most unqualified religious education teachers. While some RECs encountered a very small minority of religious education teachers expressing interest in undertaking tertiary studies they acknowledged that most were reluctant to do so. Resistance to undertaking tertiary studies was commented on by one REC who explored other ways of increasing the knowledge proficiencies required to teach the text-based curriculum of a religious education faculty.

> None of them [teachers] were going to do studies. I think that they're just too far down the track to commit to tertiary studies. They're not going to spend nights out studying. The school then needs to realise this and make a proactive effort to employ teachers with qualifications. As for our current teachers, I try to give them some personal confidence and show them ways of teaching and some of the teachers said that I had made them a better religious education teacher, through the professional learning experiences I was able to offer. (L)

It was not uncommon for RECs to try to help teachers gain confidence in teaching the topics in the textbooks by offering school-based professional learning experiences. Professional learning experiences are discussed later in this chapter as a factor the RECs perceived as assisting the change. While the RECs indicated that they gained professional satisfaction from facilitating professional learning experiences for teachers, they also commented on the challenge associated with finding the time to lead unqualified teachers through such experiences. Unqualified religious education teachers impeded the management and implementation of a text-based curriculum due to the amount of time being invested into organising and, in many cases, facilitating professional learning opportunities. Furthermore the deficit in religious expertise of unqualified religious education teachers placed additional time demands and responsibilities on RECs not only to organise professional learning opportunities, but also in terms of making curriculum decisions, as well as writing the curriculum and implementing it.

It is not surprising that RECs perceived lack of qualifications as an impediment to the implementation process. The need for qualifications in religious education surfaced and was noted in the early 1980s from experiences in senior secondary religious education classrooms and Church documents. As discussed at length in Chapter one, in the early 1980s state accredited religious education courses began to be taught in senior classes in many Catholic schools. These courses were taught largely from a phenomenological perspective and revealed that the life-centred approach had not provided students with adequate religious knowledge (Engebretson, 2002). Qualified teachers of religious education were sought to teach senior secondary state accredited courses in religious studies. The Congregation for Catholic Education (CCE) has repeatedly commented on the need for qualifications to teach religious education. "They [teachers] need to have the best possible qualifications and be inspired by faith" (CCE, 1982, #. 24). In 1988 the Congregation for Catholic Education again stressed the point. "Everything possible must be done to ensure that the Catholic schools have adequately trained teachers; it is vital, necessary and a legitimate expectation" (CCE, 1988, # 97).

The RECs perceived the lack of qualifications to teach religious education and teachers who are not practising Catholics, as being two key impediments to the implementation of the text-based curriculum. While there is a distinction between the knowledge gained from qualifications or training in religious education and faith practice, the relationship between the two has been explored in Church documents. The RECs suggested that the absence of either factor was clearly an impediment to implementing the change.

Rossiter (1982) has argued for "a 'creative divorce' between catechesis and religious education in Catholic schools". Moran (1991) has distinguished two processes concerning religious education. "Religious education is composed of two sharply contrasting processes: (1) teaching people religion; and (2) teaching people to be religious in a particular way" (Moran, 1991, p. 249). Teaching people religion is an intellectual pursuit open to critical academic enquiry and well suited to classroom teaching. Teaching people to be religious in a particular way is concerned with the formation of a person within a particular religious tradition and hopes for religious commitment. Within a faith-based school, both processes could be incorporated into the whole curriculum. Understanding the demarcation between the two is essential for any REC or religious education teacher.

The whole of religious education is not a terribly complex project. It requires that those of us who appropriate the term "teacher" know which of the two processes they are engaged in at a particular time and place. The tragedy would be that the lack of clarity about the distinction, institutions end up doing neither: their academic enquiry is not challenging enough and their formation is not particular enough. (Moran, 1991, p. 250)

As a leader within a Catholic school, the REC is required to take part in the two processes (Catholic Education Office, Melbourne, 1995). However, in the area of curriculum leadership the comparatively objective educational approach to teaching and learning emanating from the textbooks did not provide the impetus for the REC to prioritise qualifications over faith practice when stating the factors that impeded the curriculum change.

## Capacity to Articulate a Paradigm Shift

Another factor that impeded the change was the difficulty RECs encountered in articulating the paradigm shift from a life-centred approach which underpinned the pre-existing curriculum based on *Guidelines* (1995) to an educational approach that emphasised the acquisition of knowledge through the achievement of learning outcomes. The RECs did not explicitly state this as a factor, as they had done with other factors outlined in this chapter. However, the examples that follow later in this section indicate the limited ability of RECs to articulate this paradigm shift.

The approaches underpinning *Guidelines* (1995) and the text-based curriculum have been discussed at length in Chapter one. However, a brief outline here will assist in contextualising the RECs' limited capacity to articulate the paradigm shift. *Guidelines* (1995) were based on theological principles (Engebretson, 1997; see also, Amalorpavadass, 1971 & 1973) which underpinned a life-centred approach to religious education in the Melbourne Archdiocese. The curriculum schema was founded on a catechetical process that involved four interactive elements aimed at helping students to reflect on their experience as a means to understanding the Christian tradition. This was commonly known as the "four-point plan" and consisted of four movements: a) experienced shared (we share our experiences); b) reflection deepened (we reflect together); c) faith expressed (we come to know our Catholic faith); and d) insights reinforced (we gain further insights and respond) (Catholic Education Office Melbourne, 1995, pp. 27-29).

In contrast the text-based curriculum was founded on an outcomes-based educational model (Buchanan, 2004; Pell, 2001). Particular cognitive and affective outcomes and strategies to achieve such outcomes were articulated in the *To Know Worship and Love Teacher Companions* (Elliott, 2002c). The educational approach implied in the Church-sponsored textbooks, had a distinct emphasis on the acquisition of knowledge as a potential channel to faith formation (Rossiter, 1981a; 1981b, see also Buchanan, 2003; Buchanan, 2004). Educational outcomes were emphasised in this approach (Elliott, 2002c).

Some RECs grappled with language to try to explain the paradigm shift between the pre-existing curriculum developed from the *Guidelines* (1995) and the approach taken in the text-based curriculum. One REC who commented on the attitude of some religious education teachers as a factor impeding the change, provided an example of an REC's inability to find appropriate language to identify the paradigm shift.

Teachers were used to the *woolly woolly approach* taken to teaching our course based on *Guidelines*. It was easy for them to discuss experiences and feeling with students. But the textbooks demanded a more *concrete approach* to curriculum planning and teaching. I think the staff found this really difficult and it made it harder for me to manage the change. (B)

While one REC referred to the life-centred catechetical approach which had an emphasis on discussing life experiences as the "woolly woolly approach" another identified it as the "fluffy stuff".

> I think *Guidelines* were addressing religious education within Catholic schools at a time where it got a little bit 'fluffy'. We were talking about spirituality, we were talking about prayer and meditation, and there was little theological background. Now, I think that the textbooks try to address a shift from the *fluffy stuff* in religious education. (J)

The absence of an Archdiocesan initiative to convey a context and a curriculum framework in which to understand the text-based curriculum initiative, made it difficult for RECs to clearly articulate the paradigm shift and the implications of this shift to learning and teaching and the implementation of the text-based curriculum. Another REC attempted to explain the paradigm shift as follows.

> I think now, *To Know Worship and Love*, is coming out of a different context, where we are being mandated to ensure that our students in schools now know the Catholic faith, the Catholic traditions, the Catholic dogma and the doctrine. And I think that's what they're ensuring that students have an understanding of. (O)

Without any directives or explanations from the Archdiocese about the rationale, context and implications of the change, the RECs struggled to fully understand and find language to adequately explain a context to distinguish the text-based curriculum from the pre-existing curriculum based on *Guidelines* (1995). There was a tendency amongst RECs to incorporate the content of the textbooks within their pre-existing curriculum rather than to start afresh and develop a new curriculum consistent with the paradigm shift in which the textbooks were situated.

In summary the Archdiocese did not effectively explain the rationale, context and implications of the change to the RECs who were responsible for implementing it. The RECs struggled with the use of language while trying to articulate an understanding of the change. Lack of understanding of the implications of the change resulted in many instances of RECs inappropriately fusing pre-existing courses underpinned by the life-centred paradigm, with the textbooks that emphasised a knowledge-centred outcomes based educational approach. While this fusion may seem understandable, it was based on a limited capacity to articulate an adequate understanding of the paradigm shift stemming from the text-based curriculum to that emanating from pre-existing curricula based on *Guidelines* (1995). An ability to understand the paradigm shift from the life-centred approach in *Guidelines* to the outcomes based knowledge-centred approach emanating from the textbooks would have been beneficial.

It was apparent that some RECs were unable to articulate the differences between the approaches they were using. This difficulty in articulating the paradigm shift compounded the lack of coherent preparatory discussions about the approach underpinning the textbooks in the lead up to the change. In addition to this, the Archbishop who had directed the change referred to it as a change to a text-based curriculum (Pell, 2001, p. 5) but the textbooks were not supported by a curriculum outline explaining the curriculum theory in which the textbooks were situated. While some RECs could recognise the educational approach from reading the textbooks, their ability to articulate the change was impaired because the theory underpinning the change was neither explained nor reported. In the absence of the theoretical and pedagogical implications being adequately communicated to the RECs it is no wonder that numerous impediments emerged which affected the management and implementation of the change. In this climate it is understandable that some RECs did not distinguish between the relevance of inadequate qualifications and not practising the Catholic faith as impediments to the curriculum change. It may also account for the perspective by some RECs that the language of the textbooks was also a factor that impeded the change.

As discussed in Chapter two, some religious education textbooks have been written with catechesis as the primary intention and others with education as the primary focus. The lack of coherent discussion about the theoretical and pedagogical context underpinning the textbooks made it more difficult to discern where the emphasis should be.

## *Difficulties Associated with Textbooks*

Another factor identified as impeding the implementation of the *To Know Worship and Love* textbooks concerned the language of the Year 7 and 8 textbooks. The RECs suggested that the language was too difficult for Year 7 and 8 students (aged between 12 and 13) to understand and consequently limited or compromised the use of the textbooks. The following comment by a REC reflected the general opinion of those involved in the study:

> I found that the language in the Year 7 and 8 textbooks was not conducive to independent learning. It is very hard for a teacher to leave students to work independently and complete a lesson based entirely on using the textbook. Teachers have to take the text, read it and put it into a language that the students understand. (G)

Although the RECs stated that the difficult language in the Year 7 and 8 textbooks impeded the management of change, they could not identify examples of religious education textbooks or textbooks from other curriculum areas that demonstrated an appropriate use of language for students at these levels. This may suggest a limited understanding of the use of textbooks in education by the RECs. Garner and Biewer (1983) indicated that the language of textbooks used in other Year 7 and 8 curriculum areas was also of concern to teachers. The RECs involved in this study suggested that difficult language alienated students from developing as independent learners and encouraged teacher dependency in the learning process. Another REC indicated that teachers tended to use the textbook as a teacher resource rather than a student textbook.

> The language is a difficulty; the presupposition, and the assumptions are too heavy. So I see the textbook as a resource book. It's almost like a teacher resource. There are some parts of the textbook that I think can be a student resource but on the whole I use the textbook as a teacher resource. (L)

The allegation of difficult language may be a symptom of teacher inexperience with the use of textbooks in religious education, and this inexperience may be an impediment to curriculum change. Most of the RECs involved in this study were not able to clearly identify clearly the perceived difficulties associated with the language in the textbooks. Judgements about the language were not based on a comparison with other textbooks from the field of religious education or other curriculum areas. Furthermore, the data collected from the interviews did not indicate that the RECs were aware of the use of differences in the language styles between primary school and secondary school textbooks, and the evident challenges even for students who are proficient readers.

During the transition years, from primary to secondary school, many students struggle to use textbooks effectively even by the end of Year 7 (Garner & Biewer, 1983).

The biggest 'hidden' problem faced by students in the transition years is the change in writing style of textbooks – whereas in the primary years students become accustomed to the story or narrative form, in the post-primary school they are expected to extract meaning from a descriptive or expository form of writing. (Garner and Biewer, 1983, p. 5)

There are variables other than reading proficiency that influence a student's ability to gain meaning from texts. "Students need to be made familiar with a variety of patterns and structures in textbooks if they are to use them effectively" (Garner and Biewer, 1983, p. 8). Students may become overwhelmed with the quantity of material to be learned from textbooks (Crawford & Carnine, 2000) and even "good students may come to view their task as one of learning many details... less able students may come to view their task as simply impossible" (Kinder & Bursuck, 1991, p. 271). Pepper (1981) suggested that textbooks should be written for students and stressed the importance of the use of examples as a mechanism for 'bridging the gap between the expert and the novice' (pp. 259-269). It is beneficial for students to become familiar with vocabulary and stylistic structures relevant to a particular subject discipline (Garner & Biewer, 1983). The role of the skilled teacher is important in the learning process and "teachers must draw to the attention of students the language of their own subject if textbooks are to be a realistic tool for the classroom" (p. 10).

Despite the perceived difficulties relating to the language in the textbooks, none of the RECs saw this as an area where teachers of religious education would benefit from professional development experiences. The text-based curriculum placed much emphasis on a knowledge-centred outcomes-based approach to religious education.

The absence of textbooks in religious education in the Melbourne Catholic Archdiocese meant professional experience concerning the use of textbooks in religious education was neglected. Consequently RECs and teachers had comparatively limited experience in effectively using textbooks in religious education. A limited knowledge about the use of textbooks seems to have influenced the perspective of RECs that difficult language impeded the management of this particular change to a text-based curriculum.

From either perspective, concerns about the language of the textbooks were further exacerbated in the hands of unqualified teachers of religious education. A religious education teacher with minimal qualifications to teach religious education, and minimal knowledge about the content contained in the textbooks would find the language of the textbooks challenging. This no doubt would be the case in any discipline where textbooks were used and the teacher was not qualified in that specialist area. Some RECs expressed concern that the difficult language of the textbooks did not encourage independent learning because the teacher could not set the whole lesson from the textbook. This perspective failed to consider the responsibility a teacher has to be a mediator between the textbook and student learning, a role expected of any subject teacher where textbooks are used (Garner & Biewer, 1983). It is arguable that lack of experience religious education teachers and RECs had in using knowledge-centred textbooks may have been a greater problem than the actual language style presented in the textbooks.

## *RECs' Perspectives on Self as a Leader of Curriculum Change*

In some instances the REC considered that he/she impeded the process of curriculum change. This consideration was presented as a lack of confidence in their ability to make professional demands on members of the faculty.

> And perhaps in myself too, in my way of leadership, I may lack a bit of confidence in persuading teachers to take part in a major review of the RE course. Many staff members say they have no time or don't know about RE and it is difficult to make demands on them. All those little things can be impediments to change. (I)

In situations where the RECs lacked confidence in their abilities to make professional demands on members of their faculty, there was a tendency to justify this by expressing sympathy for the work demands placed on the average teacher. In some cases this type of sympathy acted as a justification for not making professional demands on religious education teachers by the REC. However it was more likely to be a way of camouflaging their own lack of confidence in making such demands. In some situations this lack of confidence resulted in RECs undertaking all the tasks involved to bring about the desired change. Some RECs tended to design, develop and document a text-based curriculum for their school with almost no input from other members of their faculty. Lack of confidence resulted in RECs giving religious education teachers copies of a curriculum they had prepared based on the textbooks. The only demand made on the teacher was to teach it.

Some RECs considered that their perspectives of themselves as curriculum leaders may have been a factor impeding the curriculum change. Fleming's (2002) research demonstrated that from the beginning the role of RECs was regarded predominantly as one of Church ministry. Crotty (2005) indicated that RECs perceive their role as both within education and within Church ministry. However, it appeared that RECs gave greater priority to the Church ministry aspects of the role, preferring to ignore classroom religious education curriculum responsibilities (Crotty, 2005, p. 54). Inexperience in curriculum leadership in religious education may have posed some challenges for RECs who were likely to be more experienced and more willing to pursue the aspects of the role commonly associated with Church ministry rather than the educational issues that the text-based curriculum demanded.

## Factors That Assisted Curriculum Change[11]

Figure 15 shows the sub-categories associated with category seven, factors that assisted the curriculum change. In total there were five sub-categories associated with category seven.

*Figure 15.* Category 7: Factors that assisted the curriculum change.

### Time to Reflect on Practice

The RECs involved in this research suggested that time to reflect on practice assisted the management of this curriculum change. It provided opportunities for religious education teachers to reach an understanding about the reasons for the change, to share their responses to the change and to identify and express any difficulties they had with the change. The following comment was a common view expressed by the RECs.

> Reflection time provided opportunities for adequate communication between members of staff. Staff members were able to discuss issues concerning the reasons for the change and share their responses. It provided an opportunity for them to express their concerns and difficulties and find a way forward. This process was particularly important because concerns about the changes not only raised educational questions but also questions relating to the personal or religious faith concerns of many teachers teaching RE. (A)

Time to reflect and discuss was not only valuable for the teaching staff involved in the change but also for the RECs leading the change. This time enabled teachers to share pedagogical experiences about how the curriculum innovation was being translated to the classroom. Opportunities to celebrate success, express concerns and find ways to improve the learning and teaching approaches

---

[11] Parts of this section have been published in:
Buchanan, M. T. (2006c) Factors that assist curriculum change. *Journal of Religious Education, 54* (1), 18-26.

provided opportunities for teachers to learn from each other. Johnson (2000, 2001) has reported on the value of reflective practice, suggesting that it enabled teachers to focus on the needs of their real work situation. This study revealed that the time devoted to reflecting on and discussing practice provided opportunities for teachers to professionally learn from each other.

Another significant insight revealed by the RECs was that discussion about practice was not only beneficial for teachers but also for RECs as curriculum leaders. Because of their role as curriculum leaders, RECs were able to gain insights into the real needs of teachers from the time set aside to discuss the link between theory and practice. The insights gained by the RECs were: a) insights concerning staff development needs; b) insights concerning the potential for "faith formation"; and c) insights concerning resources. The insights RECs gained assisted the management of the curriculum change as it enabled RECs to identify the needs of their religious education teachers and to respond in a constructive way to those needs.

*Staff Development Needs*

Time to reflect on practice provided opportunities for RECs to consider and organise for staff development needs relevant to the teachers' current situation. The following comment by a REC was indicative of the sentiments shared by others:

> By allowing opportunities for staff to share their experiences in the religious education classroom and reflect on the level of success or failure of that lesson helped me [REC] to identify the needs of individual teachers as well as the collective needs of faculty members. I would attempt to address these issues by providing staff members with relevant literature, organising professional learning and peer support opportunities, and guest speakers. I

The approach enabled the RECs to identify the specific needs of the teachers and to respond. In adopting this approach the RECs were able to create environments where, according to Johnson (2000a), teachers learn best. He suggested that when the staff development opportunities are focussed on the real needs of the teacher it enables teachers to perceive them as an integral part of their work.

## Potential for Faith Formation

In the Catholic school context in the Archdiocese of Melbourne, the approach to religious education was based on a faith-nurturing model which is common in many faith based school systems (Grimmitt, 2000). The curriculum innovation studied in this research had an emphasis on knowledge as a channel to faith (Rossiter, 1981a; 1981b; see also, Buchanan, 2003; Elliot & Rossiter, 1982; Engebretson, Fleming & Rymarz, 2002; Hart, 2002; Pell, 2001). The interviews with RECs suggested that time to reflect on practice in religious education had the potential to provide opportunities for classroom teachers to reflect on their own "faith formation". One comment by an REC provided an example of what some RECs perceived, according to their own words, as the "faith-forming" potential emanating from the discussion time.

> Yesterday I met with the Year 10 teachers and we evaluated what we had taught about Mark's Gospel. Before teaching the unit, their understanding of scripture was predominantly literal, rather fundamental. I decided to provide them with an understanding of the historical background and the structure of the text. I thought this would be a good starting point for

their classroom teaching. As they reflected on the content I was leading them through, they began to comment on passages from Mark's Gospel and what the messages actually mean to them. It was a very personal experience where their own understanding of Jesus was being enriched by their reflections. It was a faith-forming experience for some. (L)

The RECs interviewed considered the likely influence the textbooks could have upon the personal and "faith formation" of a teacher. The RECs interviewed were sensitive to the impact of the Church-sponsored textbooks on the personal and "faith formation" of some of their religious education teachers. Given the ecclesial and ministerial perceptions of the role of the REC discussed earlier as well as in Chapters two and five of this book, it is understandable that RECs would perceive staff development experiences as having the potential to enrich a religious education teacher at a personal and faith forming level. It also suggests that within a faith-based Catholic school system RECs do not separate catechesis from education in religious education for teachers or students.

## Resources

The RECs involved in the study saw part of their role in the management of curriculum as providing appropriate learning and teaching resources. When time was allocated for classroom teachers to discuss practice some RECs were able to gain insights into the needs of the religious education teachers and disseminate appropriate resources to them.

On-going reflection time helped me to understand the needs of the teachers. I gained insights about the types of resources they needed. As articles, books and videos came my way I would pass the relevant ones on and suggest how they could be used. (G)

Those resources provided by some RECs assisted the curriculum change by enabling opportunities for religious education teachers to become less reliant towards the use of textbooks in conjunction with other learning and teaching resources.

Time to discuss the interplay between the new curriculum and practice provided an opportunity for members of the faculty to meet and express their concerns and understandings relating to the curriculum change. In so doing the learning and teaching needs associated with the curriculum innovation were articulated. Consequently it enabled RECs to respond to the needs of the classroom teacher by providing professional learning opportunities and appropriate curriculum resources for the teachers to use. The insight into the pastoral/ministry concerns of the teachers also influenced the actions of the RECs, particularly in taking responsibility for the professional development/learning opportunities they provided for members of their faculty.

## *Professional Development / Learning Experiences for Teachers of Religious Education*

A second factor that assisted the change was the provision made by the RECs to offer school based opportunities for professional learning (Johnson 2000b, 2001) and development. This was also problematic in that it took away curriculum management time in an already under-resourced and demanding role (Liddy, 1998). However, the RECs perceived this as an important aspect of their role in managing the change.

The transition to a knowledge-centred text-based curriculum in religious education exposed deficiencies in the religious knowledge and skills of many religious education teachers. Most RECs indicated that providing professional learning and development opportunities helped religious education teachers to become more proficient, and this assisted the management of the curriculum change. Johnson (2000a; 2000b) has emphasised the importance of professional learning cultures in schools. In some instances RECs claimed that it was imperative that they facilitate and lead the professional learning/development opportunities for the religious education teachers in their faculty.

Most indicated that members of their faculties seemed vulnerable when teaching religious education. This sense of vulnerability stemmed from being inadequately qualified or not sufficiently connected to the Catholic faith tradition. Thomas (2000) has commented on the implications of unqualified teachers of religious education in terms of impeding the quality of teaching and learning in religious education. The RECs were committed to supporting vulnerable teachers of religious education by facilitating and leading professional learning/development opportunities.

The RE teachers feel threatened when experts from outside the school lead professional development seminars in religious education. They just sit there and they are reluctant to interact or ask questions. At first I thought it was because they did not care about the subject. Then I realised that they felt vulnerable, so I began to organise and lead the professional development seminars. The staff felt more relaxed because they know me. They asked questions, shared ideas, began to try things in the classroom. (B)

Fleming (2002) indicated that RECs in secondary schools in the Melbourne Archdiocese were generally well qualified in both education and religious education. The highly specialised and unique nature of the role may be pivotal in understanding why RECs accepted responsibility for organising and leading religious education teachers through professional development and learning experiences.

So part of my task is to provide on-site professional development or survival for the religious education teachers. So in teaching them how to prepare lessons in religious education and lesson content they feel personally and professionally supported. They feel more confident to take risks and to talk about what they are experiencing in the classroom. (L)

The RECs suggested that the professional development experiences they provided helped staff members to gain proficiency in teaching and learning and to develop knowledge about the content of the text-based religious education curriculum. Growth in teacher confidence and a willingness to try new teaching and learning approaches in the classroom, as well as a willingness to share their successes and failures with other members of the faculty, was identified as one of the positive aspects of professional learning experiences. According to the RECs, the professional learning experiences they offered helped religious education teachers to grow personally and professionally. One REC measured the growth in personal and professional confidence of religious education teachers by their willingness to attend professional development experiences beyond the school context. "As their confidence escalated from the professional development experiences I was offering at school, they became more willing to participate in professional development organised in a wider educational context" (G).

Literature about curriculum change and the value of professional learning experiences organised by school personnel at a school based level has been discussed in Chapter two (Fullan, 1993; Johnson, 2000, 2001; Hargreaves, 1998; Marsh, 1997; Smith & Lovat, 2003). The RECs demonstrated a sympathetic understanding of how vulnerable many religious education teachers were because of lack of qualifications in and lack of personal commitment to the Catholic faith tradition. RECs were able to recognise how such issues might have an impact on a teacher's level of confidence in the religious education classroom. It is understandable that RECs perceived themselves as being key persons, able to be responsible for facilitating and leading professional learning experiences of religious education teachers in their faculty.

*Teamwork*

The RECs perceived that teamwork among members of the faculty was a factor that assisted the management of the curriculum change. It provided opportunities for members of the faculty to audit the content of existing curriculum against the content of the textbooks and their own understanding of the content of the textbooks. The development of effective professional relationships and expertise amongst staff members was enhanced by the experience of teamwork. Teamwork helped to develop proficiencies in teaching and curriculum planning amongst teachers. "The teachers are building confidence and competence in planning the curriculum in religious education through sharing their ideas and concerns at the team meetings" (A).

This accords with Johnson's (2000a) notion of professional action-learning teams (PLTs). Such teams respond to actual workplace needs and thus have a reason to come together. They engage in professional conversation and collaborative practices. Members of the team share collective responsibility for producing effective learning for all students as well as each other (Healy, 2003). In many situations RECs encouraged teamwork opportunities particularly in year levels rather than at a faculty level. Year level teams provided opportunities for teachers at particular year levels to explore creative ways of developing and implementing the curriculum, as well as discussing issues about the faith tradition emanating from the content of the textbook at their particular year level. "We work quite well in teams. I [REC] make sure that each year level has a team leader who is creative and pushes the others along to be more creative" (O).

Some RECs were able to negotiate as part of the teaching load a timetabled meeting for teams to meet. Teams in other schools arranged meeting times after school. According to Thomas (2000) the vulnerability experienced by many teachers of religious education can be attributed to two broad issues, these being a lack of personal familiarity with the religious tradition to which the faith-based school belongs, and limited or no qualifications in religious education. The RECs regarded teamwork as an opportunity to develop positive working relationships with other faculty members by trying to address the professional concerns of the staff. "It sounds strange but the development of a positive relationship between staff members happens when they feel that their contribution is valued and important. So it is the development of these relationships within teams that helps to create effective teams" (J).

In the process of managing curriculum change some RECs undertook the responsibility to provide opportunities for religious education teachers to work in teams. Teamwork helped to encourage faculty members to accept ownership of the implementation of the text-based curriculum.

> The most important thing for me was to make sure that everything was done in terms of relationships between team members in order to allow effective dialogue amongst colleagues. I did not want a situation where I was telling people what to do. I wanted teachers to come up with some ideas and solutions as well by working together to plan and implement the curriculum. I

Teamwork promoted a collaborative partnership (Smith & Lovat, 2003) which assisted the management of curriculum change in the following ways. It enabled opportunities for curriculum planning, auditing and development to occur. Teamwork fostered the development of positive professional relationships amongst colleagues. It also provided opportunities to build up professional confidence amongst members of the faculty particularly for vulnerable religious education teachers.

## *Support from School Leadership / Administration*

Some RECs indicated that support from the school leadership / administration team was a factor that also assisted in the management of the curriculum change. Support was identified in terms of the display of a genuine interest concerning the change from members of the leadership team. In addition an eagerness to be informed about the process of managing the change was interpreted as a measure of support for the initiatives.

> I think the support from the leadership team was very positive. In addressing the issue of change and thinking about the processes that needed to be put in place to bring about the change, I think the support of the leadership team helped significantly. (A)

Most RECs commented on the importance of keeping the leadership / administration team informed about the curriculum change and their progress in managing the change. To some extent keeping the leadership / administration team informed helped to generate support and interest in how the REC was progressing with the change.

> I felt that the leadership team were willing to support my initiatives to manage the change but I also felt it was important for me to keep them informed about the text-based curriculum and its implications, especially for our school. I was always encouraged by the leadership team. You know, they would say 'well done, congratulations, if you need anything let me know.' But that's about it. It never went any further. (J)

In addition to encouraging comments from leadership / administration teams, some RECs identified support from the leadership / administration team as a willingness to provide them with additional classroom time release in order to manage the curriculum change implementation. However due to the demands placed on the REC in this role, none took up the offer of time release.

The demands of the role of REC meant that time release for managing the curriculum change would prove costly in terms of completing all the other aspects of the role for which the REC was accountable.

> If I wanted extra time then there certainly was support for that. I would just have to ask the principal and I would get it. But I did not ask because there is so much else to do in the role and it seemed easier to do the curriculum tasks during my holidays, than to ask for time release. (O)

Smith and Lovat (2003) have emphasised that the principal and other leaders within the school need to actively support the change if it is to be successful. Crotty (2005) has indicated that specifically in relation to religious education, the REC is most effective in the role if she/he is supported by the principal. Support was certainly apparent and demonstrated in a genuine interest in the curriculum change, and RECs believed this to be a factor that assisted the management of that change.

## *Attracting Qualified Teachers of Religious Education*

The RECs suggested that attracting qualified religious education teachers assisted the curriculum change. The text-based curriculum emphasised a knowledge-centred approach to teaching religious education as a channel to faith formation (Rossiter, 1981a). Concerns were raised by some RECs about the ability of some teachers to teach religious education without any background knowledge or qualifications in religious education. Some RECs were able to encourage the principal of the school to advertise for the appointment of qualified teachers of religious education. "The Principal has definitely made it a priority to attract qualified teachers of religious education and the employment of such teachers has really helped to develop and implement the text-based curriculum" (L).

Some RECs also suggested that the transition to a text-based curriculum exposed deficiencies in the religious knowledge of many teachers. This revelation provided the impetus for some teachers to seek tertiary qualifications in religious education. One REC suggested that the studies undertaken by a few religious education teachers from her/his school have assisted the management and implementation of this knowledge-centred text-based curriculum change.

> The text-based curriculum has made people realise that they do not know enough about what they are teaching. This curriculum initiative has made teachers want to know more about what they are teaching. It has made some of the teachers want to take on some studies in religious education, not all of them, but some of them. They bring what they are learning from their courses into the school and our curriculum development has really benefited. (G)

The transition to a text-based curriculum provided the impetus for appointing qualified teachers of religious education in Catholic schools in the Archdiocese of Melbourne. It also encouraged some existing teachers of religious education to take on tertiary studies in this field. The RECs involved in this study suggested that the appointment of such teachers within their faculties has assisted the management and implementation of a text-based curriculum. Educational change challenges teachers' perceptions and beliefs about their own competencies (Smith & Lovat, 2003).

In relation to this particular curriculum change qualifications in religious education have emerged as a valuable credential for teaching the text-based curriculum.

## Conclusion

This chapter has presented the theory generated and an analysis of categories 6 and 7 and their associated sub-categories, which have emerged from the data generated from the RECs' perspectives on their management of a particular text-based curriculum change initiative. Table 12 below, provides a summary of the theory generated relevant to these categories and their associated sub-categories. Chapter seven aims to provide another dimension to the analysis in order to develop a theory about the management of this curriculum change from the perspective of the RECs that moves beyond thick description (Goulding, 2002). This will be achieved by referring to the insights gained from four experts who have commented on the theory generated. According to Glaser (1978) the grounded theory researcher can be aided in developing a theory that goes beyond thick description by considering knowledge and theory gained from outside sources such as the insights from the experts consulted in Chapter seven.

Table 13

*The theory generated relevant to categories 6 and 7 and associated sub-categories.*

| Category 6<br>Factors that impede change | Key Theory Generated |
|---|---|
| (i) Teachers of religious education not practising the Catholic faith tradition. | Regardless of the educational emphasis on the acquisition of religious knowledge through outcomes-based learning, RECs perceived that such knowledge was meaningless without some personal faith engagement from the classroom religious education teacher. It was held by the RECs that religious education teachers who were not practising the Catholic faith in their own lives were likely to impede the management of a curriculum change. |
| (ii) Unqualified teachers of religious education. | The RECs management of the curriculum change was impeded by teachers who did not have qualifications to teach religious education. |
| (iii) Capacity to articulate paradigm shift. | RECs found it difficult to articulate the theory underpinning the curriculum change in a situation where there is a lack of coherent discussion about the theoretical position of the text-based curriculum particularly with those directing the change. |
| (iv) Difficulties associated with textbooks. | RECs have limited experiences and knowledge about the use of textbooks in religious education and they experienced difficulties using textbooks in a way that was relevant to students in the religious education classroom. |
| (v) RECs' perspectives on self as a curriculum leader. | RECs primarily perceived themselves as ministerial leaders rather than curriculum leaders. They were not as confident in their ability to exercise curriculum leadership as they were in exercising ministerial leadership. |

| Category 7<br>Factors that assist change | Key Theory Generated |
|---|---|
| (i) Time to reflect on practice. | Time to reflect on practice enabled teachers to professionally learn from each other and also enabled RECs to identify some real needs of staff such as staff development needs, "faith formation" needs, and resource needs. |
| (ii) Professional development learning experiences. | RECs were genuinely sympathetic towards teachers who lacked the qualifications to teach religious education and they would organise as well as led professional development / learning experiences to enable teachers to feel professionally and personally confident in their teaching of religious education.<br><br>RECs believed that teachers of religious education are more confident when engaging in experiences of professional development facilitated and led by the REC than by an expert from outside the school. |
| (iii) Teamwork | RECs encouraged and facilitated teamwork opportunities that fostered professional and personal growth for teachers of religious education. |
| (iv) Support from school leadership / administration. | RECs considered themselves to be supported in their management of curriculum change in situations where the principal and other members of the leadership / administration team showed a genuine interest in the change initiative. |
| (v) Attracting qualified teachers of religious education. | The employment of qualified teachers of religious education assisted the RECs in their management of the change to a knowledge-centred text-based curriculum. |

# CHAPTER SEVEN
# The Generation of Theories about Managing Curriculum Change

Chapters five and six reported on the theory generated concerning the RECs' perspectives on their management of a particular curriculum change in religious education. As discussed in Chapter four, the grounded theory researcher is interested in developing a theory that goes beyond thick description (Goulding, 2002, p. 43). The knowledge and theory gained from other sources can assist the grounded theory researcher in developing a theory beyond thick description (Glaser, 1978). In order to avoid corrupting the data, knowledge gained from outside sources should be perceived as another informant (Creswell, 1994; Glaser; 1992). For example, the researcher's voice and the views of experts in the area relating to the phenomenon being studied can be regarded as outside informants. This chapter analyses the views of outside informants who have expertise in the area of religious education curriculum. The views of the outside informants helped to develop the theory beyond thick description and provide a further level of analysis of the theory generated. Within a constructivist paradigm the views of the experts also contributed to establishing the plausibility of the study, as was discussed in Chapter four.

Chapter seven consists of the following structure: The first section provides an outline of the professional background of each of the four experts. In the second section each category of theory generated from the interviews with the RECs is analysed in the light of the opinions of the experts and the continuing presence of the researcher's voice.

## Professional Backgrounds of Experts

*Expert 1 (CA)*

CA has had many years experience as a teacher of religious education and as an REC in Catholic schools in the Archdiocese of Melbourne. She has completed postgraduate studies in theology and religious education and has been a publisher for a large publishing company that specialises in the publication of religious books. She has been involved in writing and publishing religious education textbooks and theology textbooks for Australia and New Zealand, and has also been a curriculum advisor in religious education at the Catholic Education Office, Melbourne. CA's responsibilities in this role involved organising and facilitating professional development opportunities for religious education teachers, RECs and principals in the areas of theology, religious education, curriculum design and Catholic ethos. CA also has experience in the role of Director of Religious Education and Faith Education in a P-12 Catholic College in the Archdiocese of Melbourne.

## Expert 2 (JO)

JO has been involved in religious education in the Catholic system for over 30 years and has been a religious education teacher, and an REC in Catholic schools in the Archdiocese of Melbourne, as well as a lecturer in religious education at Australian Catholic University. JO's doctoral thesis was in the area of religious education with a specific focus on the role of the REC in the Archdiocese of Melbourne. He has published in the area of religious education leadership and curriculum, and has held two leadership positions at the Catholic Education Office, Melbourne in religious education. The first position involved working with RECs in Catholic secondary schools in the role of curriculum adviser. More recently JO has held the position of Manager of religious education programs, and has been responsible for the delivery of religious education curriculum in over three hundred Catholic primary and secondary schools in the Archdiocese of Melbourne. He was recently appointed the Cardinal Basil Hume visiting scholar at Cambridge University, England.

## Expert 3 (KA)

KA has been a teacher of religious education and an REC in various Catholic secondary schools in the Archdiocese of Melbourne. She has much experience in the tertiary education sector as an academic and educator. As a lecturer in religious education, KA is involved in the training of pre-service teachers and teachers seeking post graduate qualifications in religious education and leadership in religious education. As an academic, KA has published widely in the area of religious education curriculum and religious education leadership. She is an experienced writer of religious education textbooks and has written several religious education textbooks which have been used in many Catholic secondary schools. She was seconded by the Episcopal Vicariate for Religious Education to write several of the secondary school textbooks in the *To Know Worship and Love* series.

## Expert 4 (RI)

RI has had experience as a religious education teacher and REC in Catholic secondary schools in the Archdiocese of Melbourne and has had over six years experience in tertiary education as a lecturer and academic in religious education. At tertiary level RI has been involved in planning and implementing courses concerning teaching religious education in the primary and secondary context. He has co-authored books relating to primary and secondary teaching in religious education and leadership in religious education. He has had experience in writing religious education curriculum in the Catholic and non-Catholic sector. He was seconded by the Episcopal Vicariate for Religious Education to write some of the secondary school textbooks in the *To Know Worship and Love* series.

The four experts have a great deal of expertise in religious education relevant to Catholic secondary schools in the Archdiocese of Melbourne. The theory generated and detailed in Chapters five and six were presented to each of the experts and their comments and opinions provided an outside perspective. All four experts attested to the plausibility of the theory generated. Their insights assisted the grounded theory researcher in an analysis of the data that moved the development of theory beyond thick description (Goulding, 2002, p. 42).

## Preparation for Change

Preparing for the curriculum change was perceived by the RECs as an integral part of the management of the text-based curriculum change. The theory generated and discussed in Chapter five indicated a number of ways in which the RECs endeavoured to inform themselves and staff members about the change. In order to prepare for the change, initiatives were undertaken to provide opportunities, to dialogue about the change, to explore the textbooks in light of the existing curriculum within their respective school and to develop processes for making decisions regarding how to implement the change. The theory generated suggested that the RECs perceived it as their responsibility to prepare for the change and consultation with the experts supported this view and emphasised that the potential for the RECs to become fully informed about the change was significantly compromised.

The Archbishop, as the head of the Catholic Church in Melbourne, directed the curriculum change. He established an Episcopal Vicariate for Religious Education, which was responsible for writing and implementing the textbooks, which were to comprise the text-based curriculum. In this regard it was a "top down" (Morris, 1995) curriculum initiative. The experts confirmed that a lack of communication and information available to the RECs compromised their ability to fully understand the change.

> The Episcopal Vicariate did not lead this change well at all. It was simply a matter that this change was going to happen without any consultation. The information that came out from the Vicariate was insufficient. There should have been so much more. There should have been regular meetings with RECs keeping them informed. It was in every way a top down change that did not consult the leaders in RE who were the RECs. (KA)

Information about the change and providing opportunities for access to such information was the responsibility of those leading the change. The experts agreed that those leading the change had not adequately provided opportunities for RECs and other school leaders to become appropriately informed about the change. This issue was to a large extent ignored. The Episcopal Vicariate, according to one expert, had not assigned anyone with the responsibility of informing the RECs and other leaders within Catholic school about the change and its implications.

> The process of getting information out to teachers was not extensively done in my view, because it was no one's job to do it. Speaking for myself, the maximum time I was ever employed on the textbook project was two days per week and I had to write the textbooks. As writers of the books we realised that people needed to know more about this project, and we tried as best we could to get information out and to run information sessions for people. But it was inadequate simply because there were not the personnel to do it and the mechanism was not there for it to be done. (RI)

The Catholic Archdiocese of Melbourne accommodates the third largest education system in Australia. It is responsible for a body of schools representing approximately 180,000 students

(Engebretson, 2002, p. 33). Given the size of the group upon which the curriculum change would impact, it would be reasonable to expect the highest standard of communication between those at the top directing the change, and those responsible for implementing the change. This oversight made it difficult for RECs to become adequately informed. It made it difficult for RECs to achieve a full and comprehensive understanding about the nature and extent of the curriculum change. A lack of communication resulted in a limited understanding about the change and this impacted significantly on the way in which the change was managed.

> I think the lack of communication was difficult for RECs because when an REC is trying to lead what is usually a very large curriculum team, ranging from people who are very committed to people who are not, the REC really is the main authority within the school in terms of the direction and if you don't have that information it can be very uncomfortable in RE faculty meetings. For example trying to suggest that people plan curriculum in a particular way can be difficult if the staff ask about what is happening at the CEO and the REC might not be in a position to know. (CA)

The process of preparing for the change involved RECs providing opportunities for religious education teachers to dialogue about the change. Such opportunities have the potential to inform those involved in teaching about the change. However the extent to which dialogue can inform the parties is compromised in situations where the information discussed is misinformed or inadequate. Therefore dialogue about the change under these circumstances will not lead to a fully comprehensive understanding about the change and its implications. In fact one expert suggested that dialogue between RECs and religious education teachers is often uneven dialogue in many situations.

> Very often dialogue amongst RE teachers is very uneven. You often have a large group of teachers who are just not passionate about RE and not particularly interested in seeing it as an academic subject. A lot of RE teachers bring a minimalist understanding of RE. It is not necessarily their fault because the school has to cover the RE classes and there are not enough qualified RE teachers. So when the dialogue happens it needs to be recognised that the participants in the dialogue don't bring equal commitment or understanding to the process. What is the dialogue about? Is it about educational improvement? Is it about improving RE? Is it about making sure that this change is not going to make too many demands on the teacher who is teaching RE, who in many cases is teaching RE just to fill up his/her teaching load? (RI)

Uneven dialogue with faculty members and the inability of the RECs to become fully informed about the change and its implications did not provide RECs and members of their faculty with clear understanding of what the change required. Limited access to information about the curriculum change compromised the RECs' ability to fully understand the change and its implications and this resulted in RECs attempting to fit the content of the textbooks within the context of an existing curriculum based on *Guidelines* (1995). The plausibility of this finding was confirmed by the experts and discussed earlier in this chapter.

Principals and leadership /executive teams depended on RECs, as the key source to inform them about this major curriculum change and this was problematic because the RECs' potential to fully understand the change and its implications was compromised. Therefore principals and

150

leadership teams who depended on their RECs to inform them about the change could only receive compromised interpretation to the change and its implications. "In terms of the REC I think it would have been very taxing for them to inform their principal and leadership team about the change when it was extremely hard for them to get information" (RI). The following comment by one of the experts indicated the growing desperation of some principals who sought to become informed about the change resulting from an inability to access information about the change.

I can remember going out to schools to visit pre-service teachers and sometimes the principal of the school would be waiting for me. They wanted to find out what was going on about the textbook project. They were saying, why weren't we being told what was going on, why is this a deep dark secret? I would say there is no dark conspiracy here it is just that there is no one doing it because there is no one employed to do it. It was not my job to do it. I was responsible for writing the books. (RI)

Despite the RECs' efforts to become informed about the change and encourage dialogue about the change, it did not lead to a fully comprehensive understanding about the change and its implications for the RECs or religious education teachers and their school.

The communication from the very beginning was very bad. It was extremely badly handled. There was very poor communication from the Episcopal Vicariate, who should have sent out information all the time to schools. Because the communication was very poor there was a lot of misinformation, false information. I think poor communication was a real problem with the textbook project right from the very beginning. The communication from the top was extremely bad. (KA)

Some curriculum change, as in this instance, stems from the process of adopting a curriculum initiative that has originated from a source from outside the school (Brady & Kennedy, 2003; Lee, 2001; Marsh, 1997). Teachers were expected to implement a text-based curriculum developed by the Episcopal Vicariate for Religious Education under the direction of the Archbishop. Apple and Jungck (1991) suggested that a division between curriculum development and implementation contributes to the de-professionalisation of teachers. "Instead of professional teachers who care greatly about what they do and why they do it, we have alienated executors of someone else's plans" (Apple & Jungck, 1991, p. 3). However, there appears to be little evidence of this de-professionalisation of the RECs involved in the implementation of this "top down" (Morris, 1995) text-based curriculum which is the focus of this research.

The RECs, according to one expert, appeared to manage the change in a professional manner. They sought to find out and understand as much as possible about the change. Marsh (1997) suggested that the task of the teacher (in this study, the REC) is to find out how to use the new curriculum innovation as effectively as possible. Commonly asked questions by those adopting a "top down" (Morris, 1995) curriculum initiative are: "Am I doing what the practice requires? To whom can I turn to get assistance?" (Marsh, 1997, p. 156). In situations where it is difficult to receive appropriate answers to such questions, it is possible that a difference between the prescribed curriculum and the curriculum implemented may occur. In this situation the RECs' inability to receive appropriate assistance and information about the change from those directing the change made it difficult for them to adequately determine whether or not they were doing what was required.

Several RECs tended to incorporate the context of the textbooks within their existing school curriculum in religious education based on *Guidelines* (1995). Morris (1995) suggested that there can be a difference between the curriculum innovation prescribed by a centralised body and the real curriculum implemented in the classroom. In this study the disparity between the curriculum innovation and the real curriculum has been influenced by the lack of communication from the centralised body responsible for developing the initiative with those responsible for managing the change in schools. What Morris (1995) has described as real curriculum, Brickell (1972) has referred to as curriculum adaptation. When a curriculum innovation has been developed by a centralised body there is an expectation that it will be adopted (Marsh, 1997) by the schools for which it was designed. When the curriculum innovation is modified in some way the process of implementation, adaptation is said to have occurred. According to Brickell (1972), "adaptation requires an adequate understanding of the principles and spirit underlying the innovation" (p. 399). In this study concerning RECs' management of the centralised text-based curriculum innovation, an adaptation of the curriculum occurred as a result of an inadequate understanding of the principles and spirit underlying the change.

The RECs who were ultimately responsible for managing this "top down" (Morris, 1995) curriculum change in their school endeavoured to "understand the principles and spirit underlying the innovation" (Brickell, 1972, p. 399). In this situation the centralised authority directing the change failed to adequately inform the RECs about the nature, purpose and implications of the change, therefore they explored various avenues in an attempt to become informed. The impetus to become informed was not entirely influenced by a sense of professional responsibility to fulfil a "top down" (Morris, 1995) directive to manage the change. It was to some extent driven by the dependence of all other members of the school community (from the principal to the students) on the REC to inform them about the text-based curriculum initiative and its implications for their particular school.

A school's ability to adopt (Marsh, 1997) a "top down" (Morris, 1995) curriculum change will be compromised in situations where the centralised authority directing the change has not undertaken the means to adequately communicate the nature, purpose and implications of the change to those responsible for managing the change. Inadequate communication about the principles and spirit underlying the change can lead to an adaptation (Brickell, 1972) that does not reflect the intention of the real curriculum (Morris, 1995).

## School Outlook

Each school's outlook towards classroom religious education was influenced by the REC's management of the curriculum change. The general ways in which the RECs attempted to influenced their schools' outlook was by giving particular attention to persuading the appointment of qualified religious education teachers to the faculty, and/or communicating with leadership/executive teams and/or influencing the credibility of the classroom religious education curriculum.

Most of the teachers in Catholic schools in Melbourne were familiar with the life-centred approach with its emphasis on the reflection of life experience as a means to encountering God. The life-centred approach down played the relevance of cognitive learning and teacher qualifications in religious education.

> When you have schools that are committed to that view of RE [life-centred approach], then you are going to get a whole culture within the school that says, "look as many teachers as possible should be teaching RE". It is good for their faith journey and it helps them to be pastorally caring of the students. These teachers are not selected for their knowledge or expertise in RE. I do not want to say that those aspects are not good dimensions of RE but in that scenario no one ever mentioned good education – learning about religion. (KA)

In the process of managing the change most RECs perceived that it was necessary for religious education teachers to be proficient in their understanding of the knowledge content contained in the textbooks. This emphasis on the cognitive dimension of learning in some situations marked a shift in school outlook towards religious education and many RECs responded to this shift by trying to influence the appointment of teachers who were proficient in their knowledge of the content to be covered in the text-based curriculum. The comment from another expert alludes to a staffing problem resulting from a preference for qualified teachers of religious education to teach the text-based curriculum.

> The capacity of staff required to teach RE is varied and the scarcity of people with qualifications to teach RE means that most schools find that it is just not possible to staff all the RE classes with specialist RE teachers. (CA)

The limited availability of qualified teachers of religious education may challenge the ability of an REC to promote a school outlook that favours religious education as an equally credible subject within the curriculum.

> The weakest faculty in every school I have worked in, and I have worked in a number, has been RE. This is precisely because you have RE staff where RE is not their mainstream and it is not their background of study. In schools I have also been English coordinator and History coordinator and I could have curriculum discussions assuming that every body knew exactly what we were talking about. It was not necessarily that they were committed to it. It was their academic background and their area of interest. When I was an REC, I was forever trying to convince people of the worthiness of RE. You are dealing with a significant number of RE teachers who have no specialist training and don't view it as a credible subject within the curriculum. (JO)

There are many teachers in Catholic schools who are familiar with the life-centred approach and down play the relevance of cognitive learning in religious education.

> Most teachers involved in teaching RE have been socialised in Catholic education at a time where they themselves were not exposed to a lot of content in RE, and so for them to move to a content based model of teaching is a big shift that many do not want to take. (CA)

This has a tremendous impact on the RECs' ability to influence a school's outlook towards religious education as a subject with the same academic rigour as other subjects within the curriculum (CC, 1998).

The challenge set by the Congregation of the Clergy (1998) for religious education to be taught with the same academic rigour, and to appear as a scholastic discipline with the same demands as other disciplines was taken up by RECs. The curriculum leadership focus of the RECs avoured to promote a school outlook towards classroom religious education as a credible subject and equal to other disciplines within the school curriculum. The curriculum leadership potential of RECs in Australia is one aspect of the role that has been ignored to a large extent in the existing body of literature. Buchanan (2005b), Crotty (2005; 2002), Fleming (2002), and Johnson (1989) have argued that there is a bias towards RECs fulfilling the ecclesial and ministerial functions of the role. According to Crotty (2005) and Johnson (1989) even in situations where classroom curriculum in religious education is in need of serious attention RECs ignore their responsibilities in this area in preference to fulfilling the ministerial expectations of the role.

Through the management of the curriculum change the RECs exercised curriculum leadership strategies that were aimed at influencing their schools' outlook towards religious education. Their intention was to promote a school outlook that regarded classroom religious education with the same curriculum credibility as any other discipline within the curriculum. The continued employment of qualified teachers of religious education and an emphasis on establishing religious education as a subject as equally credible as other disciplines were contributing factors that influenced school outlook.

## Staff Development

According to Marsh (1997) the most important factor concerning curriculum development and management relates to teachers having the knowledge and skills required to implement a curriculum initiative. The RECs were able to determine from the textbooks a greater emphasis on knowledge content and its implications for learning and teaching. Based on this perspective they organised staff development initiatives to provide teachers with opportunities to achieve a proficient level of understanding about the knowledge content underpinning the text-based curriculum initiative.

It is necessary that teachers develop content knowledge in order to participate effectively in the face of curriculum change (Hargreaves, 1997). However, one expert was sceptical about the effectiveness of irregular school-based staff development experiences organised by the RECs.

You cannot fix up those gaps in knowledge with some one-off morning sessions at a school or even by bringing a guest speaker in. The only way you can do it is by having the teachers really apply themselves to learning the content they need to know; for example by studying a relevant course. (KA)

The extent to which the staff development initiatives would be effective in developing staff with a proficient knowledge of the religious education content underpinning the text-based curriculum is questionable and points to an area in need of further research beyond the scope of this study. However viewed in the light of the high proportion of untrained and/or ill-qualified religious education teachers (Finlay, 2000; Thomas, 2000) the effectiveness of such staff development opportunities becomes even more questionable. School-based professional development opportunities for religious education teachers are generally compromised by time constraints.

There is not a great deal of time to offer faculty specific professional development opportunities. In most schools the religious education faculty is one of the largest faculties and it is difficult to provide staff development opportunities for all members of the faculty without interrupting other programs occurring within the school. Therefore professional

154

development is more likely to be irregular and the potential benefits of such experiences diminished in the context of these constraints. (JO)

Regardless of how many staff development opportunities are provided for religious education teachers their effectiveness depends on the individual commitment of each religious education teacher. This view was also alluded to by another expert who condoned staff development opportunities but questioned their effectiveness.

> We do need to offer as many staff development opportunities as possible for teachers in the area of RE content. I also think teachers have a responsibility to really research and learn the skills to develop that necessary repertoire of content themselves. In my experience this des not happen in school-based professional development forums. School based staff development opportunities are rare and few people participate in a way that really benefits them. (CA)

The relevance of staff development opportunities aimed at building up teachers' understandings about curriculum theory in religious education and its significance to the text-based curriculum change were underestimated by the RECs in their management strategies.

> These textbooks represented a whole change in the way that RE was to be done in the classroom and I really don't think that the RECs understood that. I find it surprising that there was an emphasis on PD regarding knowledge and nothing on theory or pedagogy. I think it goes back to the problem that we had regarding RE teachers in Victoria not really knowing anything about theories in RE, other than the life-centred approach. (KA)

The RECs' inability to comprehend the theoretical position underpinning the *To Know Worship and Love* series stands in contrast to Ryan's (2000) contention that textbooks are able to help teachers identify the particular curriculum theory underpinning them. Grimmitt (2000) has argued that each approach to religious education is interrelated and an awareness of this provides a means by which to understand the relevance of the particular change initiative in question. Ryan (2000) stressed the relevance of understanding the theoretical position by emphasising that a teacher who knows the curriculum theory is able to convey it through the learning activities employed to engage the student in the learning process.

School based staff development experiences focussed on the development of knowledge pertaining to the content contained in the textbook was likely to have little impact on preparing teachers to teach the text-based curriculum. As a change management strategy, staff development experiences emphasising this point have ignored the relevance of knowing and understanding the theory underpinning the text-based curriculum and its application to teaching and learning. One-off school based staff development experiences down play the benefits of continuous on-going study and reflection required to understand new concepts. When there is an expectation that teachers attend staff development sessions it is inappropriate to assume that all are willing participants open to learning new information and skills.

## Attitudes and Perspectives

Most RECs perceived that managing the change to a text-based curriculum involved blending the contents of the *To Know Worship and Love* textbook series within their schools' existing curriculum. Managing the change in this way supported the view that the RECs were not fully aware of the theoretical shift and its implications for learning and teaching, and curriculum development in classroom religious education.

As discussed in Chapter one pre-existing classroom religious education curriculum was based on *Guidelines* (1995) and based on a theological theory that held that a person could encounter God in life experiences and therefore there was a strong focus on reflecting on life experience. This catechetical theory differed from the theoretical position underpinning the text-based curriculum. It was not the intention of the text-based curriculum to presume that all students had experiences of a personal encounter with God. The theory underpinning this curriculum initiative was influenced by typology (Engebretson, 2000) and situated classroom religious education within an educational paradigm that embraced a knowledge-centred outcomes based approach to learning and teaching (Pell, 2001). Any REC who managed the change by incorporating the contents of the textbooks into an existing curriculum based on *Guidelines* (1995) was not fully aware of the theoretical shift underpinning classroom religious education. The following comment from one of the experts suggested that RECs did not distinguish between curricula according to the theory underpinning it.

> With RE, people grab an existing curriculum and when something new comes out they just throw the existing curriculum in with the new. You cannot blend the pedagogy of *Guidelines* [1995] with that of *To Know Worship and Love,* but that is what the majority of RECs did. They had not known that or appreciated or understood the paradigm shift and the inappropriateness of trying to blend new in with the old curriculum. (JO)

The incorporation of the contents of the textbooks into the existing curriculum based on *Guidelines* (1995) indicated that the RECs were not fully aware of the theoretical position of the text-based curriculum and its implications for curriculum development and learning and teaching in classroom religious education.

The text-based curriculum was to mark a major turning point in the approach to learning and teaching in religious education in Melbourne (Engebretson, 2002). However a lack of awareness about the curriculum theory underpinning the text-based curriculum had an impact on the RECs' perspectives on the textbooks. In many situations, as the theory generated in Chapter five indicated, RECs perceived the textbooks as a resource. The misuse of the textbooks was confirmed by some of the experts. "Many of the RECs who approached me about the textbooks regarded them as being just another resource to fit into the curriculum they were already teaching" (KA). The experiences of another expert also attest to this misuse.

> In the many schools I was involved with RECs would see the topics covered in the books and consider where they would fit within their existing curriculum. They would substitute some of their handouts and use the books. So in these situations the RECs were using the textbooks to resource a curriculum they had developed in the past. (CA)

Tyson-Bernstein (1989) argued that, "textbooks compensate for the weaknesses of teachers" (p. 74). However, embedded within the body of Australian literature on religious education textbooks is the contention that, the extent to which textbooks can be used effectively depends on the skill and competence of the teacher (Crotty & Crotty, 2000; Finlay, 2000; Reilly, 1998; Rossiter, 2000; Thomas, 2000). This study supports this view.

Some RECs commented on the "faith formation" of religious education teachers. The theory generated discussed in Chapter five indicated that these RECs perceived classroom religious education in a Catholic school as being suited to teachers who were formed in the Catholic faith tradition and who demonstrated their commitment to public prayer and worship. This view, held by some RECs, has been reflected in many Catholic education documents which address religious education and coordination throughout Australia (Catholic Education Commission, Queensland, 2002; CEO, Canberra & Goulburn, 2003; CEO, Archdiocese of Hobart, 1984; CEO, Melbourne, 1995; 2005; CEO, Sydney, 2005; CEO, Broken Bay, 2001; CEO, Darwin, 1998; Commission for Catholic Schools South Australia, 1993). Concerns about the "faith formation" of religious education teachers emanate from three decades of classroom religious education based on the catechetical model of the life-centred approach (Amalorpavadass, 1973; 1971). The relevance of the religious education teachers' personal faith is questionable when the curriculum is underpinned by a typological theory (Hill, 2004).

> Back in the 1970s when they were bringing in a life-centred approach it depended on the teacher being able to lead the students to see the presence and action of God in their life. Now if a teacher cannot reflect in that way in themselves, if a teacher cannot catch a glimmer of the presence and action of God in their own life, it is going to be very hard for them to help students to do that. So in the 1970s I would have thought it was absolutely appropriate when we were using a life-centred approach, to be giving faith development activities to RE teachers because that theory depended on the teachers being reflective about their own faith. Now the theory in these new books doesn't require that. It is quite clear that the emphasis in these books is on the communication of a certain amount of knowledge. That is why I am always puzzled when the RECs say we are concentrating on the faith formation of the teachers. Well it is a very good thing to do but it is not going to help them to teach the knowledge that is in the textbooks. (KA)

Misunderstandings about the theoretical position underpinning the text-based curriculum may have contributed to the concern that some RECs had for the "faith formation" of religious education teachers and its relevance to teaching. However, another factor bearing upon this perspectives has been the tradition of catechesis, underpinning religious education which was discussed in Chapter one. This view has been supported by the experts.

> I think for too long RE has been seen more as faith than as education. That it is faith stuff therefore it is about the personal, it is about the mysterious, about discussion and reflection. It is about life, about you, so it is personal and it is not about the professional, about the educational and pedagogical. I think a healthy academic pedagogical approach is enlivening. I just think it is the faith aspect of religious education that stops people from bringing a general educational approach to the RE classroom. (JO)

Fleming (2002) reported a bias towards the appointment of RECs who displayed ecclesial and ministerial traits. Crotty's (2005) research indicated that these dimensions of the role were given the highest priority by RECs. Against this backdrop the RECs' perception of the relevance of the "faith formation" of religious education teachers to teaching the text-based curriculum has been analysed.

The RECs' attitude towards blending the text-based curriculum into their existing curriculum suggested an inability to perceive a significant theoretical distinction between the new curriculum and its predecessor. The attitude of some RECs was that the personal faith position of the religious education teacher had a bearing on their ability to teach the text-based curriculum. This perspectives is perhaps more indicative of the inability of those RECs to distinguish between the theory underpinning the life-centred approach and the text-based curriculum.

## Curriculum Leadership

While an existing body of literature has portrayed the view that RECs have tended to ignore the curriculum demands of this key leadership role (Crotty, 2005; 2002; Johnson, 1998; 1989), this research has focussed on a select number of RECs who have actively exercised their curriculum leadership responsibilities.

A finding reported in Chapter five revealed that the RECs accepted responsibility for writing and documenting the curriculum based on the *To Know Worship and Love* textbook series. The impetus for the RECs to fulfil curriculum leadership responsibilities was based on their perspective that in general religious education teachers did not have the time or expertise to be involved in writing and documenting the curriculum. The following comment by one expert attested to the plausibility of this finding.

In our secondary schools we have RECs who are exceptionally theologically and religiously competent. When they have a faculty where there are a lot of RE teachers who don't have the capacity in terms of their professional knowledge, the trend is to rely on the RECs to write the curriculum and tell the RE teachers what to teach. (JO)

In the process of leading this aspect of the curriculum change the RECs' decision to write and document the curriculum did not suggest an intention to foster a collaborative culture where teachers could become more aware of the change and its implications (Frost & Durrant, 2002). According to Durrant and Holden (2006), "Schools can be surprisingly uncollaborative places. Teachers with little time to spare fall back on their own resources and ideas in planning" (p. 163). From one perspective, the decision made by RECs to undertake the responsibility for writing and documenting the curriculum may suggest an uncollaborative nature amongst some RECs. Viewed from another angle, collaborative cultures in the face of educational change can be fatal if only a small percentage of the teachers have the capacity to pursue the initiative (Fullan, 2001b). This research suggested that the RECs perceived a limited capacity on the part of the religious education teachers in terms of time and expertise to write and document the curriculum initiative, and therefore they made the decision to undertake that responsibility.

The RECs' management of this aspect of the change is inconsistent with Elmore's (2000) view of large scale reform, where the responsibility for change shifts from control to direction and guidance. In light of Elmore's (2000) view, the transition from the RECs' control of the management of the change, to one of directing and guiding the school through the change may be stultified in situations where teacher capacity to change is very low or inactive (Fullan, 2001b). The RECs perceived the teachers as lacking in their capacity to respond to the change by writing and documenting the curriculum, due to their lack of expertise in religious education and lack of time available to devote to curriculum writing.

In situations where the REC was perceived as the only expert in religious education within the school, much control was bestowed upon them in shaping and determining the structure and content of the text-based curriculum. One expert attested to the influence a REC has been able to have over shaping the religious education curriculum.

> The RECs have an enormous amount of autonomy regarding how they prepare courses and curriculum for RE. At the very least the textbooks gave RECs an idea of the level of content they should be including in their curriculum and the sort of scope regarding the areas they could cover. (RI)

The RECs had the autonomy to determine the content areas to be taught at each year level. This type of autonomy can create a situation where religious education teachers become dependent on the REC to determine what should be taught at each year level.

> A dependency model is easy to build in where the RE teachers rely on the REC to write the curriculum and tell them what to teach. That dependency model is very difficult to break when an REC has a faculty where half or more of the RE teachers don't know much about RE. (CA)

In the absence of an Archdiocesan curriculum statement or outline and guidelines about how to implement the text-based curriculum, as well as the lack of religious education expertise amongst teachers, the RECs were bestowed with a great deal of autonomy in making decisions about the content, structure and documentation of their school's text-based curriculum.

The extent to which RECs promote collaborative cultures in the face of curriculum change is influenced by their perspectives on the religious education teachers' capacity for change. In situations where the REC perceives a limited capacity among faculty members to bring about change or an aspect of change, the REC will do the work and make the decisions to effect change. They will also negotiate with members of the education community to develop structures and processes to enable teachers to participate in the change process.

## Introduction to Factors that Impede and Assist Curriculum Change

The RECs discussed their perspectives on the factors that impeded (Category 6) and assisted (Category 7) their management of the curriculum change. Some of the sub-categories reported in category six and seven overlapped with some aspects of categories one to five. The repetitions or overlaps were mechanisms that helped to confirm that the knowledge reported on in Chapter five and Chapter six emerged according to grounded theory principles (Glaser, 1998) as discussed in Chapter four. In addition, the experts confirmed the plausibility of the theory generated from all categories including category six and seven but, in order to limit repetition of the theory generated in the latter two categories, reference is now made to the sub-categories where outside knowledge provided by the experts and the voice of the researcher added a further level to the analysis.

## Factors that Impeded Change

The RECs' perspectives on religious education teachers not practising the faith tradition impeded the change was expressed several times. However the RECs were not clear about what they meant by this concern. Participant (I) suggested that not attending Mass amounted to a religious education teacher not practising the faith tradition. This perspectives or summation is open to debate. There can be several reasons why a person may not be able to attend Mass yet still be committed to practising the faith tradition. This view was emphasised by one expert.

I think we have got some very good RE teachers who are faithful Catholics, who don't place as high priority on going to Church every Sunday as some others do. An REC who thinks that such teachers are not practising the faith may be wrong. (KA)

The RECs' concern about religious education teachers not practising the Catholic faith being a factor that impeded the change has been discussed earlier in this chapter and in Chapter five. The typological theory underpinning the text-based curriculum (Engebretson, 2000) does not require a teacher to give witness to a particular faith tradition. The education system in England provides examples of approaches to religious education that do not require a faith stance to be evidenced by the teacher (Jackson, 2004). Concerns about the "faith commitment" of religious education teachers in the process of managing the change might have been alleviated if the RECs had been appropriately informed about the theoretical position underpinning the change. The following comment from one of the experts also suggested that a teacher's commitment to the Catholic faith tradition was not essential to teaching the text-based curriculum. "I think that RE teachers can still teach RE in a really positive and effective way even if they are not practising. It would only concern me if they were really negative about the Catholic faith tradition or any religious tradition" (CA).

In addition to the discussion that has already taken place about the language of the textbooks being a factor that impeded the change one expert who has had much experience in writing religious education textbooks argued that the language of the textbooks in the *To Know Worship and Love* series was similar to the level of language used in other school textbooks.

The textbooks are at exactly the same level of language as any other textbooks relevant to those year levels. It is just that teachers and RECs are not used to using reasonably sophisticated language in talking about    religion. (KA)

The life-centred approach to religious education required the religious education teacher to place much emphasis on providing opportunities for students to discuss and reflect on their life experiences. A knowledge content based curriculum placed a greater demand on religious education teachers to know and understand religious content and language. This paradigm shift may have contributed to this perspective about the language of the textbooks as one expert suggested.

If an RE textbook comes out which comparatively speaking places significant educational demands on everyone [students and teachers], it could seem to a lot of RECs that the book is missing the audience. Traditionally the audience has been used to a typical life-centred approach group where at the classroom level RE does not place the same demands on students and teachers as other subjects. (RI)

A religious education curriculum or approach that placed new educational knowledge-centred demands on students and teachers marked a significant shift. This would have been difficult for those who had not undertaken training or qualifications in religious education. Each discipline has its own way of using language and its own vocabulary (Garner & Biewer, 1983) and if a teacher is not trained or qualified in that tradition then it can be very difficult to understand the language of that discipline.

Some RECs expressed a lack of confidence in their perspective on themselves as a curriculum leaders. One expert indicated that many principals do not perceive the REC as a curriculum leader.

Some principals have said we don't want our REC to be on the school leadership team because they are not good leaders. They are great at liturgy, at organising social justice campaigns and retreats but they do not have an understanding of curriculum. (JO)

Fleming's (2002) research into the role of the REC in the Melbourne Archdiocese indicated that employment interviews for the position were geared towards employing a REC who was suitable for ecclesial and ministerial leadership. Most RECs recalled employment interview experiences where they were questioned about their life of faith and worship. In many cases applicants for the position of REC were not asked any questions regarding their curriculum skills or educational qualifications. Downplaying the educational and curriculum leadership aspects of the REC role support a bias to the appointment of ministerial leaders.

The text-based curriculum initiative challenged RECs to reconsider their perspectives on REC leadership and demanded they exercise curriculum leadership in order to manage the change. One expert suggested that the shift to a text- based curriculum has challenged perspectives on the role of the REC.

I think the textbooks have created a different model of leadership for the RECs. It is just not enough to just be a nice faithful person that people can come to talk to, or to run a few prayer services. I think it has challenged what leadership in RE means (CA).

What it has emphasised more than ever before is the educational dimension of the role and in particular the curriculum leadership aspect. According to Durrant and Holden (2006), all teachers should be "supported in exercising leadership of learning, whatever their professional situation" (p. 1). The position of the REC is regarded as a senior leadership position in Catholic education (CEO, Melbourne, 2005). While it is acknowledged that principals play a crucial role in fostering educational leadership (Frost & Durrant, 2004), the development of the educational and curriculum leadership capacity of the REC has been ignored by many principals in preference to employing RECs who demonstrate ministerial leadership capacity (Fleming, 2002).

The RECs' biases towards religious education curriculum and leadership have a significant influence on their perspectives on the factors that impede curriculum change. These biases are more influential than their understanding about the nature, purpose and intention of the change. For example, RECs who have a bias towards faith expression as an integral part of a religious education curriculum are likely to perceive teachers who are not practising the Catholic faith tradition as impediments to change. They are also likely to view textbooks that focus on content knowledge as irrelevant. If an REC perceives his/her role as solely a ministerial one (Crotty, 2005; Fleming, 2002) then their willingness and confidence as a curriculum leader may be underdeveloped.

**Factors that Assisted Change**

In addition to the discussion and analysis in Chapter six of this book regarding the factors that assisted the change, the experts provided two further insights. The RECs who were responsible for managing this "top down" (Morris, 1995) change were not adequately made aware of the theoretical position underpinning the text-based curriculum. One expert, who was also the writer of some of the secondary textbooks in the *To Know Worship and Love* series indicated that those instigating the change did not have an adequate understanding either.

> We're seeing the results now of this top down change as being brought in without any clear explanation of the theoretical perspective from which it was coming. The reality was the people who instigated the change and were responsible for communicating it to schools did not really understand it either. (KA)

The interplay between production use of (producer-user) knowledge has influenced the way and pace at which teachers adopt innovation (Windeen, Mayer-Smith & Moon, 1996). This research suggests that producers who develop knowledge can influence the pace and way in which an innovation is adopted by the users who implement it, by clearly communicating the knowledge to the user (in this case the REC).

The feeling of being supported by the leadership / executive team was also perceived as a factor assisting the change. One expert suggested that if the REC "feels" supported by the leadership team this feeling can enable the REC to remain motivated.

> The support of the leadership team is critical to the role of REC. If the REC feels that the leadership team is on her/his side and that they are helping and encouraging the REC to do a good job then the REC is motivated to do a good job. (RI)

As the theory generated and discussion in Chapter five suggested, the support of the leadership / executive team did not have to be demonstrated in practical terms. Even though the leadership / executive teams may have been genuine in trying to support the REC through time release, they did not understand that the RECs could not fulfil the constant demands of their role by accepting the time release offered to work on the curriculum. Beaudoin and Taylor (2204) provide another perspective by which to consider the impractical though genuine offer of time release for the REC. They suggested that the hierarchical nature of school leadership can cause leadership /executive teams to become disconnected from the realities of teachers and in this case RECs. Regardless of the practicalities of the offer the RECs appreciated and felt supported by it.

Those responsible for producing "top down" (Morris, 1995) curriculum change have a capacity to influence the way and pace of the change as well as the extent to which the change will be adapted (Marsh, 1997) or adopted (Brady & Kennedy, 2003). The way and pace in which the change will be taken up will depend upon the ability of those producing the change to clearly communicate knowledge about the change to those responsible for managing the change.

## Conclusion

The insights gained from the experts referred to in this chapter have been used to provide a further level of analysis of the categories that have emerged from the interviews with the RECs who actively aimed to manage the curriculum change directed by the Archdiocese. In Chapters five and six, tables 11 and 12 provided a summary of the theory generated from each sub-category. The theory generated from the analysis of the interviews with the RECs and the experts have been merged into one table, that is table 13 below.

Based upon the theory generated and analysis presented in Chapters five, six and seven which explored the RECs' perspective on their management of the change to a text-based curriculum, the following chapter will, by way of conclusion, make some recommendations for the future management of curriculum change in religious education in the Archdiocese.

Table 14

*Summary of the theory generated relevant to categories 1- 7 and associated sub-categories.*

| Category 1    Preparation for Change |
| --- |
| **Key Theory Generated** |

A school's ability to adopt (Brady & Kennedy, 2003) a "top down" (Morris, 1995) curriculum change will be compromised in situations where the centralised authority directing the change has not undertaken the means to adequately communicate the nature, purpose and implications of the change to those responsible for managing the change. Inadequate communication about the principles and spirit underlying the change can lead to an adaptation (Brickell, 1972) that does not reflect the intention of the real curriculum (Morris, 1995).

| | |
| --- | --- |
| (i)   RECs informed about the change | In situations where a comprehensive understanding about a "top down" (Morris, 1995) curriculum change is difficult to achieve from the centralised authority initiating the change, those responsible for managing the change in their local school context explored other avenues in order to become informed about the change. |
| (ii)  Staff informed about the change | RECs who were responsible for managing the change perceived that it was necessary to ensure that teachers responsible for teaching the text-based curriculum were informed and up-dated about the change.<br><br>The RECs explored a variety of ways to enable religious education teachers to be informed about the change and its implications. |
| (iii) Dialogue about the change | Change affects people and RECs facilitated formal and informal opportunities for teachers involved in the change to dialogue about their feelings, concerns and possible strategies for managing the change. |
| (iv) Exploration of textbooks in light of pre-existing religious education curriculum. | In the absence of an informed understanding about the different theories underpinning various curriculum approaches, RECs managed a text-based curriculum change by blending the contents of the textbooks into a school's existing curriculum. |
| (v)  Decisions regarding implementing the curriculum change. | Working in collaboration with religious education teachers, RECs as curriculum leaders ultimately managed the implementation of the change by making the key decisions about the structure and content of the new curriculum based on the textbooks. |

| | Category 2 | School Outlook |
|---|---|---|

| **Key Theory Generated** | | |

Through the management of the curriculum change RECs exercised curriculum leadership strategies that were aimed at influencing their school's outlook towards religious education. Their intention was to promote their school's outlook that regarded classroom religious education with the same curriculum credibility as any other discipline within the curriculum. The continued employment of qualified teachers of religious education and an emphasis on establishing religious education as a subject as equally credible as other disciplines are key factors that influence school outlook and the management of the change to a knowledge-centred text-based curriculum.

| (i) Appointment of religious education teachers. | Direct involvement: In situations where the REC has direct involvement in the employment of teachers of religious education the REC was more likely to establish a faculty where a shared philosophy about learning and teaching in religious education and the role of the teacher were compatible. |
|---|---|
| | Negotiated involvement: In situations where the REC has "negotiated involvement" in the selection and appointment of religious education teachers, a biases towards the recruitment of qualified teachers as well as those committed to teaching more than one class was preferred. |
| | No Involvement: In situations where the REC has no involvement in the selection and appointment of religious education teachers it was more difficult to promote a cohesive school outlook towards religious education and the role of the religious education teacher. |
| | Employment of religious education teachers: The RECs' management of the text-based curriculum change has revealed a preference for qualified teachers of religious education and teachers who are willing to teach more than one class of religious education. |
| (ii) Communication with school leadership/executive. | Communication with the leadership/executive team about the management of the change to a text-based curriculum helped to emphasise an educational outlook towards classroom religious education, distinct from a ministerial outlook. |
| (iii) Curriculum credibility. | Through the management of a curriculum change RECs utilised other change processes happening within the school to promote classroom religious education as a discipline holding the same curriculum credibility as other subjects. |

| Category 3 | Staff Development |
| --- | --- |

**Key Theory Generated**

School based staff development experiences focussed on the development of knowledge proficiencies pertaining to the content contained in the textbook is likely to have little impact on preparing teachers to teach the text-based curriculum. As a change management strategy, staff development experiences emphasising this point have ignored the relevance of knowing and understanding the theory underpinning the text-based curriculum and its application to teaching and learning. One-off school based staff development experiences down play the benefits of continuous on going study and reflection required to understand new concepts. When there is an expectation that teachers attend staff development sessions it is inappropriate to assume that all are willing participants open to learning new information and skills.

| | |
| --- | --- |
| (i)   Faith formation. | Some RECs managed the change to a knowledge-centred text-based curriculum by providing staff development experiences that focussed on the personal faith formation of religious education teachers. |
| | Some RECs managed the change to a knowledge-centred text-based curriculum by providing staff development opportunities that focussed on developing knowledge content proficiencies while at the same time aware that the development of such proficiencies had the potential to probe personal faith issues for some teachers. |
| (ii)  Professional development. | To prepare teachers for the change to a knowledge centred text-based curriculum RECs organised professional development experiences where teachers could develop proficiencies in content knowledge relevant to the curriculum. |
| | The preferred professional development option was guest speakers with expertise in topics relevant to the content covered in the textbooks. Guest speakers were preferred because they were cost effective and provided an opportunity for all teachers to be involved in the professional development experience. |
| | Teachers who became interested in pursuing tertiary qualifications in religious education sought the advice of the REC about which course to study. |
| (iii) Professional learning. | RECs organised professional learning teams and fostered professional learning presentations to enable teachers to learn from each other and develop their proficiencies in relation to the content knowledge associated with the text-based curriculum. |

| Category 4 | Attitudes & Perspectives |
|---|---|
| **Key Theory Generated** | |

The RECs' attitude towards blending the text-based curriculum into their existing curriculum suggested an inability to perceive a significant ideological distinction between the new curriculum and its predecessor. The attitude of some RECs was that the personal faith position of the religious education teacher had a bearing on their ability to teach the text-based curriculum. This perspective reflects an inability to distinguish between theory underpinning the life-centred approach and the text-based curriculum.

| (i) Perspectives on the change. | Where the management of a curriculum change was influenced by misunderstandings about the theoretical position underpinning the curriculum, RECs managed the change based on their existing experience and knowledge of classroom religious education curriculum. Discrepancies between the theoretical position of the curriculum change and the REC's curriculum knowledge can trivialise the management of the change. |
|---|---|
| (ii) Perspectives on the textbooks. | RECs' previous experiences of textbooks in religious education can influence their perspective and attitude towards the books associated with the text-based curriculum. |
| (iii) Perspectives on religious education teachers. | RECs generally adopted a sympathetic attitude towards members of their faculty who are unqualified and RECs will undertake a greater workload in order to compensate for the limited capabilities of their staff members. |
| (iv) Perspectives on the religious education curriculum. | Perspectives on the text-based curriculum as an emphasis on teaching Church doctrine was sometimes influenced by the RECs' view of the Archbishop as an authoritarian, mandating a "top down" (Morris, 1995) change. |

| Category 5 | Curriculum Leadership |
| --- | --- |
| **Key Theory Generated** | |

The extent to which RECs promote collaborative cultures in the face of curriculum change is influenced by their perspectives on the religious education teachers' capacity for change. In situations where the REC perceives a limited capacity among faculty members to bring about change or an aspect of change, the REC will do the work and make the decisions to effect change. They will also negotiate with members of the education community to develop structures and processes to enable teachers to participate in the change process.

| | |
| --- | --- |
| (i) Structure and content of religious education courses. | RECs successfully negotiated time within the school timetable to be allocated for teachers to meet and develop strategies and proficiencies to accommodate the management and implementation of the text-based curriculum. |
| (ii) Documentation of courses. | The RECs managed the curriculum change by documenting the text-based curriculum in a fashion similar to other curriculum areas. This enabled the classroom religious education curriculum to be more accessible to untrained religious education teacher because they were able to draw upon their general curriculum educational expertise. |
| (iii) Negotiating educational issues with school leaders. | RECs negotiated with school leaders the employment of qualified teachers of religious education in order to manage the implementation of the knowledge-centred educational focus of the text-based curriculum. |

| Category 6 | Factors that impede change |
|---|---|

**Key Theory Generated**

The RECs' biases towards religious education curriculum and leadership have a significant influence on their perspectives on the factors that impede curriculum change. Their biases are more likely to influence their perspectives on the factors that impede change in situations where their understanding of the nature, purpose and intention of the change is obscured or misinformed.

| | |
|---|---|
| (i) Teachers of religious education not practising the Catholic faith tradition. | Regardless of the educational emphasis on the acquisition of religious knowledge through outcomes-based learning, RECs perceived that such knowledge was meaningless without some personal faith engagement from the classroom religious education teacher. It was held by the RECs that religious education teachers who were not practising the Catholic faith in their own lives were likely to impede the management of a curriculum change. |
| (ii) Unqualified teachers of religious education. | The RECs management of the curriculum change was impeded by teachers who did not have qualifications to teach religious education. |
| (iii) Capacity to articulate paradigm shift. | RECs found it difficult to articulate the theory underpinning the curriculum change in a situation where there is a lack of coherent discussion about the theoretical position of the text-based curriculum particularly with those directing the change. |
| (iv) Difficulties associated with textbooks. | RECs have limited experiences and knowledge about the use of textbooks in religious education and they experienced difficulties using textbooks in a way that was relevant to students in the religious education classroom. |
| (v) RECs' perspective on self as a curriculum leader. | RECs primarily perceived themselves as ministerial leaders rather than curriculum leaders. They were not as confident in their ability to exercise curriculum leadership as they were in exercising ministerial leadership. |

| Category 7 | Factors that assist change |
|---|---|

**Key Theory Generated**

Those responsible for producing "top down" (Morris, 1995) curriculum change have a capacity to influence the way and pace of the change as well as the extent to which the change will be adapted (Marsh, 1997) or adopted (Brady & Kennedy, 2003). The way and pace in which the change will be taken up will depend upon the ability of those producing the change to clearly communicate knowledge about the change to those responsible for managing the change.

| (i) Time to reflect on practice. | Time to reflect on practice enabled teachers to professionally learn from each other and also enabled RECs to identify some real needs of staff such as staff development needs, "faith formation" needs, and resource needs. |
|---|---|
| (ii) Professional development learning experiences. | RECs were genuinely sympathetic towards teachers who lacked the qualifications to teach religious education and they would organise as well as led professional development / learning experiences to enable teachers to feel professionally and personally confident in their teaching of religious education.<br><br>RECs believed that teachers of religious education are more confident when engaging in experiences of professional development facilitated and led by the REC than by an expert from outside the school. |
| (iii) Teamwork | RECs encouraged and facilitated teamwork opportunities that fostered professional and personal growth for teachers of religious education. |
| (iv) Support from school leadership / administration. | RECs considered themselves to be supported in their management of curriculum change in situations where the principal and other members of the leadership / administration team showed a genuine interest in the change initiative. |
| (v) Attracting qualified teachers of religious education. | The employment of qualified teachers of religious education assisted the RECs in their management of the change to a knowledge-centred text-based curriculum. |

# CHAPTER EIGHT
# Conclusion and Recommendations

The purpose of this study has been to explore the perspectives of religious education coordinators' in secondary schools in the Archdiocese of Melbourne regarding their management of a particular curriculum change in religious education. As a qualitative study situated within the epistemology of social constructionism, it has drawn upon symbolic interactionism as the theoretical perspective, and utilised unstructured in-depth interviews with RECs from Catholic secondary schools. These unstructured in-depth interviews were audio-tape recorded, transcribed and interpreted according to the principles of grounded theory. As a result of this undertaking, this study categorised and analysed several issues concerning the management of a curriculum change from the perspective of the RECs involved in this study. It has also identified factors that impeded and assisted the curriculum change. The theory generated was discussed with four experts in the field of religious education enabling a further level of analysis. This final chapter begins by briefly summarising the discussion of the key theory generated of the research. It then proposes some recommendations as a result of the study and considers the significance and limitations of the research. Prior to the conclusion of this book some recommendations for further research are made.

## Summary of the Theory Generated

Three of the research aims outlined in the introduction of this book were to study and analyse the RECs' perspectives on the issues involved in the management of the text-based curriculum change, including factors that assisted and impeded the change. This summary of the discussion of the theory generated is presented in the light of these aims, under the following categories: preparation for change, school outlook, staff development, attitudes and perspectives, curriculum leadership, factors that impeded change, and factors that assisted change. The research also revealed certain ambiguities and paradoxes about the RECs' perspectives on classroom religious education curriculum which had bearing upon the issues involved in their management of the curriculum change.

### Preparation for Change
The RECs were required to manage the adoption (Brady & Kennedy, 2003) of a particular "top down" (Morris, 1995) text-based curriculum change that was directed by a centralised authority. This study revealed that inadequate communication about the nature and purpose of the change diminished the RECs' chances of adopting (Brady & Kennedy, 2003) the change and increased the likelihood of adaptations (Brickell, 1972) of the curriculum initiative by those responsible for

managing the change. Therefore, this study shows that curriculum adaptations will not always reflect the spirit and intention behind a curriculum initiative especially in situations where there is inadequate communication between the authority developing and directing the change and those managing the change.

## School Outlook

The nature of classroom religious education as either an academic discipline or a "faith-formation" subject emerged as an ambiguity in this study. The RECs' perspectives, in this regard, influenced the management of the curriculum change. This challenged the RECs to promote a school outlook that regarded classroom religious education as a subject as equally credible as other academic disciplines within the curriculum. From the perspective of some of the RECs, the establishment of equal curriculum credibility for classroom religious education was achievable if the subject was given the same time allocation as other subjects, had the same assessment and reporting procedures and practices and had the same curriculum documentation format as other disciplines. Some RECs regardless of their intention to promote classroom religious education as an academic subject with equal credibility to other academic disciplines, seemed more concerned about religious education teachers' faith practice than their curriculum skills. The educational/ministerial ambiguity was not resolved by some of the RECs. On the one hand they wanted to promote a school outlook towards classroom religious education that perceived it as a subject like any other, yet at the same time they emphasised the ministerial or faith-in-action expectations of the teacher.

## Staff Development

The staff development activities organised by the RECs also showed ambiguous perspectives towards classroom religious education and the role of the religious education teacher. RECs perceived many of their staff members as not having the knowledge background relevant to the contents of the textbooks, thus suggesting that they understood the text-based curriculum to be knowledge-centred. While most RECs organised professional development experiences to enable teachers to develop knowledge proficiencies pertaining to the content in the textbooks, they continued to emphasise the personal faith formation of the teachers. In fact some professional development experiences were extremely biased towards providing "faith formation" experiences for teachers despite the general perspective that most teachers did not have adequate religious knowledge to teach the contents of the textbooks. Some perceived that knowledge-based professional development could also enhance faith formation (a view held by Rossiter, 1981a; 1981b). Therefore it is uncertain whether or not some RECs saw the text-based curriculum as knowledge centred or ministerial. This ambiguity was not resolved by some RECs and the consequence of this was that they invested resources into providing "faith formation" experiences for teachers who would have benefited more from staff development opportunities that enabled them to develop knowledge about the content in the textbooks.

172

## Attitudes and Perspectives

The RECs in this study perceived the management of this curriculum change as a process of blending the contents of the textbooks into their existing religious education curriculum based on the life-centred approach. This perspectives on curriculum blending as a means to managing the change perhaps accounted for the RECs' preference for religious education teachers to be practising Catholics and to be formed in the Catholic faith tradition. The emphasis on sharing life experiences as a means to knowing God was integral to the life-experience approach and the Congregation for Catholic Education (1977; 1982; 1988) and the Congregation for the Clergy (1998) have repeatedly emphasised the importance of religious education teachers practising the Catholic faith as an example to students. It was not the intention of this book to argue that a faith commitment from teacher in faith-based schools is not relevant. Nevertheless this study showed that RECs did not know or understand the theoretical shift to an educational approach underpinning the text-based curriculum which called for a whole new approach to curriculum development and the role and expectations of teachers.

The attitudes towards the textbooks also suggested that teachers did not understand the theoretical shift associated with the text-based curriculum. Some RECs perceived that the language of the textbooks limited student and teacher use of the books. After almost three decades of the life-centred approach with its emphasis on life experience, it is arguable that teachers and RECs were not familiar with the language of the discipline or competent in using textbooks in religious education within an educational context that was knowledge centred. Had this context and theoretical position been explained to the RECs who were responsible for managing the change, then perhaps it would have provided the RECs with the necessary background and skills to help teachers use the textbooks as an effective learning and teaching tool.

## Curriculum Leadership

Another paradox disclosed in this study was that RECs claimed to have a bias towards promoting collaborative cultures and managing the change through the process of collaborative decision making. However, they would suspend this preference and arbitrarily make decisions, particularly in situations where they perceived that those involved in a collaborative process did not have the capacity to make decisions relevant to the management of this curriculum change.

In many situations a dependency model of REC curriculum leadership evolved and further contributed to the RECs making the decisions despite their expressed preference for collaborative decision making. Principals and leadership teams were dependent upon RECs for information about the "top down" (Morris, 1995) curriculum change and for advice about how the change should be managed. Many teachers who were not qualified to teach religious education depended on the RECs for direction. Those who taught only one religious education class did not have the time to invest in curriculum planning in religious education and relied on the RECs' curriculum decisions. All these factors contributed to staff members being dependent upon the REC to make the curriculum decisions in order to manage the text-based curriculum change. Each school was largely dependent upon their REC's knowledge and understanding about the nature and purpose of the change in order to manage the change.

## Factors that Impeded Change

This study also aimed to identify factors that impeded and assisted the RECs management of the curriculum change. Those RECs who viewed their role as primarily ministerial displayed a lack of confidence in exercising curriculum leadership. This impeded their ability to require the religious education teachers to share the workload involved in implementing the text-based curriculum. They were reluctant to make the same requests as coordinators of other disciplines generally make of their teachers. The first phase of the implementation of the text-based curriculum took place in 2001 during a time in which Crotty (2005) and Fleming (2004) reported a ministerial bias towards the selection, appointment and preference for the duties carried out by the REC. Both Crotty and Fleming argue that this continues to be the case. Consequently, it is arguable that RECs with a preference for fulfilling the ministerial functions of this demanding leadership role (Liddy, 1998) will not develop strong curriculum leadership skills and this is likely to impede the management of curriculum change.

The study also indicated that RECs who did not understand the theoretical position underpinning the text-based curriculum perceived issues such as teachers not practising the Catholic faith tradition as a factor impeding the change. Yet paradoxically the study also showed that RECs perceived a lack of qualifications to teach religious education as a factor impeding change. Teachers who did not have the qualifications to teach religious education were perceived as an impediment to the change because they did not have the knowledge to understand the contents in the textbooks. This was viewed as an impediment to the management of the change because such teachers could not adequately contribute to curriculum planning and were likely to struggle in their teaching of the content. While they did not fully understand the change and the implications of the change they were able to identify inadequate content knowledge as a factor impeding change. However, the RECs' preoccupation with their teachers' level of faith commitment as a factor impeding the change shows an inability to fully understand the nature and purpose of the change towards classroom religious education.

## Factors that Assisted Change

The study uncovered several factors that the RECs perceived as assisting the management of the curriculum change. These factors involved opportunities to reflect on teaching practices associated with the text-based curriculum as well as the opportunity to work collaboratively in teams. Other factors were the employment of qualified teachers of religious education and participating in professional development / learning experiences and feeling supported by the principal and other members of the leadership team.

The theory generated exposed an apparent contradiction between some of the factors that impeded and assisted the change. For example, teachers not practising the Catholic faith tradition was perceived as a factor impeding the change but practising teachers were not identified as a factor assisting the change. The theory generated also uncovered factors that impeded and assisted the change which were in support of each other. For instance unqualified teachers of religious education were perceived as impeding change and the employment of qualified teachers was viewed as a factor assisting change.

Two overarching theories emerge from this study:

1. The RECs' understanding of curriculum theory associated with approaches to religious education will have a significant bearing upon their exercise of curriculum leadership and their management of curriculum change. It will also influence their perspectives and judgements about the factors that impede and assist the management of curriculum change.

2. The RECs' perspectives on the role will have a considerable impact on the priority they give to the curriculum leadership aspect of the role. It will also influence the judgments they make about what is important in the process of managing curriculum change.

## Links between the Research and the Literature

Another key aim of this research was to analyse the theory generated from this research against the existing knowledge about curriculum change in education. This study provided insights into the management of curriculum change brought about by forces from outside the school (Brady & Kennedy, 2003). It showed that adopting a "top down" (Morris, 1995) curriculum change can be difficult to achieve particularly in situations where the theoretical position underpinning the curriculum change has not been adequately communicated to those responsible for managing the change. Misunderstandings about the nature and purpose of the change can lead to curriculum adaptations (Brickell, 1972) that do not reflect the spirit and intention of the "top down" (Morris, 1995) change.

People's attitudes towards change can have an impact upon how a change is implemented (Marsh, 1997) and this study has reported on how RECs' attitudes and perspectives on the change in religious education has influenced their management of the change. It confirmed the literature on attitudes towards change and the difficulties, constraints and tensions associated with change (Hargreaves, 1998). It also showed how misunderstandings about the intention and context of the change can impact upon the way in which the change is managed.

This study supported a view held in the literature which suggested that while curriculum change is challenging for the teacher (as well as in this case the REC) it can also lead to professional growth (Hargreaves, 1995; Johnson, 2000a; Marsh, 1997). The management of the change challenged RECs to exercise their curriculum leadership skills by dealing with similar curriculum management issues dealt with by other curriculum leaders.

The importance of professional learning cultures was another area explored in the literature (Johnson, 2000b) and this study showed that while RECs encouraged collaborative cultures and decision-making, they would ultimately make the decisions in situations where they perceived that the staff members did not have the capacity to do so.

This study supported the view that a school's previous history of change can have a significant impact on a school's ability to manage and implement new change initiatives (Smith & Lovat, 2003). The theory generated from this research also indicated that RECs managed the curriculum change by drawing upon the skills and strategies being utilised in other change initiatives occurring at the same time within the school.

"Top down" (Morris, 1995) curriculum change directed by a centralised authority places a great deal of pressure on schools to keep up with the change. This study confirmed that the management of curriculum change leads to an increased work load. It also revealed that RECs would fulfil the additional work demands in their own time, particularly in school holidays and during weekends. While this was not their preferred time for responding to the additional workload generated by a centralised authority, they argued that the other demands of the REC role prevented them from utilising school time.

Two major studies about RECs in Australia (Crotty, 2002; Fleming, 2002) reported that REC leadership had a significant bias towards fulfilling the ministerial aspects of the role. It was also suggested that even in situations where the curriculum was in need of urgent attention, RECs would ignore the curriculum demands of their role in preference for the ministerial challenges (Crotty, 2005). This study which reported on a select group of RECs who had actively undertaken to manage the change, indicated that in a particular situation of "top down" (Morris, 1995) curriculum change some RECs will give attention to the curriculum demands of their role while at the same time maintaining their commitment to the other demands of the role. It also revealed that in most situations this select group of RECs will give attention to the curriculum aspects of the role at the personal cost of working on holidays and on weekends.

The literature suggested that teacher reliance on textbooks varies according to the experience of the teacher (Britton & Woodard, 1993; Crotty & Crotty, 2000; Finlay; 2000; Vespoor, 1989). However this study suggested that a teacher's familiarity with using textbooks and their understanding of the discipline were also contributing factors influencing a teacher's level of reliance on textbooks.

## Recommendations from the Theory Generated

### Role of the REC

The role of the REC is very demanding and complex (Crotty, 2002) and perhaps too big for one person to manage (Liddy, 1998). There is a significant bias towards REC leaders who can carry out the ministerial functions of the role (Fleming, 2002). It is recommended that the role be divided enabling one person to have specific responsibility for religious education curriculum leadership and another to have responsibility for religious education ministerial leadership. It would be necessary to establish distinct criteria for both roles. If each role is to be considered a significant leadership position within Catholic education then a minimum level of qualifications and experience should be part of the criteria. A minimum level of knowledge and understanding about curriculum theory and about different approaches to classroom religious education should be expected of a religious education curriculum leader.

### Archdiocesan Responsibility for Religious Education

This "top down" (Morris, 1994) curriculum change directed by the Archdiocese has caused a division between curriculum development and implementation and diminished the role of the teacher and by association the REC as a curriculum writer. It is recommended that those responsible for directing the "top down" (Morris, 1995) curriculum change provide the ways and means to adequately communicate the change and its implications to those responsible for managing the change at the school level. It is further recommended that the Catholic Education Office, Melbourne be given the responsibility for ensuring that those responsible for curriculum leadership and in particular curriculum leadership in religious education in Catholic schools be adequately informed about curriculum change initiatives and their implications and be involved in the writing of the textbooks.

## Understandings about Curriculum Theory

Knowledge and understandings about curriculum theory have played a major part in the way the RECs managed the curriculum change. It is recommended that the Catholic Education Office, Melbourne support or provide professional development experiences for RECs and teachers of religious education that will enable them to learn and know about curriculum theory underpinning approaches to religious education. It is further recommended that RECs and teachers who receive sponsorship from the Catholic Education Office, Melbourne, to study for qualifications in religious be required to undertake a unit within the course that focuses on curriculum theory in religious education.

## Textbook Usage

The inclusion of a uniform textbook series into the learning and teaching process in religious education in Catholic schools is the first of its kind since the 1960s. Given that textbooks will be a prominent feature in classroom religious education for some time to come it is recommended that the Catholic Education Office, Melbourne provide professional development opportunities for teachers and RECs who are not familiar with using textbooks in religious education. Such professional development programs could include opportunities to consider ways of using textbooks to plan lessons and curriculum as well as provide insights into ways in which students can interact with textbooks at different age levels. Such professional development programs on textbook usage could also explore what a textbook can and cannot do.

## Text-based Curriculum

The *To Know Worship and Love* series was introduced into the Archdiocese of Melbourne as a "text-based curriculum" (Pell, 2001, p. 5), however it was not supported by a uniform curriculum. It was assumed that each school would develop its own text-based curriculum based on the contents of the textbook. This study has shown that attempts to do this mainly involved incorporating the content of the textbooks into a school's existing curriculum. This process did not reflect the spirit and intention underpinning the text-based curriculum. It is recommended that the Catholic Education Office, Melbourne develop a curriculum document to support the teachers' use of textbooks.[12] It is further recommended that the curriculum be designed to give teachers direction about the scope and sequence of content to be learned by students as well as an understanding of the theoretical position underpinning the text-based curriculum.

---

[12] The document *Coming To Know Worship and Love,* (Elliott, 2005) makes some progress in this direction.

## Qualifications in Religious Education

The implementation of the text-based curriculum was hampered by the lack of qualified teachers of religious education. If religious education is to "appear as a scholastic discipline with the same systematic demands and the rigour as other disciplines" (CC, 1998, # 73) then it is recommended that the Archdiocese ensure that they have the "best possible qualified teachers of religion" (CCE, 1977, # 52). Only individuals who are qualified to teach religious education should be given that responsibility. If for some reason teachers who are not qualified are appointed to teach religious education then the school with the support of the Catholic Education Office, Melbourne should assist the teacher in obtaining the qualifications as soon as possible.

## Significance and Limitations of this Study

This present study has been limited in terms of participant numbers as it focussed on a select number of participants who were actively involved in managing the curriculum change directed by the Archdiocese. It was also limited to RECs in Catholic secondary schools because, as discussed in the introduction of this book, the process of managing the change and the theoretical position underpinning the primary textbooks differed significantly from that of the secondary school context.

However, having noted the above limitations, it is valid to claim that this study is significant. This research is beneficial to those responsible for curriculum change in classroom religious education – RECs, Catholic schools and the Catholic Education Office, Melbourne – where the insights gained from the RECs' perspective on the management of curriculum change can be drawn upon to advance thinking and practice in the highly specialised area of classroom religious education. This research is also significant because it has the potential to be applied beyond its immediate context, that of the Archdiocese of Melbourne. In recent times the Archdiocese of Sydney and other New South Wales diocese have implemented a text-based curriculum based on the *To Know Worship and Love* textbook series, therefore this research may have the potential to improve practice in the management of curriculum change in other dioceses throughout Australia.

This research is the first major study undertaken to explore the management of curriculum change in the highly specialised area of classroom religious education in Catholic schools in Melbourne. This book advances knowledge through the presentation of new research in this area. It has applied existing knowledge about curriculum change to the area of religious education in Catholic schools therefore it produces knowledge upon which advances may be built.

## Recommendations for Further Research

In any research project there are areas of interest that must be left to other researchers. In this study the management of curriculum change was analysed from the perspective of the REC. Further research could explore the management of curriculum change in classroom religious education from the perspective of the Principal and / or leadership team. Another research direction could be to concentrate on classroom teachers of religious education. This study did not focus on evaluating the effectiveness of the REC in their management of curriculum change. Future research could collect data on the effectiveness of RECs as managers of curriculum change. Given that a major curriculum change in religious education has also taken place in Catholic primary schools throughout Melbourne, research could also be undertaken to explore how RECs in these schools manage curriculum change.

## Conclusion

From the perspective of the REC this study has identified and analysed the RECs' management of a particular curriculum change in classroom religious education in Catholic secondary schools in the Archdiocese of Melbourne. The theory generated provided insights into the way in which RECs managed this curriculum change as well as the factors that assisted and impeded their management of the change. Recommendations were made in the light of the theory generated from this research with a view to improving the RECs' management of curriculum change. If this study assists those who are responsible for classroom religious education at both the levels of curriculum development and implementation then it will have made a significant contribution to the ongoing task of curriculum management in classroom religious education.

# *Figures*

categories.

# *Tables*

# *Abbreviations*

| | |
|---|---|
| AEC | Australian Episcopal Conference |
| ACSSO | Australian Council of State School Organisations |
| APC | Australian Parents Council |
| CC | Congregation for the Clergy |
| CCE | Congregation for Catholic Education |
| CEOB | Catholic Education Office, Brisbane |
| CEOCG | Catholic Education Office, Canberra & Goulburn |
| CEOD | Catholic Education Office, Darwin |
| CEOH | Catholic Education Office, Hobart |
| CEOM | Catholic Education Office, Melbourne |
| CEOS | Catholic Education Office, Sydney |
| CEOP | Catholic Education Office, Parramatta |
| CEOWA | Catholic Education Office, Western Australia |
| DOCE | Declaration on Christian Education |
| GDC | General Directory for Catechesis |
| RDECS | The Religious Dimension of Education in a Catholic School |
| RE | Religious Education |
| REC | Religious Education Coordinator |

# Bibliography

Abbott, W. M. (Ed.). (1966). *The documents of Vatican II.* London: Geoffrey Chapman.

Amalorpavadass, D. S. (1971). *Theology of catechesis.* (Keynote address delivered at the World Congress of Catechesis), Rome.

Amalorpavadass, D.S. (1973). *Theology of catechesis.* National Biblical Catechetical and Liturgical Centre, Bangalore.

Apple, M. & Jungck, S. (1991). Is participating enough? Gender, teaching, and technology in the classroom. *Curriculum Perspectives, 11* (12), 114.

Australian Catholic Bishops. (1964). *My way to God.* Australia: Dwyer.

Barker, R.G. (1968). *Ecological psychology: Concepts and methods for studying the environment of behaviour.* Stanford, California: Stanford University Press.

Beaudoin, M. & Taylor, M. (2004). *Creating a positive school culture: How principals and teachers can solve problems together.* Thousand Oaks, California: Corwin Press.

Berman, H. (1980). *Towards and implementation paradigm of educational change.* San Francisco: Far West Laboratory for Educational Research and Development.

Bezzina, M., Gahan, P., McLenaghan, H. & Wilson, G. (1997). Shared Christian praxis: The Paramatta experience. *Word in Life, 45* (3), 3-11.

Bilmes, J. (1975). Misinformation in verbal accounts: Some fundamental considerations. *Man, 10,* 60-71.

Blahut, L. and Bezzina, M. (1998). The primary religious education coordinator: Role demands and job turnover in the diocese of Parramatta. *Journal of Religious Education, 46* (2), 2-7.

Blumer, H. (1969). *Symbolic interactionism: Perspective and method.* Englewood Cliffs, NJ: Prentice Hall.

Board of Studies. (1999). *Religion and study design 2001-2005.* Victoria: Board of Studies.

Board of Studies. (1999). *Texts and traditions study design 2001-2005.* Victoria: Board of Studies.

Boomer, G. (1982). *Negotiating the curriculum: A student-teacher partnership.* Sydney: Ashton-Scholastic.

Bowers, B. (1989). Grounded theory. In B. Starter (Ed.), *Paths to knowledge: Innovative research methods in nursing.* (pp. 33-59). National League of Nursing.

Brady, L. and Kennedy, K. (2003). *Curriculum construction* (2nd ed.). N.S.W. Australia: Pearson/Prentice Hall.

Brickell, H. M. (1972). Two local change strategies. In R. Hooper (Ed.), *The curriculum: context design and development* (pp. 399-410). Great Britain: Open University Press.

Britton, B.K. and Woodard, A. (Ed.). (1993). *Learning from textbooks: Theory and practice*. New Jersey: Hillsdale.

Brodrik, J. (1928). *Blessed Robert Bellarmine Vol 1*. London: Burns, Oates and Washbourne.

Bryman, A. (2001). *Social research methods*. Oxford: Oxford University Press.

Buchanan, M. T. (2003). Survey of current writings on trends in religious education. *Journal of Religious Education, 51* (4), 22-30.

Buchanan, M. T. (2004). An outcomes based educational approach to using *To know worship and love* in religious education in the Archdiocese of Melbourne. *Catholic School Studies: A Journal of Catholic Education, 77* (1), 36-40.

Buchanan, M. T. (2005a). Pedagogical drift: The evolution of new approaches and paradigms in religious education. *Religious Education, 100* (1), 20-37.

Buchanan, M.T. (2005b). The REC: Perspectives on a complex role within Catholic education. *Journal of Religious Education, 53* (4), 68-74.

Buchanan, M. T. (2006a). A brief history of approaches to RE in Catholic schools. In R. Rymarz, (Ed.). *Leadership in Religious Education* (pp. 11-29). Australia: St Paul Publication.

Buchanan, M. T. (2006b). Curriculum management: Influencing school outlook towards religious education. *Journal of Religious Education, 54* (2), pp. 71-78.

Buchanan, M. T. (2006c). Factors that assist curriculum change. *Journal of Religious Education, 54* (1), 18-26.

Buchanan, M. T. (2006d). Factors that impede curriculum change: A preliminary report. *British Journal of Religious Education, 28* (1), 51-64.

Buchanan, M. T. (2006e). Textbooks in religious education. In M. de Souza, K. Engerbretson, G. Durka, R. Jackson, & A. McGrady (Eds.). *International handbook of religious, moral and spiritual education* (pp. 747-760). Netherlands: Springer.

Buchanan, M. T. & Engebretson, K. (2006). *The religious education in Australian Catholic schools: A review of the literature*. Unpublished paper for the Primary RECs Project, Catholic Education Office, Melbourne. Australian Catholic University, Australia.

Burgess, R. G. (1982). *Field research: Sourcebook and field manual*. London: Allen & Urwin.


Burns, R. B. (1997). *Introduction to research methods* (3rd ed.). NSW, Australia: Longman.

Carnine, D. (1991). Curricular interventions for teaching higher order thinking to all students: Introduction to the special series. *Journal of Learning Disabilities, 24* (5), 261-269.

Carr, W. and Kemmis, S. (1986). *Becoming critical: Knowing through action research*. Geelong: Deakin University Press.

Catechism of the Catholic Church. (1994). *Catechism of the Catholic Church*. Strathfield, NSW: St Pauls.

Catholic Education Office, Archdiocese of Brisbane. (1997). *APRE in the Catholic school*. Brisbane: Catholic Education Office, Archdiocese of Brisbane.

Catholic Education Office, Archdiocese of Canberra & Goulburn. (1979). *The religious education coordinator in Catholic schools*. Canberra and Goulburn: Catholic Education Office.

Catholic Education Office, Archdiocese of Hobart. (1984). *The religious education coordinator.* Tasmania: Catholic Education Office, Archdiocese of Hobart.

Catholic Education Office, Archdiocese of Melbourne. (1972). My first day at school. *Let's Go Together, 5* (1), 4.

Catholic Education Office, Archdiocese of Melbourne. (1973). *Guidelines for religious education of students in the archdiocese of Melbourne.* Melbourne: Catholic Education Office.

Catholic Education Office, Archdiocese of Melbourne. (1975). *Guidelines for religious education of students in the archdiocese of Melbourne.* Melbourne: Catholic Education Office, Archdiocese of Melbourne.

Catholic Education Office, Archdiocese of Melbourne. (1977). *Guidelines for religious education of students in the archdiocese of Melbourne.* Melbourne: Catholic Education Office, Archdiocese of Melbourne.

Catholic Education Office, Archdiocese of Melbourne. (1984). *Guidelines for religious education of students in the archdiocese of Melbourne.* Melbourne: Catholic Education Office, Archdiocese of Melbourne.

Catholic Education Office, Archdiocese of Melbourne. (1995). *Guidelines for religious education of students in the archdiocese of Melbourne.* Melbourne: Catholic Education Office, Archdiocese of Melbourne.

Catholic Education Office, Archdiocese of Melbourne. (2005). *Leadership in Catholic schools: The role of the religious education coordinator.* Melbourne: Catholic Education Office, Archdiocese of Melbourne.

Catholic Education Office, Archdiocese of Sydney. (1983). *The religious education coordinator: A handbook.* Sydney: Catholic Education Office, Archdiocese of Sydney.

Catholic Education Office, Archdiocese of Sydney. (1988). *Policy statement: The religious education coordinator in Catholic systemic schools in the Archdiocese of Sydney.* Sydney: Catholic Education Office, Archdiocese of Sydney.

Catholic Education Office, Archdiocese of Sydney. (1989). *Religious education: place in Catholic secondary education.* Sydney: Catholic Education Office, Archdiocese of Sydney.

Catholic Education Office, Archdiocese of Sydney. (1996). *Religious education coordinators: Conditions of appointment and employment.* Sydney: Catholic Education Office, Archdiocese of Sydney.

Catholic Education Office, Diocese of Darwin (1998). *Conditions of employment leadership positions other than principal.* Darwin: Catholic Education Office, Diocese of Darwin.

Catholic Education Office, Diocese of Parramatta, (1997). *Religious education coordinators: Conditions of appointment and employment.* Parramatta: Catholic Education Office, Diocese of Parramatta.

Catholic Education Office, Western Australia. (1986). *The religious education coordinator: A handbook.* Western Australia: Catholic Education Office, Western Australia.

Charles, C. M. & Mertler, C. A. (2002). *Introduction to educational research* (4th ed.). Boston: Allyn & Bacon.

Clandinin, D. J. & Connelly, F. M. (1994). Personal experience methods. In N. K. Denzin & Y. Lincoln (Ed.). *Handbook of qualitative research*. Thousand Oaks: Sage.

Colombo, C. (1970). From the President of the Episcopal commission of the doctrine of the faith and catechesis. In Australian Episcopal Conference, *The renewal of the education of faith* (pp i- xvi) Sydney, Australia: Dwyer.

Come Alive. (1970). *Come alive.* Sydney: E.J. Dwyer.

Congregation for Catholic Education. (1977). *The Catholic school.* Australia: Society of Saint Paul.

Congregation For Catholic Education. (1982). *Lay Catholics in schools :Witnesses to faith.* http://www.vatican.va/roman_curia/congregations/ccatheduc/documents/rc_con_ccatheduc _doc_19821015_lay-catholics _en.html (March 5th 2004).

Congregation for Catholic Education. (1988). *The religious dimension of education in a Catholic school.* Homebush: St. Paul's.

Congregation for the Clergy. (1998). *General directory for catechesis.* Australia: St Paul's.

Constable, C. (1992). A parent reflects. *Word in Life, 40* (4), 1-14.

Cornbleth, C. (1990). *Curriuclum in context.* London: Falmer Press.

Crawford, D. B. and Carnine, D. (2000). Comparing the effects of textbooks in eighth-grade U.S. History: Does conceptual organisation help? *Education and Treatment of Children,* 23 (4), 387. Retrieved June 28, 2004, from Questia database, http://www.questia.com.

Creswell, J. W. (1998). *Qualitative inquiry and research design: Choosing among five traditions.* London: Sage.

Crotty, L. (1998). The religious education coordinator: Evolution and evolving agendas. *Journal of Religious Education, 42* (2), 8-14.

Crotty, L. (2002). *Religious leadership in the Catholic school: The position of the religious education coordinator.* Unpublished doctoral dissertation, The University of Sydney, Australia.

Crotty, L. (2005). The REC and religious leadership. *Journal of Religious Education, 53* (1), 48-59.

Crotty, M. & Crotty, R. (2000). Assessing the role of the RE textbook. Journal of Religious Education, *48* (2), 23 – 27.

Crotty, M. (1998). *The foundations of social research: Meaning and perspective in the research process.* NSW, Australia: Allen Urwin.

D'Orsa, T. (1998). The religious education coordinator as leader. *Journal of Religious Education, 42* (2), 33-37.

Dalton, A. (1988). *The challenge of curriculum innovation: A study of ideology and practice.* Great Britain: The Falmer Press.

De Souza, M. (2005). Engaging the mind, heart and soul of the student in religious education: Teaching for meaning and connection. *Journal of Religious Education, 53* (4), 40-47.

Declaration on Christian Education. In A. Flannery (1995). *The Basic Documents of Vatican Council II: Constitutions, Decrees, Declarations* (pp. 575-592). New York: Costello Publishing Company.

Denzin, N. K. & Lincoln, Y. S. (1998). *Collecting and interpreting qualitative materials.* London: Sage.

Dick, R. (2002). *Grounded theory: A thumbnail sketch.* [On line] Retrieved on 26/02/03 from http://www.scu.edu.au/schools/gcm/ar/arp/grounded.html.

Doyle, A. (1972). *The story of the Marist Brothers in Australia 1872-1972.* Sydney, Australia: E.J. Dwyer.

Durrant, J. & Holden, G. (2006). *Teachers leading change: Doing research for school improvement.* London: Paul Chapman Publishing.

Dwyer, B. (2000). Wanted; Textbooks with 'Hilaritas". *Journal of Religious Education, 48 (2),* 17 – 18.

Eisner, E. W. (1975). Can educational research inform educational practice? *Phi Delta Kapan, 65,* 447-452.

Elliot, J. (1998). *The curriculum experiment: Meeting the challenge of social change.* Great Britain: Open University Press.

Elliot, R. & Rossiter, G. (Ed.). (1982). *Towards critical dialogue in religious education: A collection of conference papers and case studies which raise issues for religious education in Australian schools.* Australia: Australian Association for Religious Education.

Elliott, P. (Ed.). (2001a). *To know worship and love (Years 7).* Melbourne, Australia: James Goold House.

Elliott, P. (Ed.). (2001b). *To know worship and love (Years 9).* Melbourne, Australia: James Goold House.

Elliott, P. (Ed.). (2001c). *To know worship and love teacher companion level 3a.* Melbourne, Australia: James Goold House.

Elliott, P. (Ed.). (2002a). *To know worship and love (Years 8).* Melbourne, Australia: James Goold House.

Elliott, P. (Ed.). (2002b). *To know worship and love (Years 10).* Melbourne, Australia: James Goold House.

Elliott, P. (Ed.). (2002c). *To know worship and love teacher companion year 10.* Melbourne, Australia: James Goold House.

Ellis, C. & Berger, L. (2003). Their story/my story/our story: Including the researcher's experience in interview research. In J. F. Gubrium & J. A. Holstein (Eds.). *Postmodern interviewing* (pp. 157- 186). London: Sage.

Elmore, R. (2000). *Building a new structure for school leadership.* Washington DC: The Albert Shanker Institute.

Engebretson, K. (1991). The approach to religious education in the Victorian certificate of education. *Journal of Religious Education, 39* (2), 9-11.

Engebretson, K. (1997). The four point plan of the Melbourne guidelines and shared praxis: Two distinct and different methodologies. *Word in Life, 45* (3), 25-29.

Engebretson, K. (1998). Structural arrangements for the role of religious education coordinator in Australian dioceses. *Journal of Religious Education, 46* (2), 23-26.

Engebretson, K. (2000). The Melbourne archdiocesan textbook project: An innovation in Australian religious education. *Journal of Religious Education, 48* (2), 28-32.

Engebretson, K. (2002). Writing church-sponsored religious education textbooks. *British Journal of Religious Education 25* (1), 33-45.

Engebretson, K. (2004). *Introduction for section three: Religious education: Theoretical approaches to curriculum.* Unpublished.

Engebretson, K. (2006). A framework for effective religious education leadership in the catholic secondary school. In R. Rymarz, (Ed.). *Leadership in Religious Education* (pp. 135-151). Australia: St Paul Publication

Engebretson, K., Fleming, J., Rymarz, R., (2002). *Thriving as an RE teacher: A handbook for secondary religious educators.* Australia: Social Science Press.

Engebretson, K. & Rymarz, R. (2002) *Report on the first stage of the implementation of the Melbourne archdiocesan textbook series, To know worship and love, books 7-10.* Unpublished. A joint project of the Archdiocese of Melbourne and the School of Religious Education, Victoria, Australian Catholic University.

Engebretson, K. & Rymarz, R. (2004) *Report on the second stage of the implementation of the Melbourne archdiocesan textbook series, To know worship and love, books 7-10.* Unpublished. A joint project of the Archdiocese of Melbourne and the School of Religious Education, Victoria, Australian Catholic University.

Everitt, N. & Fisher, A. (1995). *Modern epistemology: A new introduction.* New York: McGraw-Hill.

Ferning, L. R. McDougal, J. F. and Ohlman, H. (1989). Will textbooks be replaced by new information technologies? In J. Farrell, and S. P. Heyneman, (Ed.). *Textbooks in the developing world: Economic and educational choices* (pp. 197-205). Washington: The World Bank.

Finlay, G. (2000). Why textbooks? A reflection on New Zealand experience. *Journal of Religious Education, 48 (2),* 58-61.

Fleming, G. P. (2002). *An analysis of religious education coordinators perceptions of their role in catholic secondary schools in the archdiocese of Melbourne.* Unpublished doctoral dissertation, Australian Catholic University, Australia.

Fleming, G. P. (2004). Religious education coordinators' perceptions of the challenges in their role in Catholic schools. *Journal of Religious Education, 52* (2), 48-54.

Fleming, J. (2001). Religious education coordinators in catholic schools. In M. Ryan (Ed.). *Echo and Silence: Contemporary Issues for Australian Religious Education* (pp. 104-116). Katoomba NSW: Social Science Press.

Flick, U. (2002). *An introduction to qualitative research* (2nd ed.). London: Sage.

Frost, D. & Durrant, J. (2002). Teachers as leaders: Exploring the impact of teacher-led development work. *School Leadership and Management, 22* (2), 143-161.

Fullan, M. (1982). *The meaning of educational change.* New York: Herder & Herder.

Fullan, M. (1993). *Change forces: probing the depths of educational reform.* New York: Falmer.

Fullan, M. (1999). *Change forces: The sequel.* London: Falmer Press.

Fullan, M. (2001a). *Leading a culture of change.* San Francisco: Jossey Bass.

Fullan, M. (2001b). *The new meaning of educational change* (3$^{rd}$ ed.). London: RoutledgeFalmer.

Fullan, M. (2004). *Personal action guide and workbook: Leading in a culture of change.* San Francisco: Jossey Bass.

Fullan, M. and Hargreaves, A. (Ed.). (1992). *Understanding teacher development.* London: Cassell.

Fullen, M. and Stiegelbauer, S. (1991). *The new meaning of educational change.* London: Cassell.

Garner, N. and Biewer, M. (1983). *Talking about textbooks.* Victoria: Publication and Information Branch, Education Department of Victoria.

Glaser, B. & Strauss, A. (1967). *The discovery of grounded theory: Strategies for qualitative research.* New York: Adeline.

Glaser, B. (1978). *Theoretical sensitivity: advances in the methodology of grounded theory.* Mill Valley, California: Sociology Press.

Glaser, B. (1992). *Basics of grounded theory analysis: Emergence v forcing.* Mill Valley, California: Sociology Press.

Glaser, B. (1998). Doing grounded theory: Issues and discussions. Mill Valley, California: Sociology Press.

Gopinathan, S. (1989). And shall the twain meet? Public and private textbook publishing in the developing world. In J. Farrell, and S. P. Heyneman, (Ed.).*Textbooks in the developing world: Economic and educational choices* (pp. 61-71). Washington: The World Bank.

Goulding, C. (2002). *Grounded theory: A practical guide for management, business and market researchers.* Great Britain: Sage Publications Ltd.

Gouldner, A. (1970). *The coming crisis in western sociology.* New York: Basic Books.

Grimmitt, M. (2000). Contemporary pedagogies of religious education: What are they? In. M. Grimmitt (Ed.). *Pedagogies of religious education: Case studies in the research and development of good pedagogic practice in RE* (pp. 24-52). Great Wakering, England: McCrimmon.

Groome, T. (1980). *Christian religious education: Sharing our story and vision.* New York: Harper & Row.

Groome, T. (1991). *Sharing faith: A comprehensive approach to religious education and pastoral ministry.* San Francisco, USA: Harper.

Habel, N & Moore, B. (1982). *When religion goes to school: A typology of religion for the classroom.* South Australia: South Australian College of Advanced Education.

Hargreaves, A. (1994). *Changing teachers, changing times.* London: Cassell.

Hargreaves, A. (1997). The four ages of professionalism and professional learning. *Unicorn, 23* (2), 99-100.

Hargreaves, A. (1998). The emotions of teaching educational change. In A. Hargreaves (Ed.), *International Handbook of Educational Change* (pp. 558-575). London: Kluwer Academic Publishers.

Hart, D. (2002). From the Archbishop. In Elliot, Peter (Ed.). *To Know Worship And Love Teaching Companion Year 8* (p. 6). Melbourne, Australia: James Goold House Publications.

Hatoss, A. (2004). A model for evaluating textbooks. *Babel,* 39 (2), 25-32.

Healy, H. (2003). Sustaining and building good practice in religious education: Using a school-centred model for educational change and teacher development. *Journal of Religious Education, 51* (4), 13-21.

Hill, B. V. (2004). *Exploring religion in school: A national priority.* Adelaide: Openbook Publishers.

Hirsch, E. D. Jr. (1996). *The schools we need and why we don't have them.* New York: Double-day.

Hofinger, J. (1966). *The art of teaching Christian doctrine.* London: Sands & Co.

Hoyle, E. (1972). How does curriculum change? In R. Hooper (Ed.), *The curriculum: Context, design and development* (pp. 375-398). Great Britain: Open University Press.

Hull, J. M. (1984). *Studies in religion and education.* London: Falmer Press.

Issitt, J. (2004). Reflections on the study of textbooks. *History of Education, 33* (6), 683-696.

Jackson, P. (1968). *Life in classrooms.* New York: Holt, Rinehart & Wilson.

Jackson, P. (Ed.). (1992). *Handbook of research on curriculum.* New York: Macmillan.

Jackson, R. (2004). *Rethinking religious education and plurality: Issues in diversity and pedagogy.* London: RoutledgeFalmer.

Janesick, V. J. (2003). From the individual interview to the interview society. In F. J. Gubrium & J. A. Holstein (Eds.), *Postmodern interviewing* (pp. 21-51) London: Sage.

Johnson, H. (1989). *The religious education coordinator – mission and ministry.* Unpublished Masters thesis, Sydney: Catholic College of Education.

Johnson, H. (1998). The role of the religious education coordinator: Mission and ministry. *Journal of Religious Education, 42* (2), 44-46.

Johnson, N. (1995). *Schools As Learning Communities: Curriculum Implications.* Melbourne University. Conference Paper. No 31, presented at the Australian Curriculum Studies Association Biennial Conference. Melbourne.

Johnson, N. (1996). Becoming learning communities. *Learning Matters, 1* (1), 7-11.

Johnson, N. (2000a). *Supporting school and classroom improvement and change.* Unpublished resource booklet from Connections Educational Consultancy.

Johnson, N. (2000b). *Sustaining and building good practice in schools.* Unpublished resource booklet from Connections Educational Consultancy.

Jungmann, J. A. (1957). *Handing on the faith*. Germany: Herder.

Keats, D. M. (1993). *Skilled interviewing* (2nd ed.). Australia: The Australian Council for Educational Research Ltd.

Kerin, R. & Nixon, H. (2005). Middle years English/literacy curriculum: The interface of critical literacy and digital texts. *Literacy Learning: The Middle Years, 13* (1), 20-35.

Kinder, D. and Bursuck, W. (1991). The search for a unified social studies curriculum: Does history really repeat itself? *Journal of Learning Disabilities, 24* (5), 270-275.

Kools, S., McCarthy, M., Durham, R. and Robrecht, L. (1996). Dimensional analysis: Broadening the conception of grounded theory. *Qualitative Health Research, 6* (3), 312-330.

Kvale, S. (1996) *InterViews: An Introduction to qualitative research interviewing*. Thousand oaks, California: Sage Publications.

Lee, J. (2001). School reform initiatives as balancing acts: Policy variation and educational convergence among Japan, Korea, England and the United States. *Educational Policy Analysis Archives, 9* (13) 1-14 Retrieved 25/08/04 from http://epaa.asu.edu/epaa/v9n13.html.

Leiberman, A. (Ed.). (1990). *Schools as collaborative cultures: Creating the future now*. London: Falmer Press.

Lewis, M. E. (1988). Continuation of a curriculum innovation: Salient and alterable variable. *Journal of Curriculum and Supervision, 4* (1), 52-64.

Liddy, S. (1998). Key issues for the REC. *Journal of Religious Education, 42* (2), 27.

Liddy, S. (2002). Children's spirituality, *Journal of Religious Education, 50* (1), 13-19.

Lincoln, Y. S. (1997). Self, subject, audience, text: Living at the edge, writing in the margins. In W. G. Tierney & Y. S. Lincoln (Eds.), *Representation and the text: Re-framing the narrative voice*. Albany: State University of New York Press.

Lincoln, Y. S. and Guba, E. G. (1985). *Naturalistic inquiry*. Beverly Hills, California: Sage Publications Ltd.

Lincoln, Y. S. and Guba, E. G. (1994). Competing paradigms in qualitative research. In N. Denzin and Y. Lincoln (Eds.), *handbook of qualitative research* (pp. 105-117). Thousand oaks, California: Sage.

Lovat, T. (1989). *What is this thing called religious education?* Social NSW, Australia: Science Press.

Lovat, T. (1995). *Teaching and learning religion: A phenomenological approach*. Australia: Social Science Press.

Lovat, T. (2002). *What is this thing called R. E. A decade On?* (2nd Ed.). Australia: Social Science Press.

Mackenzie, A. (1998). Crisis or opportunity. *Journal of Religious Education, 46* (2), 38-43.

Malone, P. & Ryan, M. (1996). *Exploring the religion classroom: A guidebook for catholic schools*. Australia: Social Science Press.

Mannix, D. (1937). *Catechism.* Melbourne: Australian Catholic Truth Society.

Marsh, C. J. (1997). *Planning, management and ideology: Key concepts for understanding curriculum* (2nd Ed.). London: The Falmer Press.

Marsh, D. D. and Bowman, G. A. (1987). *Top-down versus bottom-up reform in secondary schools.* Unpublished paper, University of California, Los Angeles.

McBrien, R.P. (Ed.). (1995). *Encyclopaedia of Catholicism.* USA: Harper Collins.

McCarthy, M. (2004). Leadership in religious education: Addressing three elements: Teacher, student and subject matter. *Journal of Religious Education, 52* (4), 26-30.

McInerney, P. (2004). *Making hope practical: School reform for social justice.* Australia: Post Pressed.

McLaughlin, M. W. (1987). Learning from experience: Lessons from policy implementation. *Educational Evaluation and Policy Analysis, 9* (2), 171-178.

Mead, G. H. (1934). *Mind, self and society.* Chicago: University of Chicago Press.

Miles, M. B. & Huberman (1994). *Qualitative data analysis: An expanded source book* (2nd ed.). Thousand Oaks, Calafornia: Sage.

Minichiello, V., Aroni, R., Timewell, E. & Alexander, L. (1995). *In-depth interviewing: Principles, Techniques, Analysis* (2nd ed.). Australia: Longman.

Moran, G. (1991). Understanding religion and being religious. *Professional Approaches for Religious Educators, 21(9), 459-252.*

Morris, P. (1995). *The Hong Kong school curriculum: Development, issues and policies.* Hong Kong: Hong Kong University Press.

Mudge, P. (2000). Four foundational dimensions of the religious education textbook. *Journal of Religious Education, 48 (2), 2 – 7.*

Neumann, P. H. (1989). Publishing for schools in France, the Federal Republic of Germany, the United Kingdom, and the United States. In J. Farrell, and S. P. Heyneman, (Ed.). *Textbooks in the developing world: Economic and educational choices.* Washington: The World Bank pp. 115-129.

New South Wales Government. (1980). *Religion in education in NSW government schools: The Rawlinson report.* Sydney: Govt. Printer.

Newport, P. (1992). Teacher thinking and beliefs: Parent-teacher partnership: A case study. *Curriculum Perspectives, 12* (1), 45-54.

O'Farrell, P. (1992). *The Catholic church and community: An Australian history* (3rd Ed.). Kensington NSW, Australia: NSW Press.

Patton, M. Q. (1987). *How to use qualitative methods in evaluation.* Newbury Park, California: Sage Publications.

Paxton, R. (1998). Coordinating the religious dimension at Normanhurst. *Journal of Religious Education, 42* (2), 47-50.

Pell, G. (2001). From the Archbishop. In P. Elliot (Ed.). *To Know Worship and Love Teaching Companion Year 7* (p. 5). Melbourne: James Goold House.

Pepper, J. (1981). Following students' suggestions for rewriting a computer programming textbook. *American Educational Research Journal, 18* (3), 259-269.

Reilly, G. (1998). Stirring the human heart – the task of religious education. *The Furrow, 49 (3),* 137 – 142.

Rennie, D. L. (1998). Grounded theory methodology: The pressing need for a coherent logic of justification. *Theory of Psychology, 8* (8), 101-119.

Richardson, L. (2003). Poetic representation of interviews. In J. F. Gubrium & J. A. Holstein (Eds.). *Postmodern interviewing* (pp. 187-283). London: Sage.

Rossiter, G. (1981a). *Religious education in Australian schools.* Australia:Curriculum development centre Australia.

Rossiter, G. (1981b). The gap between aims and practice in religious education, *Word in Life 29* (1), 24.

Rossiter, G. (1988). Perspectives on change in Catholic religious education since the second Vatican council. *Religious Education, 83* (2), 264-276.

Rossiter, G. (2000). The qualities of an excellent student text in religious education. *Journal of Religious Education, 48 (2),* 13-16.

Rummery, R. M. (1975). *Catechesis and religious education in a pluralist society.* Sydney: E. J. Dwyer.

Ryan, M. (1997). *Foundations of religious education in Catholic schools; an Australian perspective.* NSW, Australia: Social Science Press.

Ryan, M. (1998). An evaluation of outcomes based approaches in religious education curriculum guidelines. *Word in Life: Journal of Religious Education, 46* (1), 14-19.

Ryan, M. (2000). Religious educator as curriculum maker. *Journal of Religious Education, 48 (2),* 19 – 22.

Rymarz, R. (1998). The religious education coordinator (REC): A four fold approach. *Journal of Religious Education, 42* (2), 28-32.

Rymarz, R. (2000). Religious education textbooks for Catholic secondary schools: some practical issues. *Journal of Religious Education, 48 (2),* 41 – 44.

Sarantakos, S. (1998). *Working the social research.* South Yarra, Australia: Charles Sturt University.

Schroder, H.J. (1941). *Canons and decrees of the Council of Trent.* St Louis: Herder.

Scott, G. (1999). Change matters: making a difference in education and training. Sydney: Allen & Unwin.

Settelmaier, E. & Taylor, P. (2002, July). *Using autobiography to map an interpretive researcher's sensitivities towards her subject(s).* Presented at the annual conference of the Australasian Science Education Research Association. Townsville, Queensland.


Smart, N. (1968). *Secular education and the logic of religion.* London: Faber & Faber.

Smart, N. (1974a). *The teaching ministry of the Church.* Philadelphia: Westminster.

Smart, N. (1974b). *The science of religion and the sociology of knowledge.* New Jersey: Princeton University.

Smart, N. (1978). *The phenomenon of religion.* London: McMillan.

Smart, N. (1979). The phenomenon of Christianity. London: William Collins Sons & Co Ltd.

Smart, N. (1998). *The worlds religions (2nd ed.).* Cambridge: Cambridge University Press.

Smith, D. L. & Lovat, T. J. (2003). *Curriculum: Action on reflection* (4th ed.). Tuggerah, NSW, Australia: Social Science Press.

South Australian Government. (1973). *Religious education in state schools: The Steinle report.* Adelaide: Department of Education.

Stenhouse, L. (1975). *An introduction to curriculum research and development.* London: Heinemann Educational.

Stern, B. (1994). Classical and vignette television advertising dramas: Structural models, formal analysis and consumer effect. *Journal of Consumer Research, 19,* 601- 615.

Strauss, A. & Corbin, J. (1990). *Basics of qualitative research.* Newbury Park, London: Sage.

Taba, H. (1962). *Curriuclum development: Theory and practice.* New York: Harcourt, Brace and World.

Taylor, S. J. & Bogdan, R. (1984). *Introduction to qualitative research methods,* (2nd ed.). New York: Wiley.

Thomas, J. (2000). Survival without texts. *Journal of Religious Education, 48 (2),* 54 – 57.

Tyson, H. and Woodward, A. (1989). Why students aren't learning very much from textbooks. *Educational Leadership, 47* (3), 14-17.

Tyson-Bernstein, H. (1989). Textbook development in the United States: How good ideas become bad textbooks. In J. Farrell, and S. P. Heyneman, (Ed.). *Textbooks in the developing world: Economic and educational choices* (pp. 71-87). Washington: The World Bank.

Vespoor, A. M. (1989). Using textbooks to improve the quality of education. In J. Farrell, and S. P. Heyneman, (Ed.). *Textbooks in the developing world: Economic and educational choices* (pp. 52-58). Washington: The World Bank.

Victorian Curriculum and Assessment Authority. (2001). *Curriculum Standards Framework II.* Melbourne: Victorian Curriculum and Assessment Authority.

Victorian Government. (1974). *Report on the committee on religious education: The Russell report.* Melbourne: Department of Education.

Watson, H. (2004). Classrooms of the future. *Teacher, 153,* 54-55.

Werner, W. (1987). Training and curriculum implementation. *Pacific Education, 1* (1), 40-53.

Western Australian Government. (1977). *Religious education in the government schools of Western Australia: The Nott report.* Perth: Department of Education.

Wiersma, W. (2005). *Research methods in education* (8th ed.). Boston: Allyn and Bacon.

Windeen, M. F., Mayer-Smith, J. A., Moon, B. J. (1996). Knowledge, teacher development and change. In I. G. Goodson & A. Hargreaves (Ed.). *Teachers' professional lives*. London: Falmer Press.

Woodard, A. and Elliot, D.L. (1990). Textbook use and teacher professionalism. In D.L. Elliot and A. Woodard (Ed.). Textbooks and schooling in the United States. Chicago IL: National Society for the Study of Education.

Woods, P. (1992). Symbolic interationism: Theory and Method. In M. D. LeCompte, W. L. Millroy, & J. Preissle (Eds.), *The handbook of qualitative research in education*. San Diego: Academic Press, Inc.